ETHICS AND PROFESSIONAL CONDUCT

For 2027 exams

Edited by Mark Thomas

Series editors: Amy Sixsmith and David Sixsmith

REVISE SQE

First published in 2022 by Fink Publishing Ltd
This edition published in 2026

Impression number 10 9 8 7 6 5 4 3 2 1

British Library Cataloguing in Publication Data
A catalogue record for this book is available from the British Library
ISBN: 9781807730123

This book is also available in various ebook formats.
Ebook ISBN: 9781807730147

Production and typesetting by Westchester Publishing Services (UK)
Cover and text design by BMLD (bmld.uk)

Revise SQE
Fink Publishing Ltd
E-mail: hello@revise4law.co.uk
www.revise4law.co.uk

Notes from the publisher

1. This book reflects the SQE1 assessment specification (updated April 2026) applicable for assessments from 1 September 2026.

2. While Fink Publishing has made every attempt to ensure that advice on the qualification and its assessment is accurate, the official specification and associated assessment guidance materials are the only authoritative source of information and should always be referred to for definitive guidance. See the SRA website at https://sqe.sra.org.uk. Note that the SRA may amend their assessment guidance (including the contents of the assessment specifications) at any point.

3. Fink Publishing has robust editorial processes to ensure the accuracy of the content in this publication, and every effort is made to ensure this publication is free of errors. We are, however, only human, and occasionally errors do occur. Fink Publishing is not liable for any misunderstandings that arise as a result of errors in this publication, but it is our priority to ensure that the content is accurate. If you spot an error, please do contact us at revise4law.co.uk so we can make sure it is corrected.

Contents

Contributors

THE EDITOR

Mark Thomas is a practising barrister and has taught law for several years at both undergraduate and postgraduate levels, including the Legal Practice Course and the SQE-preparation courses. Mark has published academic textbooks in the field of criminal law and evidence, and has extensive experience in writing revision-style books for law students. He is the co-author of *Revise SQE: Criminal Law, Revise SQE: Criminal Practice* and *Revise SQE: Oral Skills for SQE2: Advocacy*. He is also the editor of *FLK1 Practice Assessments* and *FLK2 Practice Assessments*. Mark acts as MCQ adviser and reviewer for the Revise SQE series.

CHAPTER AUTHORS

James J Ball is a practising barrister on the Midland Circuit and teaches on the undergraduate and postgraduate courses, including the SQE-preparation courses, at Nottingham Law School, Nottingham Trent University. He is the co-author of *Revise SQE: Criminal Practice* and *Revise SQE: Oral Skills for SQE2: Advocacy*.

Richard Clements has taught law at a number of universities including the University of the West of England and the University of Exeter. He is the author of *Revise SQE: Constitutional and Administrative Law*.

Benjamin Jones is a senior lecturer in law at the University of South Wales. He is the author of *Revise SQE: Business Law and Practice* and *Revise SQE: Property Practice*.

Tina McKee is a senior lecturer in law at Lancaster University. She is the author of *Revise SQE: Solicitors' Accounts*.

David Sixsmith is co-series editor of the *Revise SQE* series (see below) and author of *Revise SQE: Dispute Resolution* and co-author of *Revise SQE: Written Skills for SQE2: Questions & Answers in Dispute Resolution*.

SERIES EDITORS

Dr Amy Sixsmith is associate professor in law at the University of Sunderland and a senior fellow of Advance HE.

Dr David Sixsmith is assistant professor in law at Northumbria Law School and a senior fellow of Advance HE.

Introduction to Revise SQE

Welcome to *Revise SQE*, a series of revision guides designed to help you in your preparation for, and achievement in, the Solicitors Qualifying Examination 1 (SQE1) assessment. SQE1 is designed to assess what the Solicitors Regulation Authority (SRA) refers to as 'functioning legal knowledge' (FLK); this is the legal knowledge and competencies required of a newly qualified solicitor in England and Wales. The SRA has chosen single best answer multiple-choice questions (MCQs) to test this knowledge, and *Revise SQE* is here to help.

PREPARING YOURSELF FOR SQE

The SQE is the relatively new route to qualification for aspiring solicitors, introduced in September 2021 as one of the final stages towards qualification as a solicitor. The SQE consists of two parts:

SQE1

- **Functioning legal knowledge (FLK)**
  - two x 180 MCQs
  - closed book; assessed by two sittings, over 10 hours in total

SQE2

- **Practical legal skills**
  - 16 written and oral assessments
  - assesses six practical legal skills, over 14 hours in total

In addition to the above, any candidate will have to undertake two years' qualifying work experience. More information on the SQE assessments can be found on the SRA's dedicated SQE website; this revision guide series will focus on FLK and preparation for SQE1.

It is important to note that the SQE can be perceived to be a 'harder' set of assessments than the Legal Practice Course (LPC). The reason for this, explained by the SRA, is that the LPC is designed to prepare candidates for 'day one' of their training contract; the SQE, on the other hand, is designed to prepare candidates for 'day one' of being a newly qualified solicitor. Indeed, the SRA has chosen the SQE1 assessment to be 'closed book' (ie without permitting use of any materials) on the basis that a newly qualified solicitor would know all of the information tested, without having to refer to books or other sources.

With that in mind, and a different style of assessments in place, it is understandable that many readers may feel nervous or wary of the SQE. This is especially so given that this style of assessment is likely to be different from what readers will have experienced before. In this *Introduction* and revision guide series, we hope to alleviate some of those concerns with guidance on preparing for the SQE assessment, tips on how to approach single best answer MCQs and expertly written guides to aid in your revision.

What does SQE1 entail?

SQE1 consists of two assessments, containing 180 single best answer MCQs each (360 MCQs in total). The table below breaks down what is featured in each of these assessments.

Assessment	Contents of assessment ('functioning legal knowledge')
FLK assessment 1	• Business law and practice • Dispute resolution • Contract • Tort • The legal system (the legal system of England and Wales and sources of law, constitutional and administrative law and European Union law and legal services)
FLK assessment 2	• Property practice • Wills and the administration of estates • Solicitors' accounts • Land law • Trusts • Criminal law and practice

Please be aware that in addition to the above, ethics and professional conduct will be examined pervasively across the two assessments (ie it could crop up anywhere).

Each substantive topic is allocated a percentage of the assessment paper (eg 'legal services' will form 12–16% of the FLK1 assessment) and is broken down further into 'core principles'. Candidates are advised to read the SQE1 Assessment Specification in full (available on the SQE website). We have also provided a *Revise SQE checklist* to help you in your preparation and revision for SQE1 (see below).

HOW DO I PREPARE FOR SQE1?

Given the vastly different nature of SQE1 compared to anything you may have done previously, it can be quite daunting to consider how you could possibly prepare for 360 single best answer MCQs, spanning 11 different substantive topics (especially given that it is 'closed book'). The *Revise SQE FAQ* below, however, will set you off on the right path to success.

Revise SQE FAQ

Question	Answer
1. Where do I start?	We would advise that you begin by reviewing the assessment specification for SQE1. You need to identify what subject matter can be assessed under each substantive topic. For each topic, you should honestly ask yourself whether you would be prepared to answer an MCQ on that topic in SQE1. We have helped you in this process by providing a *Revise SQE checklist* on our website (revise4law.co.uk) that allows you to read the subject matter of each topic and identify where you consider your knowledge to be at any given time. We have also helpfully cross-referenced each topic to a chapter and page of our *Revise SQE* revision guides.
2. Do I need to know legal authorities, such as case law?	In the majority of circumstances, candidates are not required to know or use legal authorities. This includes statutory provisions, case law or procedural rules. Of course, candidates will need to be aware of legal principles deriving from common law and statute. There may be occasions, however, where the assessment specification does identify a legal authority (such as *Rylands v Fletcher* in tort law). In this case, candidates will be required to know the name of that case, the principles of that case and how to apply that case to the facts of an MCQ. These circumstances are clearly highlighted in the assessment specification and candidates are advised to ensure they engage with those legal authorities in full. In each of our texts in the *Revise SQE* series, we detail clearly which authorities are required for that subject. Any authorities provided in addition are designed to assist in your revision by acting as an aide-mémoire.
3. Do I need to know the history behind a certain area of law?	While understanding the history and development of a certain area of law is beneficial, there is no requirement for you to know or prepare for any questions relating to the development of the law

Revise SQE FAQ (continued)

Question	Answer
	(eg in criminal law, candidates will not need to be aware of the development from objective to subjective recklessness). SQE1 will be testing a candidate's knowledge of the law as it stands four calendar months prior to the date of the first assessment in an assessment window. The SRA on the SQE website has helpfully provided the exact cut-off date for each assessment in the cycle; it is worth checking this when you are preparing for your assessment.
4. Do I need to be aware of academic opinion or proposed reforms to the law?	Candidates preparing for SQE1 do not need to focus on critical evaluation of the law, or proposed reforms to the law either.
5. How do I prepare for single best answer MCQs?	See our separate *Revise SQE* guide on preparing for single best answer MCQs below.

Where does *Revise SQE* come into it?

The *Revise SQE* series of revision guides is designed to aid your revision and consolidate your understanding; the series is not designed to replace your substantive learning of the SQE1 topics. We hope that this series will provide clarity as to assessment focus, useful tips for sitting SQE1 and act as a general revision aid.

There are also materials on our website to help you prepare and revise for the SQE1, such as a *Revise SQE checklist*. This *checklist* is designed to help you identify which substantive topics you feel confident about heading into the exam - see below for an example.

Revise SQE checklist

Ethics and Professional Conduct

SQE content	Corresponding chapter	***Revise SQE checklist***		
The purpose, scope and content of the SRA Principles	Chapter 1, pages 3–5	I don't know this subject and I am not ready for SQE1 ☐	I partially know this subject, but I am not ready for SQE1 ☐	I know this subject and I am ready for SQE1 ☐

Ethics and Professional Conduct (continued)

SQE content	Corresponding chapter	*Revise SQE checklist*		
The purpose, scope and content of the Code of Conduct • SRA Code of Conduct for Solicitors, RELs, RFLs and RSLs	Chapter 2, pages 27–29	I don't know this subject and I am not ready for SQE1 ☐	I partially know this subject, but I am not ready for SQE1 ☐	I know this subject and I am ready for SQE1 ☐
The purpose, scope and content of the Code of Conduct • SRA Code of Conduct for Firms in relation to Managers in authorised firms	Chapter 2, page 77	I don't know this subject and I am not ready for SQE1 ☐	I partially know this subject, but I am not ready for SQE1 ☐	I know this subject and I am ready for SQE1 ☐
The purpose, scope and content of the Code of Conduct • SRA Code of Conduct for Firms in relation to Compliance Officers	Chapter 2, pages 78–79	I don't know this subject and I am not ready for SQE1 ☐	I partially know this subject, but I am not ready for SQE1 ☐	I know this subject and I am ready for SQE1 ☐

PREPARING FOR SINGLE BEST ANSWER MCQS

As discussed above, SQE1 will be a challenging assessment for all candidates. This is partly due to the quantity of information a candidate must be aware of in two separate sittings. In addition, however, an extra complexity is added due to the nature of the assessment itself: MCQs.

The SRA has identified that MCQs are the most appropriate way to test a candidate's knowledge and understanding of fundamental legal principles. While this may be the case, it is likely that many candidates have little, if any, experience of MCQs as part of their previous study. Even if a candidate does have experience of MCQs, SQE1 will feature a special form of MCQs known as 'single best answer' questions.

What are single best answer MCQs and what do they look like?

Single best answer MCQs are a specialised form of question, used extensively in other fields such as in training medical professionals. The idea behind single best answer MCQs is that the multitude of options available to a candidate may each bear merit, sharing commonalities and correct statements of law or principle, but only one option is absolutely correct (in the sense that it is the 'best' answer). In this regard, single best answer MCQs are different from traditional MCQs.

A traditional MCQ will feature answers that are implausible in the sense that the distractors are 'obviously wrong'. Indeed, distractors in a traditional MCQ are often very dissimilar, resulting in a candidate being able to spot answers that are clearly wrong with greater ease.

In a well-constructed single best answer MCQ, on the other hand, each option should look equally attractive given their similarities and subtle differences. The skill of the candidate will be identifying which, out of the options provided, is the single best answer. This requires a much greater level of engagement with the question than a traditional MCQ would require; candidates must take the time to read the questions carefully in the exam.

How are single best answer MCQs structured?

For SQE1, single best answer MCQs will be structured as follows:

A woman is charged with battery, having thrown a rock towards another person intending to scare them. The rock hits the person in the head, causing no injury. The woman claims she never intended that the rock hit the person, but the prosecution allege that the woman was reckless as to whether the rock would hit the other person.

Which of the following is the most accurate statement regarding the test for recklessness in relation to a battery?

A. There must have been a risk that force would be applied by the rock, and that the reasonable person would have foreseen that risk and unjustifiably taken it.

B. There must have been a risk that force would be applied by the rock, and that the woman should have foreseen that risk and unjustifiably taken it.

C. There must have been a risk that force would be applied by the rock, and that the woman must have foreseen that risk and unjustifiably taken it.

D. There must have been a risk that force would be applied by the rock, and that both the woman and the reasonable person should have foreseen that risk and unjustifiably taken it.

E. There must have been a risk that force would be applied by the rock, but there is no requirement that the risk be foreseen.

The factual scenario. First, the candidate will be provided with a factual scenario that sets the scene for the question to be asked (known as the 'stem').

The lead in. Next, the candidate will be provided with the question that they must find the single best answer to.

The possible answers. Finally, the candidate will be provided with **five** possible answers. There is only one single best answer that must be chosen. The other answers, known as 'distractors', are not the 'best' answer available.

It will be beneficial to guide you through each aspect of the MCQ to further your understanding of the writing process.

The stem

The stem (ie scenario) will differ according to each MCQ and what it is seeking to test. If the MCQ is seeking simply to test a candidate's basic knowledge of the law, without application, then the stem is likely to be short. Where, however, the MCQ is seeking to have a candidate analyse a factual pattern, and apply it to the options available, the stem will be significantly longer.

In general, however, a stem should be a concise and clear introduction to the issue at hand. A well written stem should contain all material facts relevant to answering the question about to be asked (new facts should not be introduced in the lead in or the distractors). The stem should not be ambiguous or open to interpretation.

The lead in

The lead in will be a short question and can be phrased in a variety of ways. The lead in should provide the candidate with everything they need to answer the question. There should be no ambiguity or double meanings.

The length and nature of the lead in will vary dependent on the type of question being asked. These categories of MCQ are detailed in the table below.

Categories of MCQs	**Explanation and example**
'Knows' MCQs	To *recall* a specific answer (eg the author of X is Y)
'Shows How' MCQs	To *analyse* a fact pattern and *apply* (eg the application of X in this case is Y)
'Knows How' MCQs	To *know* the answer, and *show* the reason *why* (eg the purpose of X is Y because ...)

Most commonly, a lead in may be phrased as:

- Which of the following statements best describes ...?
- Which of the following statements best summarises ...?
- Which of the following best explains ...?

A lead in will not, however, be phrased as:

- Which of the following is true?
- What is the rule for X?
- Which one of the following is not correct?

The options

You will be provided with five possible answers and only one is correct (whether that be outright correct, or the single best).

The options will not ask a candidate to identify multiple options as being correct (eg 'A, C and D are correct; B and E are wrong'). Nor will the options feature an 'all of the above' option.

A well written MCQ will avoid vague language in the options. Words such as 'rarely', 'usually' etc should be avoided as they present too much ambiguity. On the other hand, absolute words such as 'only', 'always' and 'never' should equally be avoided because they are often obvious distractors (there rarely being a circumstance in English and Welsh law where the legal position is absolute without exception).

If written well, each option should be plausible (meaning that some candidates would choose it). Plausibility can come from drawing on faulty reasoning and common misconceptions. It may be the case that some options share identical wording save for one word (eg a change from 'may' to 'must'). You therefore need to pay close attention to the wording of the options.

To achieve that, all options will be of a fairly equal length to ensure that they are consistent with one another. It is often said that the correct answer is likely to be the longest; so the writers of the MCQs will have that in mind.

In addition, to ensure plausibility, each option is either likely to be a variation of the other, or each option will be entirely different to the others. MCQ drafters will often rely on the rule of 'Three and Two'. The idea behind this rule is that three options will be fairly similar to each other (eg starting with 'Yes'), whilst the remaining two answers will be equally similar to each other (eg starting with 'No'). If you know the answer is definitely 'Yes', that therefore removes the 'No' options immediately. If the MCQ has not adopted the rule of Three and Two, it is likely that you will be able to pick out the 'obvious' distractor.

Now that you know what the MCQs will look like on SQE1, let us talk about how you may go about tackling an MCQ.

How do I tackle single best answer MCQs?

No exact art exists in terms of answering single best answer MCQs; your success depends on your subject knowledge and understanding of how that subject knowledge can be applied. Despite this, there are tips and tricks that may be helpful for you to consider when confronted with a single best answer MCQ.

1. Read the question twice	2. Understand the question being asked	3. Select the answer if you know it outright	4. If not, employ a process of elimination	5. Take an educated and reasoned guess	6. Skip and come back to it later	7. Random guess

These tips and tricks are essential for preparing you to sit the SQE1 assessment. Each session will involve 90 MCQs, to be answered over 2 hours, 33 minutes. Answering 90 MCQs in that timescale allows *1 minute, 42 seconds per question,* under exam conditions. Of course, some questions will take more or less time to answer than others.

Please take a moment to think about that: on average, within 1 minute and 42 seconds you will have to:

- read the MCQ, including the various answers
- distil from that MCQ what the question is assessing
- work out which of the five possible answers is the correct (or 'single best') answer.

This will be an intensive assessment. You must ensure that you are properly prepared for it, in terms of your subject knowledge and also your mental resilience and time management. Your ability to navigate MCQs will also assist greatly.

1. Read the entire question at least twice

This sounds obvious but is so often overlooked. You are advised to read the entire question once, taking in all relevant pieces of information, understanding what the question is asking you and being aware of the options available. Once you have done that, read the entire question again and this time pay careful attention to the wording that is used.

- **In the factual scenario:** Does it use any words that stand out? Do any words used have legal bearing? What are you told and what are you not told?
- **In the lead in:** What are you being asked? Are there certain words to look out for (eg 'should', 'must', 'will', 'shall')?
- **In the answers:** What are the differences between each option? Are they substantial differences or subtle differences? Do any differences turn on a word or a phrase?

You should be prepared to give each question at least two viewings to mitigate any misunderstandings or oversights.

2. Understand the question being asked

It is important first that you understand what the question is asking of you. The SRA has identified that the FLK assessments may consist of single best answer MCQs that, for example:

- require the candidate to simply identify a correct legal principle or rule;
- require the candidate to not only identify the correct legal principle or rule, but also apply that principle or rule to the factual scenario;

- provide the candidate with the correct legal principle or rule, but require the candidate to identify how it should be properly applied and/or the outcome of that proper application.

By first identifying what the question is asking you to do, you can then understand what the creators of that question are seeking to test and how to approach the answers available. Many candidates actually find it beneficial to start with the lead in, before reading the scenario. This gives them the opportunity to understand what the scenario will likely entail. You need to decide what works best for you, so take the opportunity to try both ways.

3. Select the answer if you know it outright

You may feel as though a particular answer 'jumps out' at you, and that you are certain it is correct. It is very likely that the answer is correct. While you should be confident in your answers, do not allow your confidence (and perhaps overconfidence) to rush you into making a decision. Review all of your options one final time before you move on to the next question.

4. If you do not know the answer outright, employ a process of elimination

There may be situations in which the answer is not obvious from the outset. This may be due to the close similarities between different answers. Remember, it is the 'single best answer' that you are looking for. If you keep this in your mind, it will thereafter be easier to employ a process of elimination. Identify which answers you are sure are not correct (or not the 'best') and whittle down your options. Get rid of the distractors. Once you have only two options remaining, carefully scrutinise the wording used in both answers and look back to the question being asked. Identify what you consider to be the best answer, in light of that question. Review your answer and move on to the next question.

5. Take an educated and reasoned guess

There may be circumstances, quite commonly, in which you do not know the answer to the question. In this circumstance, you should try as hard as possible to eliminate any distractors that you are positive are incorrect and then take an educated and reasoned guess based on the options available. 'Always select C' will not work in this assessment; the correct answers will be randomly distributed amongst the MCQs as options A–E.

6. Skip and come back to it later

If time permits, you may think it appropriate to skip a question that you are unsure of and return to it before the end of the assessment. The assessment portal will highlight any questions that have not been answered, and you are also able to 'flag' questions for your review later on in the assessment (time permitting). If you do so, we would advise that you:

- make a note of what question you have skipped or click 'Flag for Review' on your screen, and
- ensure you leave sufficient time for you to go back to that question before the end of the assessment.

The same advice is applicable to any question that you have answered but for which you remain unsure.

7. Random guess

As a matter of absolute last resort, being unable even to take an educated and reasoned guess, you should simply choose an answer. There is no negative marking in the SQE1 assessments, so it is better for you to select an answer with the possibility, by sheer luck, of answering it correctly than it is to leave the answer blank and have no chance of scoring a point. The advice is simple: answer all of the questions, even if you have to guess at the end.

We hope that this brief guide will assist you in your preparation towards, and engagement with, single best answer MCQs.

GUIDED TOUR

Each chapter contains a number of features to help you revise, apply and test your knowledge.

Make sure you know Each chapter begins with an overview of the main topics covered and why you need to understand them for the purpose of the SQE1 assessments.

SQE assessment advice This identifies what you need to pay particular attention to in your revision as you work through the chapter.

What do you know already? These questions help you to assess which topics you feel confident with and which topics you may need to spend more time on (and where to find them in the chapter).

Key term Key terms are highlighted in bold where they first appear and defined in a separate box.

Exam warning This feature offers advice on where it is possible to go wrong in the assessments.

Revision tip Throughout the chapters are ideas to help you revise effectively and be best prepared for the assessment.

Summary This handy box brings together key information in an easy to revise and remember form.

Practice example These examples take a similar format to SQE-type questions and provide an opportunity to see how content might be applied to a scenario.

Procedural link Where relevant, this element shows how a concept might apply to another procedural topic in the series.

Key point checklist At the end of each chapter there is a bullet-point summary of its most important content.

Key terms and concepts These are listed at the end of each chapter to help ensure you know, or can revise, terms and concepts you will need to be familiar with for the assessments.

SQE-style questions Five SQE-style questions on the chapter topic give you an opportunity to test your knowledge.

Answers to questions Check how you did with answers to both the quick knowledge test from the start of the chapter and the SQE-style questions at the end of the chapter.

Key cases, rules, statutes and instruments These list the key sources candidates need to be familiar with for the SQE assessment.

SQE1 TABLE OF LEGAL AUTHORITIES

The SQE1 Assessment Specification states the following in respect of legal authorities and their relevance to SQE1:

> On occasion in legal practice a case name or statutory provision, for example, is the term normally used to describe a legal principle or an area of law, or a rule or procedural step (eg *Rylands v Fletcher*, CPR Part 36, Section 25 notice). In such circumstances, candidates are required to know and be able to use such case names, statutory provisions etc. In all other circumstances candidates are not required to recall specific case names, or cite statutory or regulatory authorities.

This *SQE1 table of legal authorities* identifies the legal authorities you are required to know for the purpose of FLK1 and 2 in respect of *Ethics and Professional Conduct*. Please remember that Ethics and Professional Conduct will be assessed pervasively across both SQE1 assessments. As such, you need to ensure that you have a strong working knowledge of how the SRA Principles and Code of Conduct apply in the various practice areas assessed on SQE1.

Legal authority	Corresponding *Revise SQE* chapter/pages
SRA Principles	**Chapter 1: SRA Principles**
SRA Code of Conduct	**Chapter 2: SRA Code of Conduct**

TABLE OF CASES

TABLE OF STATUTES

LAYOUT OF *REVISE SQE: ETHICS AND PROFESSIONAL CONDUCT*

The SQE Assessment Specification states that:

> Ethics and Professional Conduct will be examined pervasively across the two assessments and can be examined across all subject areas. As with the other subject areas, the questions will be based on realistic client-based problems and situations which can include

those set out in relevant SRA warning notices, such as those relating to Non-Disclosure Agreements (NDAs) and Strategic Lawsuits against Public Participation (SLAPPs).

Before we introduce you to the SRA Principles, it will be prudent to explain how this revision guide has been constructed to assist in your preparation for SQE1.

Chapters 1 and **2** provide you with a general introduction to the SRA Principles and Code of Conduct. These chapters allow you to experience the rules as stated by the SRA, with guidance, practice examples and key terms to assist you along the way. The subsequent chapters will then focus on ethics and professional conduct as it applies in the variety of practice areas assessed on SQE1; for instance **Chapter 5** covers ethics and professional conduct in criminal practice. These chapters have been ordered according to the FLK assessments in which the various subjects will be assessed (ie **Chapters 3** and **4** will cover the practice areas that comprise FLK1, whilst **Chapters 5–8** will cover the practice areas that comprise FLK2).

Many of the principles and rules discussed in this revision guide will feature in other books within the series. For example, many of the principles discussed here will be very relevant to legal services and the manner in which solicitors may conduct themselves in regulated activity (see ***Revise SQE: The Legal System and Services of England and Wales***).

It is vitally important, therefore, that you truly consider ethics and professional conduct as pervasive; always be on the look out for ethical issues arising.

1

SRA Principles

Mark Thomas

■ MAKE SURE YOU KNOW

This chapter will cover the purpose, scope and content of the Solicitors Regulation Authority (SRA) Principles. These Principles will be assessed pervasively across both Functioning Legal Knowledge Assessments (FLK) for SQE1 where candidates will be required to demonstrate their ability to act honestly and with integrity, and in accordance with the SRA Standards and Regulations.

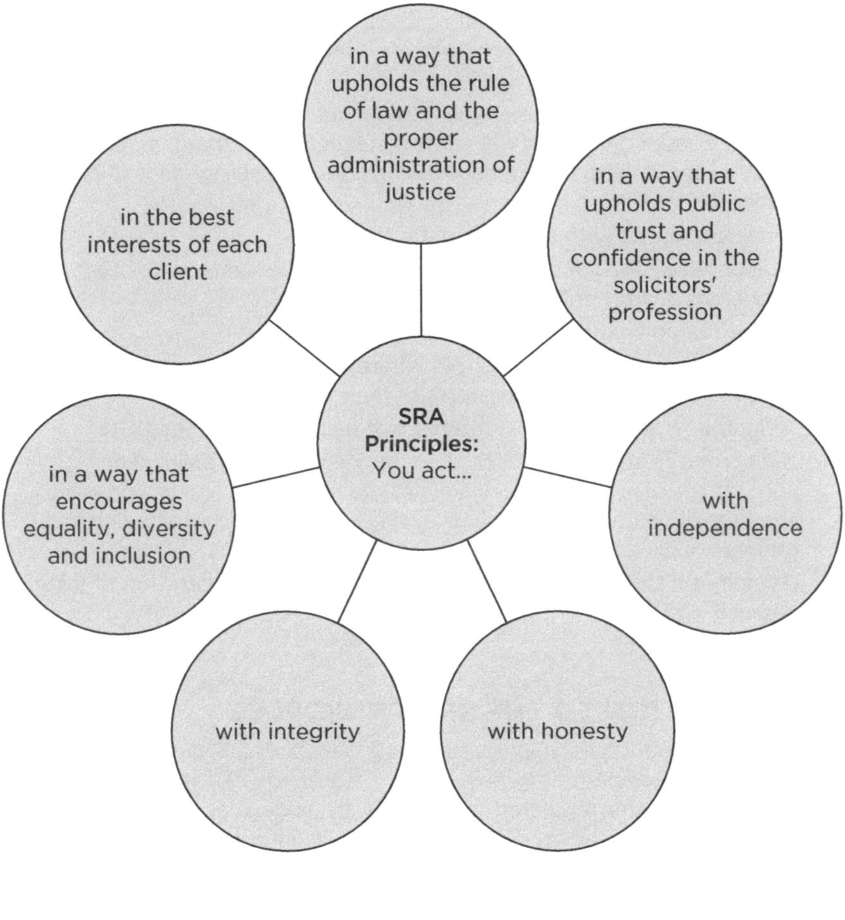

The SQE1 Assessment Specification has identified that candidates must understand the 'purpose, scope and content of the SRA Principles'. It is unlikely to be the case that candidates will need to recite or recall the exact terminology used in the Principles, nor will they need to recite or recall the paragraph numbers that equate to those Principles. The key to success in dealing with this subject matter is understanding the *application* of the Principles.

■ SQE ASSESSMENT ADVICE

As you work through this chapter, remember to pay particular attention in your revision to:

- the purpose of the SRA Principles
- the scope of those Principles and who they apply to
- the content of those Principles and their application to everyday life.

■ WHAT DO YOU KNOW ALREADY?

Have a go at these questions before reading this chapter. If you find some difficult or cannot remember the answers, make a note to look more closely at that area during your revision.

1) True or false? When assessing whether a solicitor acted dishonestly in their conduct, the SRA will apply a subjective standard, assessing whether the defendant themselves considered their conduct to be dishonest.

   [Principle 4: Act with honesty; page 11]

2) True or false? The solicitor's duty to act in the best interest of each client outweighs any other Principle and interest.

   [Introduction to the SRA Principles; pages 2–5]

3) Can you name two circumstances where a conflict may exist between the solicitor and the best interests of their client?

   [Principle 7: Act in the best interests of each client; pages 15–16]

4) Is it correct to say that a solicitor will only fail to act in a way that upholds the constitutional principle of the rule of law, and the proper administration of justice, where they have been convicted of a criminal offence?

   [Principle 1: Uphold the rule of law and proper administration of justice; pages 5–6]

INTRODUCTION TO THE SRA PRINCIPLES

The ethical conduct of a practising solicitor is detailed within the SRA Standards and Regulations, which are the standards and requirements that the SRA expects the regulated community to achieve and observe, for the benefit of the clients they serve and in the public interest.

Revision tip

To understand properly the SRA Principles and the Code of Conduct (see **Chapter 2**) you have to understand the regulatory environment in which solicitors work. You need to appreciate the workings of the SRA, its interaction with the Solicitors Disciplinary Tribunal (SDT - an independent court dealing with breaches of professional conduct), and the SRA Enforcement Strategy. In light of that, you are strongly advised to refer to ***Revise SQE: The Legal System and Services of England and Wales*** where the regulation of legal services is discussed in more detail.

The starting point for the SRA Standards and Regulations consists of the SRA Principles. The SQE1 Assessment Specification requires you to understand the 'purpose, scope and content' of the SRA Principles.

'Purpose' of the SRA Principles

To begin with, let us understand the 'purpose' of the **SRA Principles**.

Key term: SRA Principles

The SRA describes these principles as comprising 'the fundamental tenets of ethical behaviour that we expect all those that we regulate to uphold'.

'Scope' of the SRA Principles

Reference to 'those that we regulate' includes all individuals the SRA authorises to provide legal services (solicitors, registered European lawyers (RELs), and registered foreign lawyers (RFLs)), as well as authorised firms and their managers and employees. 'Employees' is a very important part of the SRA Principles. Many paralegals and legal assistants do not appreciate that these rules apply to them too.

Exam warning

What if the SRA Principles conflict? The SRA identifies that should the Principles come into conflict, those which safeguard the wider public interest (such as the rule of law, public confidence in a trustworthy solicitors' profession and a safe and effective market for regulated legal services) take precedence over an individual client's interests. A solicitor should, where relevant, inform their client of the circumstances in which their duty to the court and other professional obligations will outweigh their duty to the client.

Thinking about the above exam warning, now consider **Practice example 1.1**.

> **Practice example 1.1**
>
> Mark is a solicitor specialising in criminal law. Mark is representing David, who has been charged with burglary. David maintained his innocence to Mark up to the point of trial, providing alibi witnesses in support of his defence. At trial, David discloses that he did, in fact, commit the offence charged but would like to maintain his not guilty plea. David instructs Mark to secure an acquittal in any way possible.
>
> Can you describe how the different SRA Principles interact in this example?
>
> **Mark owes a duty to act in the best interest of his client (David). This means that Mark has a duty to attempt to secure an acquittal for David in any way possible. However, Mark must also act in a way that upholds the constitutional principle of the rule of law, and the proper administration of justice, in a way that upholds public trust and confidence in the solicitors' profession and in legal services provided by authorised persons, with independence, with honesty, and with integrity. Acting in this way will take precedence over Mark's duty to act in the best interests of David. In Chapter 5, we will learn that Mark is technically able to continue to represent David in this circumstance; however, his conduct and ability to act is severely restricted.**

To reaffirm **Practice example 1.1**, consider the following quotation from Lord Hoffmann in *Arthur JS Hall v Simons* [2002] 1 AC 615 to truly appreciate this conflict:

> Lawyers conducting litigation owe a divided loyalty. They have a duty to their clients, but they may not win by whatever means. They also owe a duty to the court and the administration of justice.

'Content' of the SRA Principles

The SRA Principles were last updated on 25 November 2019. These Principles can be located on the SRA Website, within its Standards and Regulations webpages.

There are seven Principles that all persons regulated by the SRA must comply with. The Principles are detailed below in **Table 1.1**.

Table 1.1: SRA Principles

Principle No.	Principle 'You act . . .
1	in a way that upholds the constitutional principle of the rule of law, and the proper administration of justice'
2	in a way that upholds public trust and confidence in the solicitors' profession and in legal services provided by authorised persons'
3	with independence'
4	with honesty'
5	with integrity'
6	in a way that encourages equality, diversity and inclusion'
7	in the best interests of each client'

The remainder of this chapter shall consider each Principle in turn.

Revision tip

You are not required to know the number that corresponds with a particular Principle (eg, you would not be expected to recite 'Principle 7' in SQE1), but would be required to recall that solicitors must 'act in the best interests of each client'. Despite this, it may be beneficial to memorise the corresponding Principle numbers to assist with memory recall. Certainly, this chapter will use the Principle numbers to assist with that recall.

PRINCIPLE 1: UPHOLD THE RULE OF LAW AND PROPER ADMINISTRATION OF JUSTICE

The first SRA Principle requires a solicitor to act in a way that upholds the constitutional principle of the **rule of law**.

Key term: rule of law

According to the SRA, the rule of law is 'a principle that the law is of equal application to all persons, public or private, and this is put into effect by individuals and organisations ... and through activities engaging the justice system'.

The simplest example where Principle 1 may be engaged is where a solicitor commits a criminal offence. By 'commits', we mean that the solicitor is convicted of a criminal offence. However, the SRA has made it clear in its Topic Guides for Principle 1 that Principle 1 is capable of being engaged even without a criminal conviction. In particular, the SRA identifies that '[a]ny behaviour which indicates a serious disregard for the principle that the law applies equally to all, is likely to be a breach of Principle 1'. The SRA has identified the following as examples involving a breach of the rule of law:

- Very serious, organised and premeditated offending involving terrorism, violence and/or dishonesty, showing deliberate disregard for the law.
- A sustained course of serious offending.
- Repeated convictions for the same offence.
- Involvement in or links to organised crime.
- Involvement in money laundering or the facilitation or concealment of serious or organised criminality by others.

The first SRA Principle also requires a solicitor to act in a way that upholds the **proper administration of justice**.

Key term: proper administration of justice

Whilst a solicitor owes a duty to their clients (Principle 7), they also owe a duty to the court and to the administration of justice. A solicitor must not mislead the court, must not interfere with the judicial process and must conduct themselves in such a way that they act in the interests of justice.

This requirement to uphold the administration of justice is reflected in the **overriding objective** detailed in both the Civil Procedure Rules (CPR) 1998 and the Criminal Procedure Rules (CrimPR) 2025.

Key term: overriding objective

The overriding objective details that the courts have a duty to deal with cases 'justly'. The parties to a case are required to help the court to further the overriding objective. Therefore, a failure to uphold the administration of justice would conflict with this overriding objective.

Examples of interfering with the proper administration of justice could include:

- interference with, or intimidation of, a witness (for example, attempting to force a witness to change their story or alter their evidence)
- misleading the court, or knowingly or recklessly allowing the court to be misled (for example, by allowing their client to give evidence that they know is untrue).

Use **Practice example 1.2** to apply your understanding of this Principle.

Practice example 1.2

Amy is a solicitor specialising in criminal law. Amy is representing James, who is under investigation for aggravated burglary, contrary to s 10 Theft Act 1968. Amy, aware that the police intend to search James' house, tips off James advising him as to the day and time the police intend to arrive at James' house. Amy also advises James as to how James may hide evidence from the police.

Will Amy have acted contrary to the SRA Principles here?

By impeding the lawful exercise of police powers, Amy will have acted contrary to the proper administration of justice. Amy is also likely to be liable for a criminal offence of impeding James' arrest or lawful prosecution.

PRINCIPLE 2: PUBLIC TRUST AND CONFIDENCE IN THE PROFESSION

The second SRA Principle requires a solicitor to act in a way that upholds public trust and confidence in the solicitors' profession and in legal services provided by authorised persons. You will notice immediately that the Principle distinguishes **solicitors** from **authorised persons**. Let us consider each term in turn using the definitions available in the SRA Glossary.

Key term: solicitors

A solicitor is a person who has been admitted as a solicitor of the Senior Courts of England and Wales and whose name is on the roll. This definition includes a person who practises as a solicitor whether or not the person has a current practising certificate.

Key term: authorised persons

An authorised person means any person who is authorised by the SRA or another approved regulator to carry on a legal activity.

The SRA characterises public trust and confidence as being 'at the heart of the legal system'. 'Trust and confidence' refers to (amongst other things) the integrity of the legal profession. This is an accurate reflection of the solicitor/client relationship given that clients will place their confidence in solicitors to:

- protect their interests, money, and assets
- represent their best interests, both financial and personal
- preserve information which is commercially or personally sensitive.

Without trust and confidence in the solicitors' profession, the relationship between a solicitor and a client is unworkable. A client needs to be able to trust and follow the advice of their solicitor. Otherwise, a client is likely to view advice with suspicion and is unlikely to follow legal advice best suited to their situation.

This confidence is mostly placed in legal professionals when the client is most vulnerable, for example:

- a client involved in a personal injury claim may be suffering both physical and emotional harm as a result of their injury
- a client seeking advice following the death of a family member as to the distribution of the family member's estate
- a client charged with a criminal offence may be at risk of losing their liberty.

Dishonesty, or a lack of integrity or probity by a solicitor, will fall foul of Principle 2. Even if harm is not caused to a particular individual, if a solicitor is considered as having harmed the reputation of the profession, they will breach Principle 2. Commission of a criminal offence, even if wholly unconnected with their role as a solicitor, will breach Principle 2, much like it would breach Principle 1.

In addition to dishonesty and a lack of integrity, a solicitor will also be in breach of Principle 2 where they have engaged in discriminatory conduct or behaviour involving violence or sexual harassment (see also **Principle 6**). Offensive communications, such as the making of offensive social media posts, are likely to breach Principle 2 (see the SRA's Warning Notice on *Offensive communications* (August 2017)).

Further examples of failing to uphold public trust and confidence would include:

- engaging in a high-risk, or fraudulent investment scheme
- sending offensive and derogatory emails to the opposing party's solicitor during litigation (see **Practice example 1.3**)
- sending or posting offensive content on social media (see **Practice example 1.4**).

Practice example 1.3

Mark is a solicitor with a reputation for being a cantankerous and belligerent individual to work with. During the course of litigation, Mark sends offensive emails to the opposing solicitor. Mark makes derogatory statements in his emails in an attempt to intimidate the opposing solicitor.

What do you think of Mark's conduct in this example?

Mark's conduct will be treated as a breach of the SRA's guidance in the Warning Notice on offensive communications. Whilst emails to the opposing side are likely to be robust (and perhaps even blunt), especially during litigation, the expectation is that solicitors should act professionally in conducting themselves. Mark's email is unlikely to maintain the trust the public places in solicitors and in the provision of legal services generally. Equally, Mark is unlikely to be acting in the client's best interests in conducting litigation in this fashion. This is another example of where the Principles conflict, as a client may instruct the solicitor to communicate in an offensive manner.

Exam warning

One important consideration in more recent times is the rise of Litigants in Person (LiP) or other non-legally qualified representatives. These individuals may communicate in an unprofessional manner but remember, the Code of Conduct does not apply to them! The solicitor must, however, remain professional in all communications back to the LiP.

Practice example 1.4

James is a criminal solicitor. James is quite vocal about his political views and often expresses these to anyone who will listen. One day, James sees a post on the social media platform X (formerly Twitter), which expresses a desire to hurt and injure any member of a particular political party. The post uses offensive language. Without a second thought, James shares the offensive comment.

Will the fact that James is acting in a personal capacity save him from breaching Principle 2?

James must appreciate that his duty to apply the SRA Principles, including the duty to uphold public confidence and trust, applies to his work and private life (ie both inside and outside of practice). James' sharing of the offensive post is at risk of being seen as James implicitly endorsing it. If that is the case, James will have made an offensive communication and will be in breach of Principle 2.

PRINCIPLE 3: ACT WITH INDEPENDENCE

The third SRA Principle requires a solicitor to act with **independence**.

Key term: independence

Independence refers to the independence of the solicitor and their firm. Independence is not solely related to the giving of independent advice; independence is at the heart of how the solicitor acts and conducts themselves in practice. The solicitor must act in an unbiased and objective manner without consideration for their own interests, or the interests of others.

The SRA in its Risk Outlook 2018/19 (an annual report setting out the risks and challenges faced by solicitors and law firms) explains that:

> Solicitors must put their ethical obligations first and keep their independence. This means that they must not and should not put their own, or their clients', interests above their wider professional obligations to the administration of justice, the rule of law and the

courts. Given their professional responsibilities, this means that they should be prepared to decline instructions that would conflict with their obligations.

Examples where the independence of a solicitor may be questioned include:

- where referrals are made to third parties (eg referring a client to a financial adviser and obtaining a commission or fee by making such referral) - see **Chapter 2**. This may bring into question a solicitor's independence; the solicitor must ensure that they feel free to refer clients to other providers for financial advice, and that such freedom is not restricted
- where the solicitor, acting in a case, is aware that they, or a member of their firm, may be called as a witness in the matter.

Use **Practice example 1.5** to consolidate your understanding of this Principle.

Practice example 1.5

Sheila is a solicitor, specialising in criminal law. Sheila is currently going through a great deal of financial difficulty following a messy divorce. Sheila is approached by Mark, who is charged with a string of fraud-related criminal offences. During the first interview, Mark admits that he committed the offence and offers Sheila £20,000 if she concocts a defence to explain Mark's actions. Sheila, currently feeling the pressure of mounting bills at home, accepts Mark's offer and creates a fictitious defence. To further support her finances, Sheila requests an additional £10,000 from Mark and offers to supply a false witness.

Has Sheila acted with independence?

No, of course not. Whilst Sheila may have been in a vulnerable position due to her financial circumstances, Sheila must act with independence. By allowing Mark to persuade her to create a false defence, Sheila has not acted with independence. In addition to breaching most of the SRA Principles, Sheila would also likely be liable for a criminal offence herself (eg perverting the course of justice).

Revision tip

The SRA has helpfully produced case studies on many of the Principles considered in this chapter which reflect real cases that they have investigated. Visit www.sra.org.uk and observe their Misconduct Guidance for more information. In addition, you can view decisions of the SDT. The findings of the tribunal are published on the SDT's website: www.solicitorstribunal.org.uk.

PRINCIPLE 4: ACT WITH HONESTY

The fourth SRA Principle requires a solicitor to act with **honesty**.

> **Key term: honesty**
>
> Honesty (and dishonesty) is an objective evaluation. In determining whether a solicitor's conduct is dishonest, the SRA will:
> - first, identify the state of knowledge or belief of the solicitor as to the facts at the time, and then
> - in view of their knowledge or belief at the time, assess whether their conduct was dishonest by the standards of ordinary decent people.
>
> This is the same test for dishonesty that you will see in your studies of criminal law, see ***Revise SQE: Criminal Law***.

The SRA has identified some examples of behaviour that may be considered dishonest, including:
- lying to, or misleading someone, such as telling a client that their case is going well when it has failed
- helping other people to act improperly, such as by giving credibility to a dubious or suspicious investment scheme run by others
- misleading a court, tribunal or a regulator (see **Duty to not mislead** in **Chapter 2**).

An alternative of recklessness

It is often the case that, where a solicitor is alleged to have failed to act with honesty, an alternative allegation of recklessness is made. Specifically, it will be alleged that if the solicitor was not dishonest in their particular behaviour, they were reckless.

The test for recklessness is the same as that in the criminal law, namely:

> A person acts recklessly ... with respect to –
>
> (i) a circumstance when he is aware of a risk that it exists or will exist;
>
> (ii) a result when he is aware of a risk that it will occur;
>
> and it is, in the circumstances known to him, unreasonable to take the risk. (per Lord Bingham in *R v G* [2003] UKHL 50, and as adopted in the context of regulatory proceedings by *Brett v SRA* [2014] EWHC 2974 (Admin))

Where a solicitor is found to have acted recklessly (eg recklessly misleading the court), they will not be dishonest, but will be found to have acted without integrity (see Principle 5 below). They will also likely be in breach of Principles 1 and 2.

PRINCIPLE 5: ACT WITH INTEGRITY

The fifth SRA Principle requires a solicitor to act with **integrity**.

Key term: integrity

While it is not possible to formulate an all-purpose, comprehensive definition of integrity, Jackson LJ would explain that (in *Wingate v SRA; SRA v Malins* [2018] EWCA Civ 366):

> [T]he term 'integrity' is a useful shorthand to express the higher standards which society expects from professional persons and which the professions expect from their own members. ...
>
> The underlying rationale is that the professions have a privileged and trusted role in society. In return they are required to live up to their own professional standards. ...
>
> Integrity connotes adherence to the ethical standards of one's own profession. That involves more than mere honesty. To take one example, a solicitor conducting negotiations or a barrister making submissions to a judge or arbitrator will take particular care not to mislead. Such a professional person is expected to be even more scrupulous about accuracy than a member of the general public in daily discourse. The duty to act with integrity applies not only to what professional persons say, but also to what they do.

There is a natural overlap with Principles 4 and 5 in that an individual who fails to act honestly will also likely fail to act with integrity. However, 'integrity' is considered as being a broader term than dishonesty, meaning that it is possible to behave without integrity without necessarily being dishonest (see **Practice example 1.6**). It is for this reason that Principle 5 is the most common ground on which a solicitor is said to be in breach of the SRA Principles.

Revision tip

To truly understand Principle 5, it may be easier for you to think about 'acting without morals' as opposed to 'acting without integrity'. This should make it easier to understand what a solicitor's obligations are.

Practice example 1.6

Ben is a solicitor working in a law firm. Ben recently authorised a number of payments from a client account. It is later discovered that these payments were improper and should not have been authorised. Ben did not enquire as to the reasons for the payments and transfer out of the client account, nor did he show any interest in what he was instructed to authorise.

What is your view on Ben's ethical position?

Ben has acted without integrity on the basis that he has not shown any steady adherence to any kind of ethical code. He shows a lack of care about what is required by the rules governing his profession. Whilst Ben will have acted without integrity in this case, given that he was unaware of the unauthorised nature of the transactions and payments, Ben may not be considered as being dishonest.

In **Chapter 2**, we shall discuss a solicitor's duty in respect of undertakings (ie a solicitor's enforceable promise to do something). In line with Principle 5, should a solicitor give an undertaking that they will do something, the individual to whom the undertaking was given should be able to rely on it, and on the solicitor who gave it. To fail to perform one's undertakings could be viewed as acting without integrity.

The SRA in its Guidance, *Acting with integrity* (2022), has identified a non-exhaustive list as to the types of cases where the SRA is likely to take disciplinary action for lack of integrity (see **Practice example 1.7** for a further integrity example):

- where there has been a wilful or reckless disregard of standards, rules, legal requirements, and obligations or ethics, including an indifference to what the applicable provisions are or to the impacts or consequences of a breach
- where the regulated firm or individual has taken unfair advantage of clients or third parties or allowed others to do so
- where the regulated firm or individual has knowingly or recklessly caused harm or distress to another
- where clients or third parties have been misled or allowed to be misled (except where this is a result of simple error that the regulated firm or individual has corrected as soon as they became aware of it).

Practice example 1.7

Tina is a sole practitioner specialising in chancery law. Tina is approached by David, an elderly man, to draft his will. Tina, aware that David has no knowledge of how much will drafting typically costs, charges him over £1,000 more than she would normally charge for her services.

Has Tina acted in accordance with the SRA Principles?

Tina will be treated as having breached Principle 5 in this instance. By overcharging, Tina will not be acting with integrity or honesty. In addition, Tina will have breached a number of other Principles through her conduct.

PRINCIPLE 6: ACT IN A WAY THAT ENCOURAGES EQUALITY, DIVERSITY AND INCLUSION

The sixth SRA Principle requires a solicitor act in a way that encourages **equality, diversity and inclusion**. There is an evident overlap between this Principle and Principle 2 (in that a lack of respect for equality may also undermine public trust and confidence in the profession).

Key term: equality, diversity and inclusion

These three terms have distinct meanings, according to the SRA:

- Equality is about making sure there is a level playing field and people are treated fairly.
- Diversity is about encouraging and valuing people with a broad range of different backgrounds, knowledge, skills and experiences.
- Inclusion is about accepting people for who they are and encouraging everyone to participate and contribute.

Indeed, this Principle is reflected in the SRA Code of Conduct (see **Chapter 2**), Para 1.1:

> You do not unfairly discriminate by allowing your personal views to affect your professional relationships and the way in which you provide your services.

A solicitor must comply with the law, which is laid down in the Equality Act (EA) 2010. For a full discussion of the Equality Act and its relevance to a solicitor, see ***Revise SQE: The Legal System and Services of England and Wales***. See also **Practice example 1.8**.

This does not mean that a solicitor cannot refuse to accept instructions from a client. Solicitors can choose to refuse instructions, but this must not be on the grounds of any of the protected characteristics in the EA 2010. Equally, this also means that a solicitor can cease acting on behalf of a client in certain circumstances, but this cannot be on the grounds of any of the protected characteristics in the EA 2010.

Practice example 1.8

Mark is a conveyancing solicitor who has been instructed to purchase new premises for a large family. The large family is of a non-white background and Mark has deliberately chosen to delay the process and act in a burdensome manner. Email communications between Mark and a co-worker show Mark making reference to the racial origins of the family and citing them as 'no doubt illegal immigrants'.

What do you think of Mark's conduct here?

Mark has acted in a way that does not encourage equality, diversity or inclusion. Mark's conduct is discriminatory, and along with his inappropriately held views, he has acted in a way that is not in the best interests of the client. Furthermore, Mark has acted in a manner which will fail to uphold public trust and confidence in solicitors and the legal profession.

PRINCIPLE 7: ACT IN THE BEST INTERESTS OF EACH CLIENT

The final SRA Principle requires solicitors to act in the **best interests** of each **client**.

Key term: best interests

The best interests of the client require a solicitor to act in a manner which furthers the interests of each client and does not put the client's interests in conflict, or at significant risk of conflict with either the solicitor's own interest, or those of another client.

Key term: client

A client means the person for whom a solicitor acts and may include prospective and former clients.

Principle 7 is reflected in Paras 6.1–6.2 of the Code of Conduct, which require the solicitor not to act if there is a conflict of interest, or significant risk of such (see **Chapter 2, page 53**). A conflict of interest may arise:

- between the interests of the solicitor, and of the client (known as an 'own interest conflict'), and
- between two or more clients, or a current client and a former client (known as a 'conflict of interest' – thus why you will see Principle 7 refers to the best interests of *each* client).

Use **Practice example 1.9** to consolidate your understanding of this Principle.

Practice example 1.9

James is a solicitor specialising in disputes over land. James is approached by Mark in respect of a boundary dispute that he has with Ben. Mark has instructed James to act on his behalf in respect of the dispute. Several weeks later, James is also approached by Ben to act on his behalf in respect of the same dispute.

Can James act for both Mark and Ben?

No, James is not capable of acting on behalf of both Mark and Ben. Mark and Ben are in direct conflict (ie they both wish to win the boundary dispute; if one wins, the other will inevitably lose). Suppose that Mark tells James something that could be detrimental to Ben's case. James would be conflicted in regards to using it against Ben because he would be acting for Ben at the same time. James must act in the best interests of each client; James would not be able to act in either Mark or Ben's best interests if he also acted for the opposing party. James may continue to act for Mark, but must not act for Ben.

Practice example 1.9 is a simple demonstration of the duty to act in the best interests of a client. In addition, the best interests of a client will also require a solicitor to:

- observe their duty of confidentiality to the client
- consider whether they have the appropriate expertise to deal with the issues presented by the client
- consider whether they have the capacity to deal with the client's case with regard to their current workload
- avoid secret or unauthorised profits that might put their interests in conflict with the client's.

Revision tip

Application and adherence to the SRA Principles is largely common sense. If your conduct or actions feel inappropriate, or there is any doubt as to whether your conduct is proper in the circumstances, you should apply common sense and good judgement. If it feels wrong, it probably is wrong. If in any doubt, a practising solicitor should contact the SRA's Professional Ethics helpline. Whilst the helpline may caveat their advice, a solicitor can request a written decision.

PROFESSIONAL CONDUCT CONCERNS

Throughout this book, we shall consider examples of both good and poor professional practice. It is essential that you engage fully with these examples to assist you in applying your ethical obligations to real-life examples.

A failure to engage fully with the SRA Principles and SRA Code of Conduct can lead to wide-reaching implications. The conduct of lawyers in the now infamous Post Office Horizon scandal has been heavily criticised for failing to comply with the SRA Standards and Regulations.

The Post Office Horizon scandal has increased public scrutiny of the conduct of lawyers and is a stark reminder of the importance of acting in accordance with the SRA Principles and Code of Conduct.

As you consider the examples of poor conduct throughout this text, consider the underlying reasons or causes for such poor conduct. Examples may include:

- A lack of understanding as to the importance of what upholding professional ethics means in practice.
- A lack of understanding as to how to prioritise different principles and duties when they come into conflict (eg duties to the client, duties to act with independence, duties to the court etc).
- An overemphasis on the duty to act in the best interests of the client to the detriment of other professional ethical duties.

These are just some examples of why solicitors have been known to make poor ethical choices.

Realistic client-based problems and situations

The SQE assessment specification states that candidates must be prepared for a question that is based on 'realistic client-based problems and situations'. Throughout this text, we seek to demonstrate common scenarios and situations that may arise in practice and how best to deal with them.

Several prominent examples will be used in this text to demonstrate how the behaviours of a solicitor can undermine the public's confidence in the system, including the misuse of non-disclosure agreements (NDAs) and Strategic Lawsuits against Public Participation (SLAPPs).

Revision tip

NDAs and SLAPPs are *specifically* referenced by the SRA in the SQE1 Assessment Specification. You are highly advised to review these topics in detail and consider their application in practice. We shall approach these topics where relevant as we proceed through the book.

Materials to support you

In addition to this text, you are strongly advised to make use of all of the guidance documents produced by the SRA. Such guidance extends from issues relating to accounts and finance, to misconduct and money laundering.

The SQE1 Assessment Specification makes explicit reference to the 'SRA warning notices'. You are strongly advised to read all of the warning notices published on the SRA website in preparation for the SQE assessments.

KEY POINT CHECKLIST

This chapter has covered the following key knowledge points. You can use these to structure your revision, ensuring you recall the key details for each point, as covered in this chapter.

- The SRA Principles describe the fundamental tenets of ethical behaviour that the SRA expects all those it regulates to uphold.
- The SRA Principles apply to all individuals the SRA authorises to provide legal services (solicitors, RELs, and RFLs), as well as authorised firms and their managers and employees.
- According to the seven SRA Principles, a solicitor must act:
  - in a way that upholds the constitutional principle of the rule of law, and the proper administration of justice
  - in a way that upholds public trust and confidence in the solicitors' profession and in legal services provided by authorised persons
  - with independence
  - with honesty
  - with integrity
  - in a way that encourages equality, diversity, and inclusion
  - in the best interests of each client.
- Should the Principles conflict, those which safeguard the wider public interest take precedence over an individual client's interests.
- The SRA has produced guidance documents and warning notices for all legal professionals to assist them in upholding the Principles and the Code of Conduct.

KEY TERMS AND CONCEPTS

- SRA Principles (**page 3**)
- rule of law (**page 5**)
- proper administration of justice (**page 6**)
- overriding objective (**page 6**)
- solicitors (**page 7**)
- authorised persons (**page 7**)
- independence (**page 9**)
- honesty (**page 11**)
- integrity (**page 12**)
- equality, diversity and inclusion (**page 14**)
- best interests (**page 15**)
- client (**page 15**)

SQE1-STYLE QUESTIONS

QUESTION 1

A solicitor works in a firm, specialising in wills and probate. The solicitor is recently qualified and has little experience in practice. The solicitor is instructed by a senior partner to send drafted wills to clients, requesting their signature. When the solicitor asks about who will witness the signatures, the senior partner informs him that the solicitor and the senior partner can sign the will as witnesses when the will is returned to the firm. The senior partner identifies this as normal practice, which is affirmed by other solicitors within the firm. The solicitor does not consider his own conduct to be dishonest.

Which of the following best describes the ethical position of the solicitor?

A. The solicitor is likely to have acted without integrity in his conduct. As a result, the solicitor is treated as having also acted dishonestly according to the standards of ordinary decent people.

B. The solicitor is likely to have acted without integrity in his conduct. However, it is likely that the solicitor will be treated as having acted honestly according to the standards of ordinary decent people.

C. The solicitor is likely to have acted without integrity in his conduct. In addition, it is likely that the solicitor will be treated as having acted dishonestly according to the standards of ordinary decent people.

D. The solicitor is likely to have acted with integrity in his conduct. However, it is likely that the solicitor will be treated as having acted dishonestly according to the standards of ordinary decent people.

E. The solicitor is likely to have acted with integrity in his conduct. In addition, it is likely that the solicitor will be treated as having acted honestly according to the standards of ordinary of decent people.

QUESTION 2

A solicitor is the sole director of a company. The solicitor is on the roll but does not hold a practising certificate. Through the company, the solicitor engages in a fraudulent scheme which secures her over £20 million.

Which of the following best describes whether the solicitor has acted contrary to the SRA Principles?

A. The solicitor is not subject to the SRA Principles because she does not hold a practising certificate.

B. The solicitor has failed to act in a way that upholds public trust and confidence in companies, and the directors who work in those companies.

C. The solicitor is not subject to the SRA Principles because she was not acting in the role as a solicitor.

D. The solicitor has failed to act in a way that upholds public trust and confidence in the solicitors' profession and in legal services provided by authorised persons.

E. The solicitor has acted in a way that upholds public trust and confidence in the solicitors' profession and in legal services provided by authorised persons as her conduct was not to do with her role as a solicitor.

QUESTION 3

A solicitor is appearing in the magistrates' court defending their client, who is charged with theft, contrary to s 1 Theft Act 1968. The solicitor calls a witness to give evidence in support of their client in the knowledge that such evidence is untrue. The solicitor claims that they were acting in the best interests of their client, which was to seek an acquittal. The solicitor also claims that they were intimidated by the client. The client is convicted.

Has the solicitor acted in accordance with the SRA Principles?

A. No, the solicitor has failed to act in a way that upholds the constitutional principle of the rule of law, and the proper administration of justice.

B. Yes, the solicitor cannot be said to have acted contrary to the SRA Principles given that the client was nonetheless convicted of the offence.

C. No, the solicitor has failed to act in the best interests of his client given that the client has been convicted of the offence.

D. Yes, the solicitor has acted in the best interests of their client, which outweighs all other interests.

E. Yes, the solicitor cannot be said to have acted contrary to the SRA Principles where they have been intimidated or pressured to act in a certain way.

QUESTION 4

A solicitor has been approached by a privately funded client seeking representation in a highly contested contract dispute. The case is likely to attract a significant fee for the solicitor and his firm. The solicitor is a contract law specialist; however, he currently has a full workload and lacks the capacity to take on any more work at this time. The client has advised that if the solicitor cannot act for them, then the client will approach a different firm.

What is the best advice that can be given to the solicitor?

A. The solicitor should act for the client because it would be contrary to his firm's interests to lose a high fee-paying client.

B. The solicitor should act for the client but should seek to delay the client's case so as to allow him to complete his current workload before dealing with the new client's case.

C. The solicitor should decline to act for the client unless he can secure written consent from them that they accept he has a high workload which may limit his time spent on the client's case.
D. The solicitor should act for the client and do his best to balance the workload.
E. The solicitor should decline to act for the client because he does not have the capacity to take on any more work.

QUESTION 5

A solicitor owns a substantial number of shares in a private limited company. The solicitor has been approached by a client seeking to sue that company for negligence under the Consumer Protection Act 1987. Should the client succeed, the company is likely to suffer a great financial loss and suffer poor publicity. The client's case has merits but is weak in many regards.

Which of the following is the best advice to give to the solicitor in line with the SRA Principles?

A. The solicitor should act for the client as the solicitor can be trusted to act independently.
B. The solicitor should act for the client because he has a duty to act in his client's best interests, and not his own interests.
C. The solicitor should not act for the client as to do so would compromise his independence.
D. The solicitor should act for the client because the case is weak and the client is likely to lose regardless of the independence of the solicitor.
E. The solicitor should not act for the client as to do so would compromise his duty as a shareholder to the company.

ANSWERS TO QUESTIONS

Answers to 'What do you know already?' questions at the start of the chapter

1) False. The SRA will apply an objective test to determine whether a solicitor has acted dishonestly. The SRA will first ascertain the state of knowledge and beliefs of the solicitor, before then questioning whether, based on that state of knowledge, the solicitor was dishonest by the standards of ordinary decent people.
2) False. Whilst the solicitor owes a duty to act in the best interests of each client, this interest does not outweigh other Principles or interests. In fact, where Principles conflict, the Principles that safeguard the wider public interest should take precedence over the individual interests of a client.

3) A solicitor's duty to act in the best interests of each client may be hindered where the solicitor's own interests conflict with that of the client (known as an 'own interest conflict') or where the interests of another client conflict with the first client (known as a 'conflict of interest').
4) No, whilst criminal convictions will most certainly breach this Principle, the SRA has identified that any behaviour which indicates a serious disregard for the principle that the law applies equally to all, is likely to be a breach of Principle 1.

Answers to end-of-chapter SQE1-style questions

Question 1:

The correct answer was B. Remember from your study of wills and the administration of estates that the execution of a will must be witnessed or acknowledged at the time that the will is signed by the testator, and that the witnesses must sign the will in the presence of the testator. To sign the will without the testator being present would be to act contrary to the law. As a result, option B represents the most likely outcome should the SRA pursue a disciplinary action. Given the solicitor's belief at the time, his conduct is unlikely to be considered as being dishonest by the standards of ordinary decent people. However, given the reckless disregard for the law stated above, which he would be expected to know and apply, the solicitor is likely to be treated as having acted without integrity by blindly following the advice of the senior partner. Option A is wrong because it presupposes that a finding that the solicitor acted with a lack of integrity automatically means they are dishonest. Whilst there is a large degree of overlap, it is possible for an individual to be acting without integrity but not be dishonest. Option C is wrong on the basis that whilst the solicitor is likely to have acted without integrity, his state of knowledge and belief at the time would likely render his conduct honest according to the standards of ordinary decent people. Option D is wrong because the solicitor is unlikely to be dishonest in his conduct. Option E is wrong because it is unlikely the solicitor will be treated as having acted with integrity by recklessly disregarding the law.

Question 2:

The correct answer was D. The solicitor will have acted contrary to Principle 2: *You act in a way that upholds public trust and confidence in the solicitors' profession and in legal services provided by authorised persons.* Her position as a solicitor would likely have supplied or instilled respectability and trust in the scheme and thus she has acted contrary to that Principle even though she was not acting in the role of a solicitor (thus option E is wrong). Option A is wrong because the solicitor is subject to the SRA Principles despite not holding a practising certificate. Option B is incorrect because the focus of the SRA Principles is on her role as a solicitor, not her role as a director. Option C is wrong because the SRA Principles apply to conduct, either inside or outside of practice, which would diminish the public's trust if they knew it was done by a solicitor.

Question 3:

The correct answer was A. A solicitor is first and foremost an officer of the court. The preamble to the SRA Principles is clear that should the Principles come into conflict, those which safeguard the wider public interest (such as the rule of law, and public confidence in a trustworthy solicitors' profession and a safe and effective market for regulated legal services) take precedence over an individual client's interests (therefore option D is wrong). The conviction or acquittal of the client does not affect the solicitor's compliance, or lack thereof, with the SRA Principles (options B and C are therefore incorrect). Option E is wrong because the solicitor has chosen to act in a manner which is contrary to the rule of law and proper administration of justice; their fear of the client does not affect this.

Question 4:

The correct answer was E. The solicitor has a duty to act in the best interests of the client. If the solicitor lacks the capacity to take on the client's case, it would be contrary to the client's interests if he tried to (thus option D is wrong). Option A is wrong because the solicitor must act in the best interests of the client, and not of himself or his firm. Option B is wrong because it would not be in the best interests for the client's case to be delayed, and the solicitor is unlikely to act independently and with integrity should he attempt to delay a client's case for his own financial gain. Option C is wrong because the solicitor should not act for the client due to his high workload, and seeking such consent would be inappropriate and would put his own interest above his client.

Question 5:

The correct answer was C. The solicitor must act with independence. This means that he must act in an unbiased and objective manner without consideration for his own interests, or the interests of others. Should the solicitor accept these instructions, it is questionable whether he would be able to maintain his independence. Option A is wrong because the best advice is that the solicitor must act in the best interests of the client and with independence; it is inappropriate to accept instructions merely on the basis that we should trust people to act independently. If the risk is present, the risk should be avoided. Whilst option B is technically correct, it is misleadingly used here because the solicitor would not be acting in the client's best interests if the solicitor chose to act for the client. Option D is wrong because the relative strength or weakness of a client's case does not alter the fact that the solicitor may lack independence. In fact, if the case is weaker, the solicitor may find it easier to act in a biased manner. Option E is incorrect as the solicitor's duty to the company is not a relevant consideration.

KEY CASES, RULES, STATUTES AND INSTRUMENTS

The SQE1 Assessment Specification has identified that candidates are required to understand the purpose, scope and content of the SRA Principles. Make sure that you understand the nature of each Principle and its application to practice.

The SQE1 Assessment Specification does not require you to know any case names, or statutory materials, for the topic of the SRA Principles.

2

SRA Code of Conduct

Mark Thomas

■ MAKE SURE YOU KNOW

This chapter will cover the purpose, scope and content of the Solicitors Regulation Authority (SRA) Code of Conduct for Solicitors, registered European lawyers (RELs), registered foreign lawyers (RFLs) and registered Swiss lawyers (RSLs), and the SRA Code of Conduct for Firms. The Code of Conduct will be assessed pervasively across both Functioning Legal Knowledge Assessments for SQE1 where candidates will be required to demonstrate their ability to act honestly and with integrity, and in accordance with the SRA Standards and Regulations.

The SQE1 Assessment Specification has identified that candidates must understand:

- SRA Code of Conduct for Solicitors, RELs, RFLs and RSLs (more commonly known as the 'SRA Code of Conduct for Solicitors')
- SRA Code of Conduct for Firms in relation to:
  - Managers in authorised firms
  - Compliance Officers.

Together, these are referred to as the 'Code of Conduct' or simply 'the Code'. The majority of this chapter will deal with the Code of Conduct for Solicitors. Unless otherwise stated, paragraph references throughout this guide to 'the Code' will be to the Code for Solicitors. The SRA Accounts Rules do not form part of the Code of Conduct; please consult ***Revise SQE: Solicitors' Accounts*** and **Chapter 8** of this guide for a full account of a solicitor's ethical and professional obligations when they receive or deal with client money. Lastly, please ensure you revisit ***Revise SQE: The Legal System and Services of England and Wales*** for a full discussion on overriding legal obligations (which includes discussion on equality, money laundering, and suspicious activity reports).

■ SQE ASSESSMENT ADVICE

As you work through this chapter, remember to pay particular attention in your revision to:

- the purpose of the SRA Code of Conduct
- the scope of that Code and its application to solicitors and firms
- the content of the Code and how the Code applies in everyday practice.

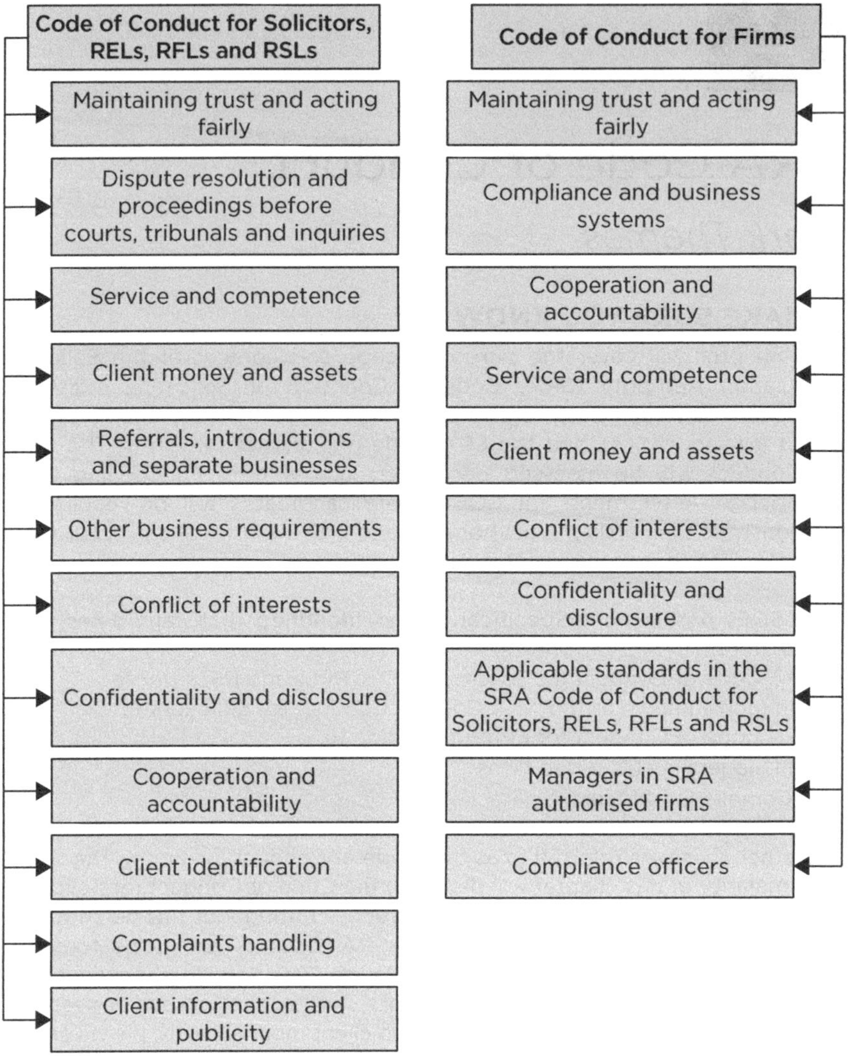

■ WHAT DO YOU KNOW ALREADY?

Have a go at these questions before reading this chapter. If you find some difficult or cannot remember the answers, make a note to look more closely at that area during your revision.

1) True or false? Mark is a newly qualified solicitor. As a result, the Code of Conduct does not expect the same standard of competence from Mark in comparison with James, who has over 15 years of experience.

   [Introduction to the Code of Conduct; page 27]

2) Fill in the blank: A solicitor must notify the SRA automatically should a particular event occur. There are four events listed in the Code of Conduct, these are ____________.

   [Para 7: Cooperation and accountability; page 61]

3) True or false? The solicitor's duty of confidentiality ceases when the client dies.

   [Paras 6.3–6.5: Confidentiality and disclosure; page 57]

4) In what circumstance may a solicitor make unsolicited approaches to members of the public in respect of the services they offer?

   [Paras 8.6–8.11: Client information and publicity; page 70]

INTRODUCTION TO THE CODE OF CONDUCT

In addition to the SRA Principles (considered in **Chapter 1**), the Code of Conduct for Solicitors, and the Code of Conduct for Firms, will be assessed pervasively on SQE1. In this chapter, we shall focus our attention on the fundamental obligations and duties owed by a solicitor, and by a firm, in the services they provide.

Revision tip

The applicable Code of Conduct was made by the SRA Board on 30 May 2018, updated on 11 April 2025, and is available on www.sra.org.uk. Previous iterations of the Code may be beneficial for interpretation and guidance but should not be relied upon as part of your engagement with the ethics and professional conduct expected of a solicitor. You are strongly advised to visit the SRA website to view the Code and its accompanying guides and glossary in full.

The SQE1 Assessment Specification requires you to understand the 'purpose, scope and content' of the Code of Conduct.

'Purpose' of the Code of Conduct

To begin with, let us understand the 'purpose' of the **Code of Conduct**.

Key term: Code of Conduct

The SRA explains that the purpose of the Code of Conduct is to describe standards of professionalism that the SRA and the public expect of individuals (solicitors, RELs, RFLs and RSLs) authorised by the SRA to provide legal services.

'Scope' of the Code of Conduct

The SRA describes that the Code of Conduct applies to conduct and behaviour relating to a solicitor's practice, and comprises a framework for ethical and competent practice that applies irrespective of the solicitor's role or the environment or organisation in which they work. See **Practice example 2.1** for a discussion as to the responsibilities involved in complying with the Code.

Practice example 2.1

James is a newly qualified solicitor. In one of James' first cases, James identifies a potential conflict of interest. James is unsure how to proceed and is unsure whose responsibility it is to ensure compliance with the SRA Code of Conduct.

Whose responsibility is it to ensure compliance with the code?

James must be advised that despite his newly qualified status, he is personally accountable for compliance with this Code - and the other regulatory requirements that apply to him. James must always be prepared to justify his decisions and actions. He must exercise his judgement in applying the Code to the situations he is in and deciding on a course of action, bearing in mind his role and responsibilities, area(s) of practice and the nature of his clients. On a practical level, every time a solicitor feels that a Code of Conduct issue has arisen or may arise, they should keep full and frank attendance notes on what happened, what they understood the Code to be and why they took a particular step.

Should a solicitor breach the Code of Conduct, the SRA may take action against them. The SRA's **Enforcement Strategy** underpins this regulatory framework and compliance with it.

Key term: Enforcement Strategy

Published in 2019, and updated in 2025, the SRA Enforcement Strategy outlines the SRA's approach to taking regulatory action in the public interest. The importance of the SRA Enforcement Strategy cannot be understated. As you will see when we observe Para 7 of the Code of Conduct (see **page 61**), the term 'serious breach' is referred to. The Enforcement Strategy, amongst other things, sets out the factors that will be taken into account when assessing seriousness. The Strategy also sets out when reports should be made, the application of the SRA Principles to private life, when enforcement action will be taken and the sanctions and controls exercisable by the SRA and the Solicitors Disciplinary Tribunal (SDT).

'Content' of the Code of Conduct

The Code of Conduct comprises two Codes:

- Code of Conduct for Solicitors, RELs, RFLs and RSLs (the 'Code of Conduct for Solicitors')
- Code of Conduct for Firms.

As you will see from the **overview figure**, these Codes are identical in many regards. Each Code is broken down into numbered paragraphs, each corresponding to a fundamental duty owed by the solicitor or firm (eg 'maintaining trust and acting fairly'). The remainder of this chapter will deal with the Code of Conduct: the next sections focus on the Code of Conduct for Solicitors, RELs, RFLs and RSLs, and the last section focuses on the Code of Conduct for Firms.

CODE OF CONDUCT FOR SOLICITORS, RELs, RFLs AND RSLs

The Code of Conduct for Solicitors, RELs, RFLs and RSLs is structured into eight paragraphs, each reflecting a key aspect of a solicitor's role. We shall consider each paragraph in turn.

Revision tip

SQE1 will assess ethics and professional conduct pervasively. This means that an ethical or professional conduct issue will be assessed within a particular practice area. This chapter focuses on the general principles and application of the SRA Code of Conduct. For specific examples of how the Code applies in different areas of practice, eg criminal law, please see the subsequent chapters of this guide.

The SQE Assessment Specification has identified that you are required to understand the Code of Conduct as it applies to 'realistic client-based problems and situations'. Throughout this chapter and the remainder of the text, we seek to present you with those realistic scenarios and how to deal with them. Some issues, such as the use of non-disclosure agreements (NDAs) and Strategic Lawsuits against Public Participation (SLAPPs), will be dealt with across multiple sections of this chapter to reflect the broad remit of your ethical duties and obligations.

PARA 1: MAINTAINING TRUST AND ACTING FAIRLY

Under this first paragraph, a solicitor must maintain trust and act fairly (which neatly summarises the SRA Principles into one clear heading). There are a number of aspects relating to this obligation; we shall deal with these in turn.

Unfair discrimination

Under this heading, a solicitor must not unfairly discriminate by allowing their personal views to affect their professional relationships and the way in which they provide their services (Para 1.1). This means that, for example:

- Whilst a solicitor does not have to accept initial instructions from a client, a solicitor *must not* refuse initial instructions based on discriminatory reasons (eg based on race, sex, religion or sexual orientation).
- Whilst a solicitor may cease to act for the client in some circumstances (eg where the **retainer** permits such cessation if the client's case is unwinnable), a solicitor must not cease to act on discriminatory grounds.
- When a solicitor is proposing to instruct counsel, they must not discriminate on the choice of advocate. This may be a particular issue with a client who requests a specific gendered barrister, or requests that the solicitor avoid a barrister of a particular race. In this case, the solicitor should discuss the request with the client and ask them to change their instructions. If the client refuses, the solicitor may need to cease to act.

Key term: retainer

A retainer simply refers to the contract that exists between a solicitor and the client. The retainer should state clearly the terms of the agreement, including what work the solicitor has agreed to undertake and the duties of the solicitor during the retainer. The retainer is governed by general contract law (as with any other contract), though a solicitor is additionally bound by their professional and ethical obligations.

Abuse of position

Under Para 1.2, a solicitor must not abuse their position by taking unfair advantage of clients or others. This obligation is fundamental to a number of the SRA Principles including Principle 2 (acting in a way that upholds public trust and confidence), Principle 4 (acting with honesty) and Principle 5 (acting with integrity). A solicitor must not abuse their position of trust and confidence, therefore. For example, a solicitor would be in breach of Para 1.2 if they presented a bill to a client for work that had not yet been carried out.

Additionally, whilst a solicitor owes a divided loyalty between their client and the court, there are also circumstances where a solicitor owes a duty to a third party (ie someone other than the client and court). As seen above, Para 1.2 particularly provides that a solicitor must not abuse their position by taking unfair advantage of clients *or others*. In many cases, the opposing party may be a **litigant in person**, represented by a McKenzie Friend (an individual who is not legally qualified but assists someone in court), or particularly vulnerable (due to age, for example).

Key term: litigant in person

A litigant in person is another term for a party engaged in litigation who does not have legal representation. The party could be an individual, a company or other organisation.

In these circumstances, a solicitor must finely balance their duty to their client to properly conduct their case with the duty to not take unfair advantage over others. This does not mean that the solicitor must legally advise their client's opponent, as that would be acting against Principle 7, but the solicitor should not act in a way to gain an unfair advantage. The SRA gives examples such as overly legalistic letters to unrepresented opponents and making threats of litigation that have no basis in law. We shall now consider two specific examples where an abuse of position may arise, namely non-disclosure agreements (NDAs) and Strategic Lawsuits against Public Participation (SLAPPs).

Non-disclosure agreements (NDAs)

The first point of concern is the use (and potential misuse) of **non-disclosure agreements**.

Key term: Non-disclosure agreements

Non-disclosure agreements (NDAs) are contracts or agreements that certain information is to be kept confidential. An NDA may have legal relevance across a broad spectrum of legal subjects including negligence claims, commercial property transactions and employment matters.

NDAs can provide legitimate means of protecting the interests of a business or an individual, by restricting the disclosure of sensitive, commercial or confidential information. However, both the Legal Services Board (LSB) and the SRA have expressed concerns at the misuse and misunderstanding of NDAs. The SRA published a Warning Notice on *Use of non disclosure agreements (NDAs)* in March 2018. This Warning Notice provides guidance and advice to practitioners on the use of NDAs and avoiding ethical issues arising.

In terms of misunderstandings, the SRA in its *Thematic Review: The use of Non Disclosure Agreements in workplace complaints* (August 2023) found that a number of practitioners held inaccurate beliefs and assumptions as to the operation of NDAs and the application of the Warning Notice. Specifically, the SRA found that solicitors wrongly assumed that the Warning Notice did not apply if:

- all parties to the NDA were legally represented;
- the agreement was not a standalone or standard NDA;
- the NDAs involved individuals rather than companies.

Furthermore, the SRA found that a low number of firms surveyed had ever questioned a client on whether an NDA was necessary or appropriate, the vast majority of NDAs were drafted using a template, and a small number of firms provided specific training on NDAs.

In terms of misuse, both the LSB and the SRA have expressed varied concerns. In March 2025, the LSB published a consultation paper on *Upholding Professional Ethical Duties*. In that consultation paper, the LSB reported concerns that vulnerable clients felt pressured to agree to the terms of the NDA by a lawyer or not having their instructions followed by their lawyer. In addition, the SRA expressed concerns that NDAs may be used to prevent reports being made to the SRA or to other regulators and law enforcement agencies or to prevent disclosures that are protected by law (see below **Para 7: Cooperation and accountability**).

Following the publication of its *Thematic Review* in August 2023, the SRA published an updated Warning Notice on *Use of non disclosure agreements (NDAs)* in August 2024. That updated Warning Notice reaffirms that whilst the use of NDAs is not prohibited by the SRA Code of Conduct, practitioners must be alive to the potential issues that may arise from using or being party to an NDA.

One of those issues is taking an unfair advantage of an opposing party, whether represented or not. The SRA considers that a solicitor will take unfair advantage if they:

- exploit their lack of legal knowledge or limited access to representation or advice, such as proposing unenforceable clauses or threatening them with litigation;
- apply undue pressure or use oppressive tactics, such as imposing artificial deadlines in NDA negotiations;
- leverage their position as a solicitor as a means of exerting power over the opposing party, for example to intimidate or discourage legal consultation;
- restrict access to an NDA or a copy of such from someone who has entered into the agreement.

The SRA in its Warning Notice provides a list of examples of what is expected of a solicitor complying with their ethical obligations. Specifically, the Warning Notice advises that a solicitor must:

- use clear, plain English tailored to relevant issues;
- define what disclosures are permitted and what are prohibited;
- provide clear written advice to prevent confusion about what is and is not permitted and protect both the client and the solicitor.

The SRA has advised solicitors to consider carefully whether an NDA is necessary at all; to ensure that firms have adequate training and support in place for those dealing with NDAs; and to avoid becoming over-reliant on NDA templates (which often do not take account of the individual circumstances of a given case).

Practice example 2.2 provides you with an example of an NDA which would cause ethical and professional conduct issues.

Practice example 2.2

Adam is a solicitor specialising in employment law. He is advising an employer on a non-disclosure agreement (NDA) intended to prevent a former employee from disclosing details of a workplace dispute. Adam drafts the NDA and includes a clause prohibiting the employee from taking legal advice or discussing the matter with legal professionals. The employee, unrepresented and unaware of their rights, signs the agreement without seeking legal advice.

Do you think Adam has complied with his ethical obligations?

Adam has likely breached his professional obligations under both the SRA Principles and the Code of Conduct by preventing the employee from seeking legal advice. By restricting the employee's ability to discuss the matter with a lawyer, and relying on the employee's lack of legal knowledge, Adam has taken unfair advantage of the employee (Para 1.2). Adam has failed to act in a way that upholds public trust and confidence in the legal profession. By preventing access to legal advice, he will have undermined transparency and fairness (Principle 1). Adam should have immediately questioned whether he could continue to act for his client, and, should his client have persisted about the NDA, Adam should have withdrawn his services.

There are a multitude of resources available for you in understanding the proper use of NDAs. We strongly advise that you consider these resources, including the SRA's *Thematic Review into the use of NDAs* (August 2023) and The Law Society's Practice Note on *Non-disclosure agreements and confidentiality clauses in an employment law context* (December 2019). The *Thematic Review* provides a number of case studies that will assist your understanding in addition to the practice examples in this text.

Strategic Lawsuits against Public Participation (SLAPPs)

The second concern, which has seen the involvement of Parliament in recent years, are so-called **Strategic Lawsuits against Public Participation**.

Key term: Strategic Lawsuits against Public Participation

The SRA in its Warning Notice on *Strategic Lawsuits against Public Participation (SLAPPs)* (May 2024) defines SLAPPs as 'a misuse of the legal system, through bringing or threatening claims that are unmeritorious or characterised by abusive tactics, in order to stifle lawful scrutiny and publication, including on matters of corruption or wrongdoing'.

You should also refer to s 195 of the Economic Crime and Corporate Transparency Act 2023 which defines the characteristics of a SLAPP in law in the context of economic crime.

The key aim of a SLAPP is to prevent publication of information that relates to a matter of public interest, such as academic research, whistleblowing or campaigning or journalism, by preventing the publication of public interest information or by removing information from the public domain. The most common cause of action that forms the basis of a SLAPP includes claims of defamation, misuse of private information and data protection breaches, and breach of confidence cases.

Parliament has provided a comprehensive list of factors that demonstrate that a claim is a SLAPP in s 195 of the Economic Crime and Corporate Transparency Act 2023. Importantly, this definition is focused on restraining the exercise of the right to freedom of speech in the context of 'economic crime'. However, the SRA adopts a wider approach to cover more behaviour that generally operates to harass, intimidate and financially or psychologically exhaust another party with the aim of preventing lawful publication of any matters relating to the public interest.

Revision tip

An SQE1 MCQ may require you to be able to identify the characteristics of a SLAPP. Things to look out for include behaviour that:

- is intended to suppress freedom of speech, rather than resolve legitimate legal disputes;
- targets individuals or organisations raising concerns on matters of public interest;
- involves behaviour that is intended to cause harassment, alarm, distress, or any other harm or inconvenience, beyond that ordinarily encountered in the course of properly conducted litigation;
- relies on excessive legal costs and procedural burdens to deter opposition;
- is often accompanied by aggressive legal threats or misuse of NDAs (see above) to stifle disclosures.

See **Practice example 2.3** for an application of these characteristics.

Practice example 2.3

1) A media outlet publishes an investigative report exposing corporate misconduct. Even though the reporting is accurate, the company responds by bringing a claim of defamation which is aimed at exhausting the outlet's resources and deter further scrutiny.
2) A community group protests against environmental damage caused by a corporation. The company brings a claim for economic

interference (a form of tort law also known as 'unlawful interference'), alleging that public demonstrations have harmed its business, with the goal of discouraging further activism.

3) An employee at a company specialising in financial transactions reports suspected money laundering to regulators. The company brings proceedings against the employee for breach of confidence, breach of fiduciary duty by misusing internal data and breach of an agreed NDA. The intent is to intimidate the employee into silence and deter other employees from coming forward.

Which of the above do you think would be characterised as a SLAPP?

All of the above could be considered SLAPPs. In all examples, an individual/organisation seeks frivolous claims to stifle legitimate publication of material in the public interest. Should a solicitor be a party to any of these proceedings, they would likely find themselves in breach of the SRA Principles and Code of Conduct.

What is your responsibility in respect of SLAPPs? In short, the SRA expects you as part of your professional obligations to:

- be able to identify proposed courses of action (including pre-action) that could be defined as SLAPPs (see above for examples of the characteristics of a SLAPP);
- advise clients *against* pursuing conduct which could be characterised as a SLAPP; and ultimately
- decline to act in any way that involves such behaviour should the client persist.

Solicitors must ensure that they do not facilitate SLAPPs. Engagement in litigation which can be categorised as a SLAPP will likely lead to disciplinary action as a breach of both the SRA Principles and the Code of Conduct. Specifically, engaging in a SLAPP will likely breach SRA Principles 1 (maintaining public trust), 2 (acting with integrity) and 5 (upholding the rule of law). Para 1.2 of the Code would be breached where a solicitor engaged in a SLAPP involving excessive legal costs, intimidating letters or aggressive legal tactics designed to pressure individuals into submission. Many other aspects of the Code would also be in jeopardy as a result of a SLAPP, and this is covered where relevant when considering other parts of the Code.

Undertakings

Under Para 1.3, a solicitor is required to perform all **undertakings** given by them.

Key term: undertaking

The SRA defines an undertaking as 'a statement, given orally or in writing, whether or not it includes the word "undertake" or "undertaking", to someone who reasonably places reliance on it, that you or a third party will do something or cause something to be done, or refrain from doing something'.

In essence, an 'undertaking' is a *promise* on the part of the solicitor. This promise can be made orally or in writing, and can be made to a client or a third party. Whilst an undertaking *can* be made orally, solicitors are best advised to avoid oral undertakings on account that disputes arise repeatedly over the terms of the undertaking.

The undertaking may be that:

- the solicitor does an act, or
- the solicitor refrains from doing an act, or
- a third party similarly does an act or refrains from doing so.

A solicitor who makes an undertaking on behalf of their client will remain personally liable for that undertaking. The solicitor should have their client's authorisation and ensure they can comply with the undertaking once given (see **Practice example 2.4**).

The solicitor must be exceptionally careful with undertakings. They must never undertake to carry out a promise which they cannot guarantee they can fulfil at the time, eg the solicitor promises (or more accurately 'undertakes') a third party to transfer funds to that third party for their client but has not yet received cleared funds from their client.

You should discover that a solicitor's firm will have a strict policy on undertakings and that undertakings can only be given in certain circumstances or by certain individuals within the firm.

Practice example 2.4

Mark is a solicitor acting on behalf of James, a landlord. James has instructed Mark that he wishes for the current tenants of his property to renew their tenancy. On the date of the tenancy renewal, however, the current tenants state that they will only renew their tenancy agreement if James agrees to redecorate the house, including installing a new shower in the bathroom. Mark attempts to contact James about this requirement but is unable to reach him.

What should Mark do in this case?

Mark is in a difficult position in this case. He has received clear instructions from James that he should try to secure the renewal of

the tenancy. However, Mark may be prevented from doing so if there is not an agreement to redecorate the house, and install a new shower. Mark should try to persuade the tenants to sign the new lease, and allow James to review the decorating requirements after the lease has been signed. This will likely be unsatisfactory for many people. Mark may consider giving an undertaking on behalf of James that he will redecorate within a prescribed time period. However, Mark must be aware that he has not received express authority from James to make this undertaking. If James refuses to comply with the undertaking, Mark will be personally liable and bound to comply with the undertaking.

An undertaking is enforceable in court, meaning that a solicitor must be cautious as to whether they should give or accept an undertaking; an undertaking can only be withdrawn by agreement with the other party to the undertaking. A solicitor must also be careful that they are not inadvertently bound to an undertaking in a court order.

Revision tip

Make use of legal databases available to you; there will be numerous precedents and examples of undertakings available therein which will assist you in considering the terms of an undertaking. However, always tailor any undertaking to suit the circumstances.

By Para 1.3, the solicitor must perform all undertakings 'within an agreed timescale'. It is advisable that the solicitor expresses a clear and manageable timescale for the undertaking. Should a solicitor agree to send documents to the opposing solicitor by a specific date, for example, they would be treated as having breached their duty if they fail to do so.

However, Para 1.3 also provides that if no timescale has been agreed, then the undertaking must be performed 'within a reasonable amount of time'. Whether a timescale is 'reasonable' will depend on the nature of the undertaking.

Exam warning

Whilst the SRA may permit an undertaking to be performed within a reasonable amount of time, such provision is ripe with difficulty and practitioners are best advised to avoid relying on such rule. A solicitor should *always* strive for certainty and ensure that there is a clear time limit on undertakings given. An MCQ may seek to test this practical application of the Code.

Furthermore, solicitors are advised to avoid undertakings where they would be reliant on a third party (on account that the solicitor has no control over whether or not that act can be achieved).

Any breach of an undertaking is a breach of Para 1.3 and may result in action being taken against the solicitor. Specifically, the solicitor may be sued personally by the recipient of the undertaking; the solicitor (or their firm) being liable to compensate the recipient personally for any loss. The solicitor may also have disciplinary action brought against them by the SRA.

Exam warning

The obligation in respect of undertakings is replicated in the Code of Conduct for Firms. This means that any undertaking given by anyone held out by the firm as representing the firm (which includes non-admitted staff and trainee solicitors) is binding on the firm. It is for this reason that many firms will have a policy in place dictating how and when an undertaking may be given. The firm may state that only certain individuals can give undertakings, or that undertakings must first be approved by an officer of the firm. Make sure you appreciate that this duty is replicated to firms and the steps taken in practice.

Duty to not mislead

Para 1.4 provides that a solicitor must not 'mislead or attempt to mislead' their clients, the court or others. This obligation links closely with Principle 2 (upholding public trust), Principle 4 (acting honestly) and Principle 5 (acting with integrity). A solicitor may mislead their clients or the court either by their own acts or omissions, or by allowing or being complicit in the acts or omissions of others (including the client).

A solicitor must be actively aware of any risk of misleading their clients or the court. Examples of such misleading include where a solicitor:

- calls a witness who they know is providing untrue evidence
- advises their client that certain necessary procedural steps have been taken, when in fact they have not
- informs the court that a document was served on a particular date, before then realising that it was served on a later date
- continues to act for a client where the solicitor has become aware that the client has committed perjury (or has otherwise misled the court)
- makes a submission to the court on instruction from their client that they know to be false or misleading
- backdates correspondence to mislead that something was served earlier than it was.

One popular example is where a solicitor has been told by their client that they are guilty of a criminal offence but wishes to plead not guilty. In this case, the solicitor may continue to act for the client so long as the solicitor does not present a positive defence. See **Chapter 5** for more information.

Revision tip

Where the possibility of misleading the court has arisen as a result of the client's behaviour, it is common for candidates to think that they must cease acting immediately. This is incorrect. Always start by asking the client to correct the position. If they refuse, then cease to act. However, remember your duty to maintain confidentiality in Para 6.3 - if you cease to act, you must not disclose the reason for it.

A further example we can consider at this stage relates to SLAPPs (see above). There is a great deal of overlap with the characteristics of a SLAPP that we have discussed above. A solicitor who makes an exaggerated claim might also adopt oppressive tactics whilst bringing a claim for an improper purpose. All of these also run the risk of misleading both the court and the opposing party.

One example in which a solicitor may mislead is through the labelling of correspondence. Such examples including 'not for publication', 'strictly private and confidential' and 'without prejudice'. Of course, there may be legitimate reasons for labelling correspondence in such a manner, and there is a long-established practice of doing so. However, such labels should not be used when the conditions for using those terms are not fulfilled and must be used in good faith. Furthermore, labels should not be used if they give the appearance of having court or legal authority where this is not warranted, for example by marking a letter as a 'Legal Notice' or similar.

The SRA advises that there is a risk that labels can cause confusion and act to inhibit appropriate disclosure. As such, consideration should be given as to whether an explanation as to the label's purpose and effect may be necessary. Furthermore, a label should not mislead an individual into believing that they cannot speak with a legal representative about the content of the letter. Likewise, a solicitor should satisfy themselves that the recipient will know they are allowed to seek legal advice on their correspondence.

Practice example 2.5

Janet is instructed to send legal correspondence on behalf of a corporate client seeking to deter David, an investigative journalist, from publishing a critical article on the client's equality and diversity record. Janet drafts a letter to David marked as 'Without Prejudice', despite knowing that the content does not relate to a genuine attempt to settle (see Part 36 CPR in ***Revise SQE: Dispute Resolution***). The letter is written in such a manner that it suggests David cannot seek legal advice.

Is Janet's letter misleading?

There is a risk that Janet's letter is misleading and in breach of Para 1.4. 'Without prejudice' is not used to signal a genuine attempt to put forward an offer, narrow issues, or settle a case. As the letter does not

offer any concessions, there should ordinarily be no need to apply it to correspondence. Furthermore, phrasing the letter in such a way that David may believe he cannot obtain legal representation is problematic; Janet should have ensured that the letter clearly set out what rights David had.

Where the risk exists that the solicitor would mislead the court if they were to proceed, the solicitor should consider the need to terminate the retainer and cease to act.

Treating colleagues fairly and with respect

Introduced in the April 2025 update, Para 1.5 provides that a solicitor must 'treat colleagues fairly and with respect'. It goes on to expand that a solicitor must not bully or harass their colleagues, or discriminate unfairly against them. Finally, the Code requires a solicitor who is a manager to 'challenge behaviour that does not meet this standard'. This provision within the Code underscores Principles 2, 4, 5 and 6 of the SRA Principles.

PARA 2: DISPUTE RESOLUTION AND PROCEEDINGS BEFORE COURTS, TRIBUNALS AND INQUIRIES

Lawyers conducting litigation owe a divided loyalty. They owe not only a duty to their client; they also owe a duty to the court and the administration of justice. We discussed this divided loyalty in **Chapter 1** when reviewing the SRA Principles (particularly Principle 1 and Principle 7). A breach of any of the provisions in Para 2 may also result in a breach of Para 1.4 (above).

Interference with evidence

Under Para 2, a solicitor owes a number of fundamental duties. In particular, a solicitor must not:

- misuse or tamper with evidence or attempt to do so (Para 2.1)
- seek to influence the substance of evidence, including generating false evidence or persuading witnesses to change their evidence (Para 2.2)
- provide or offer to provide any benefit to witnesses dependent upon the nature of their evidence or the outcome of the case (Para 2.3).

Practice example 2.6 provides you with an opportunity to apply your understanding.

Practice example 2.6

Mark is a solicitor advocate with higher rights of audience and is defending Samantha, who is charged with murder. Mark attempts to run the defence of diminished responsibility; however, he is unable to secure the evidence of an expert to support Samantha's claim. Mark contacts James, a psychiatrist, to corroborate Samantha's claim of diminished responsibility. James concludes that there is no evidence to support Samantha's claim. As a result, Mark attempts to convince James to alter his report, offering a 'substantial sum of money' to James. James refuses to change his view. As a result of his failure to convince James to change his report, Mark seeks out Adam and requests that he gives evidence to suggest that Samantha was with Adam at the time of the murder, and therefore could not have committed the murder.

What are your thoughts on Mark's conduct?

Mark has evidently not acted in a professional manner. By attempting to convince James to change his view on Samantha's claim of diminished responsibility, Mark has breached Paras 2.1, 2.2 and 2.3. By seeking out Adam and requesting that he create a false alibi, Mark has breached Para 2.1. In addition, Mark will have breached Para 1.4 in that he has attempted to mislead the court. Mark will be subject to serious consequences for his actions.

In respect of Paras 2.2 and 2.3, it is advisable to interview witnesses in the presence of a legal representative to avoid any question of impropriety. However, this is not always a possibility due to costs and expenses involved. Attendance by multiple lawyers is a common way to counter any suggestions of impropriety. More common now, however, is audio recording the evidence (with permission) and asking open questions only.

Conduct of litigation

In addition to their obligations in respect of witnesses and evidence, a solicitor owes a number of obligations to the manner in which they conduct litigation.

Properly arguable submissions

By Para 2.4, a solicitor must only make assertions or put forward statements, representations or submissions to the court or others which are 'properly arguable'. This means that a solicitor must not put forward any argument that they know to be frivolous or without a legal or factual basis. By doing so, a solicitor would waste court time (contrary to Para 2.6) and may find themselves in contempt of court (contrary to Para 2.5).

Revision tip

You are strongly advised to read the SRA's Report, *Balancing Duties in Litigation* (2019). It discusses the differing duties owed by solicitors in litigation and examines the ways in which misconduct can arise. The Report provides real-life examples of misconduct in litigation and is a fantastic resource to apply your understanding of the SRA Principles and Code of Conduct. You can access the Report on the SRA's website.

One particular example of Para 2.4 in operation is bringing a SLAPP (see above). As discussed above, one particular characteristic of a SLAPP is the making of claims or assertions without merit.

The SRA in its Warning Notice on *Strategic Lawsuits against Public Participation (SLAPPs)* (May 2024) advises that a claim is 'without merit' if it 'does not advance any arguable legal basis and/or any arguable factual basis'. Just because a claim is weak does not mean that it is without merit; weak arguments can be properly brought and tested before the courts, and there is commonly room for reasonable arguments on the law or the facts of case.

However, solicitors must ensure that they take sufficient instructions from their client and take reasonable steps to satisfy themselves that a claim is properly arguable before putting it forward, either in correspondence or via an issued claim.

The SRA advises: 'We expect you to have considered the prospects of a proposed course of action being unsuccessful or counter-productive, and to have advised your clients properly before starting. The risk of regulatory action in such cases is high if such matters operate to exclude public participation and scrutiny.'

Practice example 2.7

Ben is instructed by a high-profile client to initiate defamation proceedings against a journalist who has published investigative findings about financial misconduct. Ben is aware that the claim is weak and that the primary goal is to pressure the journalist into retracting the story through costly litigation. Ben proceeds with the claim, drafting intimidating legal correspondence threatening exaggerated financial consequences if the journalist refuses to settle.

Do you consider that Ben has acted appropriately and in accordance with the Code of Conduct?

Considering the full extent of the case, Ben has not complied with his professional obligations. The defamation proceedings have the hallmarks of being a SLAPP and Ben ought to have recognised this when commencing proceedings. The simple fact the claim is weak is not enough to breach his duty, but coupled with the primary goal, the nature of the correspondence and the exaggerated financial consequences, Ben clearly risks disciplinary action. Advancing a case without merit also means that Ben risks breaching his obligation not to mislead the court or others.

Contempt of court and wasting court time

Paras 2.5 and 2.6 provide further provision for the conduct of a solicitor whilst in court. By Para 2.5, a solicitor must not place themselves in contempt of court, and must comply with any court orders which place obligations on them. Realistically, a solicitor will only find themselves in contempt of court where they behave in an entirely inappropriate manner whilst in court. For example, a solicitor who falsely verifies a document will find themselves in contempt of court and in breach of the SRA Code of Conduct for Solicitors.

Additionally, Para 2.6 provides that a solicitor must not waste the court's time. This provision in the Code is rather broad and may be breached even where a solicitor is late attending at court, which causes court time to be wasted. In practice, wasted cost orders may be made against solicitors in such cases on top of regulatory proceedings.

Procedural irregularities

Para 2.7 provides that a solicitor must draw the court's attention to relevant cases and statutory provisions, or procedural irregularities of which they are aware, and which are likely to have a material effect on the outcome of the proceedings. This obligation arises whether the opposing party is legally represented or not. There are a number of aspects of this paragraph which require further analysis (see **Table 2.1**).

Table 2.1: Drawing the court's attention to relevant details

Element from Para 2.7	Explanation
'relevant cases and statutory provisions'	This element of the paragraph demonstrates that a solicitor must refer the court to cases and statutory provisions that are relevant, even if those cases work against the case of their client. You will notice that the materials must be 'relevant'; this means that a solicitor should equally not refer the court to *irrelevant* cases and statutory provisions.
'or procedural irregularities of which [they] are aware'	A solicitor must inform the court of any procedural irregularities that they are aware of. This may be an error made by the court, or an error made by the opposing party.
'and which are likely to have a material effect on the outcome of the proceedings'	Such disclosure is only required under Para 2.7 where the cases, statutory provisions or procedural irregularities are likely to have a 'material effect' on the outcome of the proceedings. 'Material effect' is not defined in the Code of Conduct, but refers to the situation where the outcome of the case may be changed as a result of the information. Indeed, this provision is in place to avoid a decision which is then open to appeal. If the outcome would not be changed, the solicitor may not be under an obligation to draw the court's attention to the relevant details.

Revision tip

Make sure you apply your knowledge of the Code of Conduct to the various areas of law assessed on SQE1. For instance, as detailed in ***Revise SQE: Criminal Practice***, the prosecution is obligated to disclose all material which is advantageous to the defendant's case, or detrimental to the case for the prosecution. A deliberate failure by the prosecution to comply with their duty of disclosure would breach Para 2.7.

PARA 3: SERVICE AND COMPETENCE

By Para 3.1, a solicitor must only act for clients on instructions from the client, or from someone properly authorised to provide instructions on their behalf. Whilst it is common for a solicitor to receive instructions directly from the client, a solicitor must be aware that instructions may come from other sources. For example:

- A relative may attempt to instruct a solicitor on behalf of their elderly relative.
- A family member may attempt to instruct a solicitor to attend on their relative who is currently in police detention awaiting interview.
- A wife may attempt to instruct a solicitor on behalf of themselves, and their spouse.
- A director may attempt to instruct a solicitor on behalf of a company.

In all of these circumstances, the solicitor must be satisfied that these individuals have the proper authority to provide instructions. A solicitor must not act if:

- they have suspicions that the instructions do not represent the client's wishes, and
- the solicitor has not satisfied themselves that they do.

Revision tip

In reality, a solicitor should avoid accepting third party instructions. Where they do accept them, they should have a signed authority from their client expressing precisely what the third party can instruct them on and what they can be told. Think about this advice when considering an MCQ on instructions.

See **Practice example 2.8** for an example of this.

Practice example 2.8

Mark is a solicitor specialising in land law. Mark has been approached by James, who purports to act on behalf of James' grandmother, Hyacinth. James supplies Mark with a letter, purportedly requesting that Mark transfer title to Hyacinth's holiday home to James. Hyacinth is an elderly lady who, with no other relatives, relies heavily on James.

What should Mark do in this situation?

Mark should take appropriate steps to satisfy himself that the client's wishes are genuine. He may do so by interviewing Hyacinth in the absence of James. If Hyacinth insists that her instructions are genuine, Mark may feel it appropriate to explain to her the consequences of her actions and the disadvantage she will face should her instructions be carried out. Should Hyacinth continue with her instructions, Mark should obtain her written consent to proceed.

As **Practice example 2.8** shows, a solicitor must be aware of any risk of undue influence or duress faced by their client. In this situation, the solicitor should take appropriate steps to satisfy themselves that the instructions are genuine. In any event, the solicitor is under an overriding obligation to protect the client's best interests. This is so where a solicitor has legal authority to act notwithstanding that it is not possible to obtain or ascertain the instructions of their client.

Competence of service

Under Para 3.2, a solicitor must ensure that the service they provide to clients is competent and delivered in a timely manner. Furthermore, by Para 3.3, a solicitor must maintain their competence to carry out their role and keep their professional knowledge and skills up to date. This is a personal obligation; the responsibility is on the *solicitor* who must, each year, confirm a statement of solicitor competence that they are competent to continue practising for another year. We would advise you make full use of the resources on the SRA website, including Guidance and Warning Notices. Furthermore, use of the Practice Notes from The Law Society will ensure you always remain up-to-date.

A solicitor must not, therefore, accept instructions in circumstances where the solicitor lacks:

- the appropriate competence and expertise to act for the client on that particular matter
- a sufficient amount of time to act, or
- the necessary resources to act on behalf of the client.

One particular example under Para 3.2 is the instruction of counsel. Should counsel be instructed, a solicitor must ensure that the barrister is provided with all necessary details and documentation to allow them to fulfil their role in a timely manner. To effect this, a conference with the solicitor and client may be required with the barrister. A further example is highlighted by the SRA in its Warning Notice on *Strategic Lawsuits against Public Participation (SLAPPs)* (May 2024) where the SRA advises that solicitors must have the competence to recognise and identify courses of action (including pre-action) that could be defined as SLAPPs. In that Warning Notice, the SRA emphasises that 'litigation strategy is your responsibility and understanding the ethical boundaries of it cannot be abrogated to your client'.

Finally, under Para 3.4, a solicitor must consider and take account of their client's attributes, needs and circumstances. This provision simply means that no two clients are the same, and a solicitor must be aware of the particular requirements or preferences of a client. Three examples will assist you here:

- A solicitor must consider the client's circumstances when deciding whether to enter into fee agreements to fund their legal services.
- A solicitor should arrange a face-to-face meeting with a client who is illiterate, as opposed to sending out written correspondence. There are certain rules that need to be followed in these circumstances, both for the protection of the client and to ensure that the solicitor has properly discharged their duty.
- A solicitor must tailor the content of their client care letters for vulnerable clients. For example, a solicitor could use a bigger font size, adapt the information into braille, audio or easy-read format, or offer the opportunity to discuss the content of the letter by telephone.

Supervision, management and the *Mazur* judgment

In addition to providing their own level of competent service, a solicitor may also hold a further obligation under the Code. Specifically, Para 3.5 provides that where a solicitor supervises or manages others providing legal services, the solicitor remains accountable for the work carried out through them; and the solicitor effectively supervises work being done for clients. In support of this obligation, Para 3.6 provides that solicitors must ensure that the individuals they manage are competent to carry out their role, and keep their professional knowledge and skills, as well as their understanding of their legal, ethical and regulatory obligations, up to date.

Paras 3.5 and 3.6 must now also be viewed in light of the Court of Appeal's judgment in *Mazur & Ors v CILEX & Ors* [2026] EWCA Civ 369. Overturning the decision of the High Court ([2025] EWHC 2341 (KB)), the Court of Appeal ruled that an unauthorised person, such as a trainee solicitor, paralegal, or legal executive, may lawfully perform any tasks within the scope of the 'conduct of litigation' so long as they act under the supervision of an authorised person (ie a solicitor). Specifically, such delegated tasks require 'proper direction, management supervision and control'. In response to the *Mazur* judgment, the SRA updated its guidance document *Effective supervision – Guidance* (23 November 2022; updated 12 June 2026). You are advised to read this guidance in full to understand how solicitors are to comply with paras 3.5 and 3.6.

PARA 4: CLIENT MONEY AND ASSETS

A solicitor acts in a fiduciary capacity to their clients (see ***Revise SQE: Trusts Law*** for more detail on fiduciary relationships and the obligations of a fiduciary to their principal). As a part of this fiduciary relationship, a solicitor must avoid conflicts of interest and must not make any unauthorised profits by virtue of their role. This principle is reflected through the Code of Conduct, but is particularly relevant in Para 4.

Account for financial benefit

Under Para 4.1, a solicitor must properly account to clients for any **financial benefit** they (the solicitor) receive as a result of their instructions, except where they have agreed otherwise. 'Accounting' to the client simply means either that the financial benefit be paid directly to the client, or offset against the client's fees.

Key term: financial benefit

The SRA defines financial benefit as including any commission, discount or rebate, but does not include a solicitor's fees or interest earned on any client account.

This rule is particularly important when a solicitor receives a referral fee from a third party (see also **Paras 5.1–5.3: Referrals, introductions and separate businesses** below). **Practice example 2.9** provides some examples of circumstances where a solicitor would have to account for financial benefit obtained.

Practice example 2.9

Mark is a private client solicitor and is dealing with a number of cases involving multiple clients. Mark acts for Tina in the purchase of a house and refers Tina to a surveyor. The surveyor pays Mark a £100 commission for the referral. Mark also acts for Adam, who is the executor of his mother's estate. Mark refers Adam to a specialist tax consultant due to some complexities in the mother's will. The tax consultant pays Mark a £200 referral commission.

Will Mark have to account for the commissions received?

Yes, according to Para 4.1, Mark is obligated to account to both Tina and Adam for the financial benefit he obtained as a result of the referrals. Mark must either pay the money directly to Tina and Adam, or offset his fees by use of the commission. However, Mark may ask Tina and Adam to consent to him keeping the fees.

As is evident from Para 4.1, a solicitor may retain the financial benefit *only* where the client has agreed to this (ordinarily one would find this in the client care letter, or in the terms and conditions of the retainer).

Exam warning

An MCQ may seek to test your knowledge of financial benefits and the obligation owed by a solicitor. An MCQ may suggest that the solicitor *must* pay the financial benefit directly to the client. That is incorrect given that the client *may* consent to the solicitor keeping the benefit. In practice, it is advisable to always pay/offset any commission or referral fee to clients. This ensures the solicitor acts in the best interests of the client, irrespective of the technical ability to obtain their consent.

Client money and assets

Under Para 4.2, a solicitor must safeguard money and assets entrusted to them by clients and others. 'Assets' for these purposes includes money, documents, wills, deeds, investments and other property. Under Para 4.3, a solicitor must not personally hold client money (as defined in the SRA Accounts Rules) unless they work in an authorised body.

Revision tip

Ensure that you refer to ***Revise SQE: Solicitors' Accounts*** for a more detailed discussion on a solicitor's duty when dealing with client money, including professional conduct issues arising when dealing with client money and the Accounts Rules. See also the SRA's Warning Notice on *Money missing from client account* (2024) for guidance on steps to be taken when money is discovered to be missing from the client account.

PARAS 5.1–5.3: REFERRALS, INTRODUCTIONS AND SEPARATE BUSINESSES

To ensure that the advertisement of their services is maximised, a solicitor may engage in arrangements with third parties. For example, a solicitor may enter into an arrangement with an estate agent whereby the estate agent will introduce potential house buyers and sellers to the solicitor to complete the conveyance. In line with Para 1.2 (above), a solicitor must ensure that they do not take unfair advantage of their client through such introductions or referrals.

Introductions with third parties

Para 5.1 prescribes the obligations imposed on solicitors in respect of such introductions and referrals to/from third parties. Specifically, it provides that a solicitor must ensure that clients are informed of any financial or other interest which the solicitor or their business or employer has in referring the client to another person, or which an introducer has in referring the client to the solicitor.

There are a number of aspects of Para 5.1 that must be appreciated:

- The rule covers referrals made by the solicitor to a third party, and by a third party to the solicitor.
- The rule covers both financial interests and 'other interests'.
- The financial or other interest is that of the solicitor, the firm, or to the third party.

Exam warning

The best advice is to remain cautious and vigilant. The client must be kept informed when making referrals. Therefore, should the solicitor not obtain any financial benefit from the referral, but their friend or relative is the third party in question who would receive the benefit, the client must be informed that the solicitor's friend or relative is a person or organisation being referred.

Fee sharing

Para 5.1 also applies where the solicitor and third party engage in fee sharing (eg solicitors may pay a percentage of their gross or net fees to a third party). In accordance with Para 5.1, solicitors must ensure that:

- clients are informed of any fee sharing arrangement that is relevant to their matter, and
- any such fee sharing agreement is in writing.

Introducers

Specific rules also exist under Para 5.1 in respect of **introducers**.

Key term: introducers

An introducer is any person, business or organisation who introduces or refers clients to a solicitor's business. It also includes persons who recommend the solicitor's business to clients or otherwise puts the solicitor and clients in touch with each other.

In respect of introducers, Para 5.1 provides that a solicitor must ensure that any client referred by an introducer has not been acquired in a way which would breach the SRA's regulatory arrangements if the person acquiring the client were regulated by the SRA. Putting it simply, a client must not be obtained in an unsolicited manner, eg by cold calling (see **Unsolicited approaches** later in the chapter).

Importantly, Para 5.1 also provides a restriction in respect of criminal cases: A solicitor must not receive payments relating to a referral, or make payments to an introducer, in respect of clients who are the subject of criminal proceedings.

Referral fees

It was previously the case that solicitors were restricted from paying or receiving referral fees. In the majority of circumstances, this blanket ban has been lifted. However, the payment or receipt of referral fees is not permitted in the following circumstances (see Legal Aid, Sentencing and Punishment of Offenders Act 2012 (LASPO), s 56):

- where the legal services relate to a claim or potential claim for damages for personal injury or death, or
- where the legal services relate to any other claim or potential claim for damages arising out of circumstances involving personal injury or death.

In light of this, Para 5.2 of the Code provides that where it appears to the SRA that a solicitor has made or received a referral fee, the payment will be treated as a referral fee unless the solicitor shows that the payment was not made as such (ie the onus is on the solicitor). **Practice example 2.10** identifies how this provision in the Code works.

Practice example 2.10

James is a solicitor acting for Amy in a respect of a road traffic accident where Amy suffered injury as a result of the alleged negligence of David. James receives payment from a medical agency for referring Amy to them for a medical report.

Is James in breach of the prohibition against referral fees?

Yes, this would be a breach of Para 5.2. James has received payment because he is providing legal services in the course of a personal injury matter and arranges for another person to provide services to Amy. The same outcome would be reached if James, for example, received payment from an insurance company for arranging after the event (ATE) insurance for the client.

The SRA in its Warning Notice, *Referral fees LASPO and SRA Principles* (2013) advises that where a referral is in place, solicitors should:

- inform clients about any fee-sharing agreements they have and reduce those agreements to writing. Clients must be informed where a solicitor has a financial or other interest either in referrals made to them or by them to others;
- ensure that they are satisfied and be able to evidence the fact that an arrangement with a referrer does not adversely affect their independence and their ability to advise their client;
- ensure that contracts or other arrangements between their client and a referrer are fair. The solicitor must stop dealing with a referrer whose contractual terms or whose behaviours are contrary to their clients' interests or to the rule of law.

Exam warning

The prohibition on referral fees *only* applies to claimant clients (ie the person who makes or would make the claim). It does not apply to the payment of a fee in connection with the referral of a defendant in a personal injury case (unless the defendant subsequently makes a counter-claim). Do not allow an MCQ to trick you on this point.

The SRA in its Warning Notice, *Referral fees LASPO and SRA Principles* (2013) expressed concerns about how legal professionals may set up arrangements that, whilst they do not breach s 56 of LASPO, may breach the SRA Standards and Regulations. Such concerns in the Warning Notice include:

- agreeing with an introducer to deduct money from clients' damages;
- inappropriate outsourcing of work to introducers;
- referrals to other service providers which are not in the best interests of clients;
- failure to properly advise clients about the costs and how their claim should be funded; and
- lack of transparency about the arrangement.

Separate businesses

Specific rules and obligations exist where an authorised body, or an individual who owns, manages or is employed by an authorised body (eg a solicitor) is engaged in a separate business which operates non-regulated services, eg financial services and estate agency (an unauthorised body). This term is not the most straightforward, featuring a number of different aspects. **Table 2.2** seeks to set out these aspects of the definition.

Table 2.2: Understanding separate business

Element of the definition	Explanation
1. Authorised body	Means either (i) an authorised body, or (ii) an individual who owns, manages or is employed by an authorised body.
2. Separate business which is an unauthorised body	The separate business is not an authorised body, an authorised non-SRA firm or an overseas practice.
3. Relationship to separate business	The authorised body or individual must have a relationship to the separate business by any of the following reasons: • which they own • which they are owned by • where they actively participate in the provision of its services, including where they have any direct control over the business or any indirect control over the business through another person, or • which they are connected with.

Revision tip

Focus on the authorised nature of the different parties here. The solicitor is an *authorised* body, whilst the separate business is an *unauthorised* body. The obligation arises when the authorised body and separate business are connected.

Para 5.3 stipulates specific obligations on authorised bodies who are connected to a separate business. Specifically, Para 5.3 provides that a solicitor is only permitted to refer, recommend or introduce a client to a separate business where the client has given informed consent to the solicitor or authorised body doing so. Additionally, client consent is required where the authorised body wishes to divide, or allow to be divided, a client's matter between them and a separate business.

PARAS 5.4–5.6: OTHER BUSINESS REQUIREMENTS

Under this heading, there are a number of additional requirements imposed on solicitors. The following provides a brief summary of each paragraph:

- Para 5.4: A solicitor must not be a manager, employee, member or interest holder of a business that has a name which includes the word 'solicitors', or describes its work in a way that suggests it is a solicitors' firm unless it is a body authorised by the SRA. This rule is particularly important when advertising services on letterheads, websites or by email. The SQE Annual Report 2024/25 (21 April 2026) identified this as an area that candidates tended to perform less well in. You are reminded that Para 5.4 contains an absolute prohibition; it is not dependent on factors such as the type of work undertaken, or whether the non-authorised body is a new start-up. Don't be caught out by these irrelevant factors.
- Para 5.5: A solicitor who holds a practising certificate must complete and deliver to the SRA an annual return in the prescribed form.
- Para 5.6: A solicitor carrying on **reserved legal activities** in a non-commercial body (ie a not for profit body, a community interest company or an independent trade union), must ensure that (a) the body takes out and maintains indemnity insurance, and (b) the insurance provides adequate and appropriate cover in respect of the services that they provide or have provided, whether or not they comprise reserved legal activities, taking into account any alternative arrangements the body or its clients may make.

Key term: reserved legal activity

Reserved legal activity refers to the activities that can only be carried out by a solicitor who is regulated (ie providing legal advice, assistance or representation). Such activities include the exercise of a right of audience, the conduct of litigation, probate activities, notarial activities and the administration of oaths. See ***Revise SQE: The Legal System and Services of England and Wales*** for more details on regulated activities.

PARAS 6.1–6.2: CONFLICT OF INTERESTS

There may be circumstances in which a solicitor, when acting on behalf of clients, faces a conflict of interest. The Code of Conduct prescribes two forms of conflict:

- 'Own interest conflict': This is where a conflict exists between the client's interests and those interests of the solicitor (Para 6.1).
- 'Conflict of interest': This is where a conflict exists between two or more clients' interests (Para 6.2).

In both cases, a solicitor must not act where there is such a conflict, or a 'significant risk' of such conflict.

Let us consider both types of conflict here.

Own interest conflict

Under Para 6.1, a solicitor must not act where there is an **own interest conflict**, or significant risk of such conflict.

Key term: own interest conflict

The SRA defines an 'own interest conflict' as meaning 'any situation where your duty to act in the best interests of any client in relation to a matter conflicts, or there is a significant risk that it may conflict, with your own interests in relation to that or a related matter'.

The SRA in its guidance on *Conflicts of Interest* (2019) provides the following examples of own interest conflicts:

- 'A financial interest of yours or someone close to you. For example, a client asks you to carry out due diligence on a company which you or your spouse/partner own shares in'.
- 'A personal or business relationship of yours. For example, where you are asked to advise on a claim against a relative of yours, a friend or someone with whom you are involved in a common financial enterprise'.
- 'Your role as an employee. For example, a client asks for advice in relation to a dispute involving your employer or a fellow employee'.
- 'Your own conduct (as a firm or an individual). For example, the wrong advice has been given to the client or the wrong action taken on their behalf'.

Revision tip

There are numerous examples of own interest conflicts in the subsequent chapters of this text. For example, in **Chapter 6**, we discuss the circumstances where an own interest conflict arises in the drafting of a will for which the solicitor is a beneficiary (ie a gift is made to the solicitor). Make use of the subsequent chapters and refer back to this one regularly to understand the general rule.

As should be evident from Para 6.1, there are *no* exceptions to this rule (even where, for example, the client consents or obtains independent legal advice, or where the solicitor believes they are acting in the client's best interests, or where the solicitor and the client have a substantially common interest); a solicitor must *not* act where there is, or a significant risk exists of, an own interest conflict.

Conflict of interest

Under Para 6.2, a solicitor must not act in relation to a matter or a particular aspect of it, where there is a **conflict of interest**, or significant risk of such conflict.

Key term: conflict of interest

The SRA defines a 'conflict of interest' as meaning 'a situation where your separate duties to act in the best interests of two or more clients in relation to the same or a related matter conflict'.

The most obvious example of conflict is where the matter itself concerns a dispute between two or more current or intended clients. For example, a solicitor would be prevented from acting for both a purchaser and a seller of land, or in a dispute between a landlord and tenant (see also **Practice example 1.9** in **Chapter 1**).

Exam warning

Remember that a solicitor must not act where a conflict either exists, or where there is a *significant risk* of such conflict arising. If a solicitor is satisfied that there is no conflict, and no significant risk of such, they can continue to act. Look out for significant risks in an MCQ.

The SRA in its guidance on *Conflicts of Interest* (2019) provides the following examples of conflict of interest:

- 'Two clients seeking separately to purchase a particular asset or to be awarded a particular contract.'
- 'Acting for an investor and the scheme in which they will be investing.'
- 'One client selling or leasing an asset to another client.'
- 'Agreeing a commercial contract between two clients.'

Exam warning

Importantly, a conflict can only arise where the solicitor acts, or intends to act, on behalf of two or more *current* clients. A conflict does not arise where you are dealing with a former client (though note the continuing duty of confidentiality owed to former clients in Para 6.5). An MCQ may seek to test your understanding of when a conflict of interest arises between clients.

Unlike Para 6.1, there are two exceptions to the restriction on a solicitor acting where there is a conflict of interest. These are detailed in Para 6.2(a) and (b) and are explained in **Table 2.3**.

Table 2.3: Exceptions to the conflict of interest rule

Exception	Explanation
the clients have a substantially common interest in relation to the matter or the aspect of it, as appropriate, OR	A 'substantially common interest' is defined by the SRA as meaning a situation where there is a clear common purpose between the clients and a strong consensus on how it is to be achieved. For example, a common interest exists where two clients want to instruct a solicitor to advise them on taking out a lease as joint tenants.
the clients are competing for the same objective	'Competing for the same objective' is defined by the SRA as meaning any situation in which two or more clients are competing for an 'objective' which, if attained by one client, will make that 'objective' unattainable to the other client or clients. The word 'objective' is further defined as meaning an asset, contract or business opportunity which two or more clients are seeking to acquire or recover through a liquidation (or some other form of insolvency process) or by means of an auction or tender process or a bid or offer, but not a public takeover. For example, two or more clients may instruct a solicitor to act for them as competing bidders.
If *either* of the exceptions are present, the following conditions must *also* be met:	
all the clients have given informed consent, given or evidenced in writing, to the solicitor acting, AND	The consent from the clients must be 'informed', meaning that they have been provided with sufficient information for them to understand the situation and form an independent judgement. Where a client is vulnerable, the solicitor must take additional steps to ensure that the client understands what they are being asked to consent to. The information provided should be documented clearly.

Table 2.3: (continued)

Exception	Explanation
where appropriate, the solicitor has put in place effective safeguards to protect their clients' confidential information, AND	Should a solicitor wish to continue to act for one of the clients, they must ensure that effective safeguards are put into place to protect the client's confidentiality. For example, a different solicitor at the same firm may act for the second client (so long as the solicitor can be sure that no information can pass between the two solicitors in the same firm). Alternatively, the clients may agree which information can and cannot be shared; such explicit statements may be sufficient safeguards for the purposes of Para 6.2.
the solicitor is satisfied it is reasonable for them to act for all the clients	Whether it is reasonable to act for all the clients is a judgement call for the solicitor. The SRA suggests that the following factors should be taken into account: • The respective knowledge and bargaining power of the clients. Is one party particularly vulnerable or in a relatively weak position and should be referred for independent advice? For example, one client may be an individual and the other a corporate entity with access to an in-house legal team. Or it could be that one client may be facing financial problems which would put them under pressure to reach an agreement that might not be in their best interests. • The extent to which there will need to be negotiations between the clients. The more serious any unresolved issues are, then the less it is likely to be reasonable for you to act. • Any particular benefits to the clients (eg speed, convenience, cost) from you acting for both. • Any risk of the inappropriate transmission of confidential data.

Exam warning

A conflict of interest is capable of arising in any situation. An MCQ may suggest that a conflict cannot arise in certain circumstances (eg between close family members). However, this is untrue. A conflict, or risk of such conflict, is always capable of arising. Maintain constant vigilance.

Alternatively, a solicitor may choose to restrict their retainer; expressly providing that they will only act for/advise the clients on aspects where a conflict is not likely to arise. This is a very difficult situation to be in, however, and the solicitor is not free from the dangers of a conflict arising. Each client in this situation would be required to obtain independent legal advice on the conflict areas. This must be very clearly communicated to both clients in the retainer.

See **Figure 2.1** for a summary of conflicts of interest.

Own interest conflict

- You must not act
- There are no exceptions

Conflict of interest

- You must not act UNLESS
  - the clients have a substantially common interest in relation to the matter or an aspect of it, as appropriate; OR
  - the clients are competing for the same objective, AND
    - all the clients have given informed consent, given or evidenced in writing, to the solicitor acting;
    - where appropriate, the solicitor puts in place effective safeguards to protect their clients' confidential information; and
    - the solicitor is satisfied it is reasonable for them to act for all the clients

Figure 2.1: Understanding conflicts of interest

Revision tip

In the subsequent chapters, do make sure you observe examples of conflicts of interest. For example, in **Chapter 5** we will discuss the circumstances in which a defence solicitor in a criminal case is able to act on behalf of co-defendants charged with the same offence.

PARAS 6.3–6.5: CONFIDENTIALITY AND DISCLOSURE

Perhaps one of the most well-known obligations owed by a solicitor, confidentiality is fundamental to the relationship between a solicitor and their clients.

Revision tip

Confidentiality is a separate and distinct principle from legal professional privilege. For a discussion on privilege, see ***Revise SQE: Dispute Resolution*** and ***Revise SQE: The Legal System and Services of England and Wales***

Duty of confidentiality

Under Para 6.3, a solicitor is obligated to keep the affairs of current and former clients confidential.

Revision tip

Please pay particular attention to the nature of this duty: the duty is to *keep* the information confidential, not merely to *take all reasonable steps* to do so. This is so unless disclosure is required or permitted by law, or the client consents. An MCQ may seek to test you on the extent of the duty owed.

This obligation involves a duty to not communicate the information to a third party, or misuse the information (ie use it for any purpose other than the client's best interest). For example, a solicitor should not disclose confidential information as a way of advertising their services, or the services of their firm.

Exam warning

The obligation in respect of confidentiality is replicated in the Code of Conduct for Firms. This means that all members of a firm, including support staff, owe a duty of confidentiality to clients of the firm. Keep this in your mind when you consider what systems or processes may need to be put in place to ensure that client confidentiality is maintained.

The source of the information is irrelevant; any information about the client or the matter involved is treated as confidential (whether it comes from the client or a third party). However, please note that the duty only applies where the information relates to the retainer; any information about the client that is unrelated to the retainer may not be covered by this duty.

Exam warning

Do not think that the duty of confidentiality ceases upon termination of the retainer or death of the client. The duty of confidentiality is a continuing one; the right to confidentiality passing to the client's personal representatives upon death. Do not allow an MCQ to trick you on this.

As will be evident from Para 6.3, disclosure of client information may be permitted in two circumstances (see **Table 2.4**). Before either of these circumstances are considered, a solicitor must question whether disclosure is necessary to proceed with a specific matter.

Table 2.4: Exceptions to the duty of confidentiality

Exception	Explanation and examples
Disclosure is required or permitted by law	Disclosure may be permitted or required by law. For example, disclosure will be required under terrorism legislation or where the client is committing a criminal offence, eg money laundering. Disclosure may also be required where the court orders so.

Table 2.4: (continued)

Exception	Explanation and examples
Client consents	Disclosure is permitted if the client consents to it. Even if a client has provided general consent to disclose information, a solicitor is best advised to seek specific consent for certain disclosures. The client must be informed of: • what information will be disclosed • who it will be disclosed to • when it will be disclosed • for what purpose it will be disclosed. Only if the client has this information will they be in a position to provide consent. The SRA suggests that a client, if asked about the disclosure, should be able to say: 'Yes I agreed to that information being disclosed for that purpose'. As a practice point, it is advisable to get the client to confirm in writing what information will be disclosed and get them to sign the letter which discloses the information so they have approved the content and the wording.

Outside of the circumstances where disclosure is lawfully permitted, the SRA has identified (in its guidance *Confidentiality of client information* (2019)) a number of circumstances where disclosure, although technically a breach of the Code, may be justified. The SRA notes that these justifications can be taken into account as mitigation against regulatory action. The justifications include:

- where a client has indicated their intention to commit suicide or serious self-harm
- preventing harm to children or vulnerable adults
- preventing the commission of a criminal offence.

Please note that these justifications do *not* permit disclosure after the event (ie once the circumstances justifying the disclosure have passed).

Exam warning

The duty of confidentiality does not arise where the solicitor is being used by the client to perpetrate a fraud or any other crime. The common law has long recognised that this information cannot be confidential. Do not allow an MCQ to make you think that the duty of confidentiality is absolute.

Duty of disclosure

In addition to their duty to preserve the confidential information of their client, a solicitor is also under a duty to disclose information to their client.

Particularly, Para 6.4 of the Code provides that where a solicitor is acting for a client on a matter, the solicitor must make the client aware of all information material to the matter of which they have knowledge. This duty specifically refers to information that *the solicitor* has, as opposed to information known by the solicitor's firm, or another person in the firm.

Revision tip

You will notice that Para 6.4 is very broadly drafted: 'you make the client aware of all information material to the matter of which you have knowledge.' This includes any knowledge that is obtained in the solicitor's personal life.

There are, however, a number of exceptions to this duty. These are where:

- the disclosure of the information is prohibited by legal restrictions imposed in the interests of national security or the prevention of crime
- the solicitor's client gives informed consent, given or evidenced in writing, to the information not being disclosed to them
- the solicitor has reason to believe that serious physical or mental injury will be caused to their client or another if the information is disclosed, or
- the information is contained in a privileged document that the solicitor has knowledge of only because it has been mistakenly disclosed.

Exam warning

Remember that the duty of confidentiality (Para 6.3) overrides the duty of disclosure (Para 6.4). If you have confidential information relating to one client (current or former), and that information is material to another client, you must not disclose that information to the other client.

Adverse interests (Para 6.5)

Para 6.5 deals with the common situation where a solicitor is in possession of client information relevant to another client. In particular, Para 6.5 provides that a solicitor must not act for a client (C1) in a matter where that client has an interest adverse to the interest of another current or former client (C2) of the solicitor or their business or employer, for whom the solicitor or their business or employer holds confidential information which is material to that matter.

This somewhat complex provision is explained further in **Table 2.5**. Indeed, the SQE Annual Report 2024/25 (21 April 2026) describes that candidates were unable to identify where the interests of clients/former clients were adverse to each other, or when information was 'material'. Candidates also struggled when applying the exceptions to the rule. Ensure, therefore, that you take time to review this provision and associated guidance carefully.

Table 2.5: Adverse interests and confidential information

Relevant aspect of 6.5	Explanation and example
'interest adverse to the interest of another current or former client'	A solicitor must not act for a prospective client (C1) if their interests are contrary to, or in dispute with, the interests of a current or former client (C2). This may arise, for example, where C1 and C2 may, at some point, be in litigation with each other.
'holds confidential information which is material to [the] matter'	The SRA does not define when information is 'material'. However, as with other provisions of the Code, this will mean that the information is important or relevant to the matter being dealt with. NB reference to '[the] matter' means information about C2 that is relevant to C1's case.
There are two exceptions to the prohibition contained in Para 6.5. These are that *either*:	
'effective measures have been taken which result in there being no real risk of disclosure of the confidential information', or	Effective measures (often called 'information barriers') must be in place to protect C1's information from C2. C1's information should be protected from any real risk of the disclosure. A real risk does not have to be substantial – but must be more than merely fanciful or theoretical. Appropriate barriers may include: • separate teams handling the matters, at all levels including non-fee-earning staff • separate servers (and printers) so that information cannot be cross accessed • information being encrypted, and password protected.
'the current or former client whose information [the solicitor] or [their] business or employer holds has given informed consent, given or evidenced in writing, to [the solicitor] acting, including to any measures taken to protect their information.'	The second exception is where C2 provides informed consent for the solicitor to act for C1, despite the adverse interest. The solicitor must secure C2's consent in writing, or have it evidenced in writing. In order to satisfy this exception, the solicitor must ensure that C2 has understood the issues, including any possible risks. However, please remember that the solicitor must be cautious not to breach their duty of confidentiality to C1 when ensuring that C2 understands the issues before them.

PARA 7: COOPERATION AND ACCOUNTABILITY

To ensure that a practising solicitor retains their independence and professionalism, the Code of Conduct prescribes a requirement of cooperation and accountability on the part of every solicitor. The following discusses the key obligations placed on solicitors.

Keep up to date

Under Para 7.1, a solicitor must keep up to date with and follow the law and regulations governing the way they work. This means that a solicitor must ensure their knowledge of the SRA Principles, Code of Conduct, Accounts Rules and SRA guidance is up to date. A solicitor must remain abreast with updates to the Solicitors Act 1974 and Legal Services Act 2007 (both statutes governing the way solicitors work). A particular concern in practice relates to potential money laundering. In light of that, Para 7.1 requires solicitors to understand and comply with their legal obligations under the Proceeds of Crime Act 2002, the Terrorism Act 2000 and the Money Laundering, Terrorist Financing and Transfer of Funds (Information on the Payer) Regulations 2017.

Justifying decisions and actions

Para 7.2 requires solicitors to be able to justify their decisions and actions in order to demonstrate compliance with their obligations under the SRA's regulatory arrangements. Examples of such justifications include:

- providing a good reason for the termination of a retainer by a solicitor (eg to act for a client would breach the Code of Conduct)
- maintaining effective records of when an undertaking has been given and discharged.

Record keeping, eg through attendance notes, telephone notes, confirmation of advice etc, is vital when it comes to demonstrating compliance.

Cooperation

At some point in a solicitor's career, they are bound to have *some* interaction with the SRA. By Para 7.3, a solicitor must cooperate with the SRA, other regulators, ombudsmen and those bodies with a role overseeing and supervising the delivery of, or investigating concerns in relation to, legal services. As part of this cooperation, a solicitor is obligated under Para 7.4 to:

- respond promptly to the SRA, providing full and accurate explanations, information and documents in response to any request or requirement, and
- ensure that relevant information which is held by them, or by third parties carrying out functions on their behalf which are critical to the delivery of the solicitor's legal services, is available for inspection by the SRA.

Preventing disclosure

Para 7.5 prescribes that a solicitor must not attempt to prevent anyone from providing information to the SRA or any other body exercising regulatory, supervisory, investigatory or prosecutory functions in the public interest. A specific example of Para 7.5 in practice concerns the use of NDAs to restrict disclosure to the SRA (see above **Para 1: Maintaining trust and acting fairly**). The SRA in its Warning Notice on *Use of non disclosure agreements (NDAs)* (August 2024) expressed concerns that NDAs were being used by practitioners to prevent individuals reporting to the SRA or other regulators and law enforcement agencies.

The SRA has therefore stated in clear terms that it considers that an NDA will be 'improperly used' in circumstances where it seeks to prevent, impede or deter individuals from:

- cooperating with criminal investigations or prosecutions;
- reporting offences, misconduct or regulatory breaches to the SRA and other regulatory bodies;
- making protected disclosures under the Public Interest Disclosure Act 1998;
- making any disclosure required by law;
- seeking confidential advice from legal, tax or medical professionals.

Any attempt to prevent complaints or information-sharing with the SRA is a breach of the Code, risking disciplinary action. **Practice example 2.11** seeks to put this Warning Notice into context.

Practice example 2.11

Ethan is advising a corporate client on an NDA for an outgoing senior executive. The client insists on including a clause prohibiting the executive from reporting concerns about the company's regulatory compliance to any external body, including the SRA. Ethan is aware that the executive has previously raised concerns about potential misconduct within the company, including discrimination and sexual harassment. Despite this knowledge, Ethan drafts the NDA as requested, and the executive signs it without seeking independent legal advice.

What do you think Ethan should have done?

By following his client's request, Ethan has clearly breached both the SRA Principles (Principle 2 (acting with integrity) and Principle 5 (upholding the rule of law and proper administration of justice)) and the Code of Conduct (Para 7.5). In this situation, Ethan should have refused to draft such an NDA; the conflict between his client and upholding the proper administration of justice should have been resolved against the NDA.

Finally, Para 7.9 prevents a solicitor from subjecting any person to detrimental treatment for making a report or providing information to the SRA (or proposing to do either of these things), and Para 7.10 requires a solicitor to act promptly to take any remedial action requested by the SRA.

Notification and reporting

A solicitor has a number of **notification requirements** and **reporting requirements** under the Code of Conduct (Paras 7.6–7.8).

Key term: notification requirements

There are some events or occurrences which trigger an automatic obligation to notify the SRA. These are referred to as 'notifications' and are contained in Para 7.6 of the Code.

Key term: reporting requirements

If an event does not automatically trigger a notification requirement, a solicitor must use their own judgement to determine whether they must report a matter to the SRA. These reporting obligations are contained in Paras 7.7 and 7.8 of the Code.

Table 2.6 identifies the obligations of notification and reporting.

Table 2.6: Notification and reporting requirements

Notification Requirements (Para 7.6)	Reporting Requirements (Paras 7.7 and 7.8)
A solicitor must notify the SRA promptly if: (a) they are subject to any criminal charge, conviction or caution, subject to the Rehabilitation of Offenders Act 1974, or (b) a relevant insolvency event occurs in relation to them, or (c) they become aware: (i) of any material changes to information previously provided to the SRA, by them or on their behalf, about them or their practice, including any change to information recorded in the register, and (ii) that information provided to the SRA, by them or on their behalf, about them or their practice is or may be false, misleading, incomplete or inaccurate.	A solicitor must report promptly to the SRA or another approved regulator, as appropriate, any facts or matters that they reasonably believe are capable of amounting to a serious breach of their regulatory arrangements by any person regulated by them (including the solicitor). In addition, a solicitor must inform the SRA promptly of any facts or matters that they reasonably believe should be brought to its attention in order that the SRA may investigate whether a serious breach of its regulatory arrangements has occurred or otherwise exercise its regulatory powers.

See the SRA Guidance, *Convictions arising from matters of principle or social conscience* (2022) for information on the approach taken by the SRA when dealing with solicitors convicted of offences involving 'principle or social conscience' (eg offences committed as part of protest).

Exam warning

Note from **Table 2.6** that a solicitor must disclose if they are subject to a criminal *charge*. This means that even if a solicitor is not *convicted* of an offence, but is only charged on suspicion of such, this must still be notified to the SRA. Make sure an MCQ does not trick you on this point (the SQE Annual Report 2024/25 (21 April 2026) suggests that candidates have been tricked by this and believe that the duty to notify only applies once a court or tribunal has made relevant findings against an individual).

As should be evident from **Table 2.6**, solicitors must report to the SRA any **serious breach**.

Key term: serious breach

Not every breach of the Code will result in investigation or regulatory action. The Enforcement Strategy focuses on 'serious misconduct' and may involve breaches that are serious in isolation or serious because they demonstrate a persistent failure to comply, or a concerning pattern of behaviour. The SRA will take account of mitigating but also aggravating circumstances when considering the severity of a breach and the sanction.

This means that not all breaches must be reported to the SRA. Unlike the notification requirements, which are automatic, a judgement call has to be made by the solicitor as to whether their duty under the Code obliges them to report the matter. Under Para 7.10, however, a solicitor must, if requested to do so by the SRA, investigate whether there have been any serious breaches that should be reported to the SRA.

Revision tip

To assist solicitors, the SRA has produced a guidance document on *Reporting and Notification Obligations* (November 2019). The document provides a summary of what actions involve notification obligations (Schedule 1) and what requires reporting obligations (Schedule 2). The document also provides guidance as to the factors that may affect whether a breach is considered as being serious or not. Consider reading this guidance in full.

By Para 7.12, a solicitor can satisfy their obligation to make a notification or report to the SRA if the solicitor provides the information to the firm's compliance officer (see **Para 9: compliance officers**, below). However, the solicitor will only be able to rely on this provision if they provide the information to the compliance officer 'on the understanding that' the compliance officer will report to the SRA. Where the solicitor is unsure that such report will be made, they are best advised to still make the report personally (and Paras 7.5 and 7.9 (see above) are in place to allow solicitors to feel more at ease in making these disclosures). The SQE Annual Report 2024/25 (21 April 2026) disclosed that candidates did not understand to whom reports should be made. It is vital, therefore, to remember the requirements in Paras 7.7 and 7.12.

Honesty and openness

Under Para 7.11 of the Code, a solicitor must be 'honest and open' with clients if things go wrong. If a client suffers loss or harm as a result, the solicitor must, if possible, put matters right (known as taking 'remedial action') and explain fully and promptly what has happened and the likely impact (see **Practice example 2.12**).

Practice example 2.12

Tina is a sole practitioner solicitor, specialising in private client law. In her capacity as a solicitor, Tina acts as trustee for the Ball Trust. In her role as trustee, Tina invests £10,000 in a start-up company which she had hoped would perform strongly for the Ball Trust. Unfortunately, the start-up company has recently been liquidated and the shares are now worthless.

What action should Tina take in this case?

Tina is obligated under Para 7.11 to be honest and open with the beneficiaries of the Ball Trust. Tina must explain to the beneficiaries what has happened and, if possible, take remedial action. However, as the trust has lost a substantial amount of money, Tina is likely to be in breach of trust. As Tina is in breach, an own interest conflict exists.

Tina must inform the beneficiaries of this fact and should advise them to seek independent legal advice. Tina can be advised that the beneficiaries will have a claim of negligence against her.

In addition, if requested to do so by the SRA, a solicitor must investigate whether anyone may have a claim against them. The solicitor should provide the SRA with a report on the outcome of their investigation and notify relevant persons that they may have such a claim, accordingly.

PARA 8.1: CLIENT IDENTIFICATION

Under Para 8.1, a solicitor must identify who they are acting for in relation to any matter. The SRA guidance *Identifying your client* (November 2019) explains the purpose behind this rule as follows: 'the rule is primarily to reduce the risk of being inadvertently caught up in a fraud by ensuring that you are satisfied you know who you are dealing with at the outset of each retainer'. This links closely with Customer Due Diligence under the Money Laundering Regulations 2017 (see ***Revise SQE: The Legal System and Services of England and Wales***).

The Code of Conduct does not prescribe what steps need to be taken by a solicitor or firm to identify a client. It is therefore for the firm to decide what arrangements are necessary; though it is strongly advised that appropriate steps are taken to identify the client from the outset. Such steps include obtaining and verifying two forms of identification that between them show the current address, name and date of birth of the client. On a practical level, larger firms now use agencies that carry out such identification checks.

Given the concerns relating to money laundering, the SRA has emphasised that firms should have a written risk assessment which sets out what risks their firm is exposed to and must also record the steps that have been taken to prepare the risk assessment. Consider the SRA's Warning Notice, *Compliance with the money laundering regulations - firm risk assessment* (May 2019) for guidance on what should be included in such risk assessments.

This obligation has become more prevalent following the COVID-19 pandemic where remote instructions have become, and continue to become, more common. The SRA guidance *Identifying your client* expects a 'proportionate approach' to be taken by solicitors and firms. Some relevant circumstances are detailed in **Table 2.7**.

Table 2.7: Proportionate approach to client identification

Relevant circumstances to a *solicitor* when deciding on the approach to take to identify a client	**Relevant circumstances to a *firm* when deciding on the approach to take to identify a client**
Knowledge of the client	Size of the firm
Type of work involved	The number of fee earners
Whether instructions are taken from the client in person or online	The client profile
	The different areas of work the firm does and the particular risks involved in those areas of work

Revision tip

Para 8.1 is designed primarily to avoid risks of money laundering. Make sure you read ***Revise SQE: The Legal System and Services of England***

and Wales for a full description of money laundering and the obligations on solicitors in this regard. It is also important to have regard to the SRA Warning Notice on *Money laundering and terrorist financing* (2014). This Notice provides practical advice and guidance on indicators or warning signs of money laundering and terrorist financing. Such red flags include the behaviour of the client (eg being secretive or evasive about their identity) and if the source of the funds is unusual (eg large private funding that does not fit the business or personal profile of the payer).

If red flag indicators are present in any dealings with a client, a solicitor should ask further questions and consider making a suspicious activity report to their firm's Money Laundering Reporting Officer (MLRO) or the National Crime Agency, as appropriate. As is made clear in ***Revise SQE: The Legal System and Services of England and Wales***, a solicitor should not notify a client that they have made a suspicious activity report on the basis that they may be 'tipping off' the client.

On 13 January 2025, the SRA published its guidance on *Sham litigation*. This guidance aims to bring attention to the potential threat posed by sham litigation within the legal sector, so that lawyers can take appropriate steps to protect themselves and their firms.

The SRA describes sham litigation as a scheme whereby 'criminals or their associates might orchestrate fake disputes and instruct lawyers to pursue a claim in the courts'. The purpose of such litigation is to effect the transfer of illicit funds or assets as part of a judgment or settlement agreement and thus obscure the true ownership of assets.

The SRA has identified some key indicators to spot potential sham litigation. They include:

- 'Unusual client information and identity verification': The SRA advises solicitors to scrutinise client information for unusual elements, such as inconsistency in names across emails, social media and identification documents.
- 'Clients instructing firms far from their home address': The SRA advises solicitors to consider the client's geographic location in relation to the law firm, and whether it is logical for them to instruct them rather than somebody closer.

Consider the full Guidance for further examples and indicators of sham litigation.

PARAS 8.2–8.5: COMPLAINTS HANDLING

Paras 8.2–8.5 deal with the obligations owed by a solicitor in respect of complaints handling.

Procedure for complaints

Para 8.2 provides that a solicitor must ensure that, as appropriate in the circumstances, they either establish and maintain, or participate in, a procedure for handling complaints in relation to the legal services they provide.

Information to clients

Under Para 8.3, a solicitor must ensure that clients are informed in writing at the time of engagement about:

- their right to complain to the solicitor about their services and charges
- how a complaint can be made and to whom, and
- any right they have to make a complaint to the **Legal Ombudsman** and when they can make any such complaint.

Key term: Legal Ombudsman

The Legal Ombudsman resolves complaints about legal services. They only deal with complaints of poor service (delayed communications, problems with fees or loss of documentation for example) and not breaches of the Principles or Code. The Legal Ombudsman will investigate complaints, looking at all of the facts to reach an outcome. The Legal Ombudsman has identified the steps that need to be taken by a client in respect of a complaint:

1) Tell the lawyer: The client should tell their lawyer of their complaint in order to give the lawyer the chance to resolve and remedy it.
2) Give the lawyer time to resolve things: The client should allow their lawyer up to eight weeks to resolve the complaint. If the solicitor does not deal with the complaint to the client's satisfaction in that time, the client can involve the Legal Ombudsman.
3) Bring the complaint to the Legal Ombudsman: The client has up to six months to bring the complaint to the Legal Ombudsman, but should bring the complaint as soon as they can after having tried to resolve matters with their lawyer.

Most complaints are resolved informally, and if a complaint is upheld, the options open to the Legal Ombudsman include asking the solicitor (or their firm) to give an apology, pay compensation (up to £50,000) or refund or effuse the legal fees. Do take the opportunity to read the Scheme Rules on the Legal Ombudsman's website.

The SQE Annual Report 2024/25 (21 April 2026) suggested that candidates did not appreciate the need to properly signpost complaints procedures to clients. Specifically, candidates were unable to identify when clients should be told about their rights to complain. Furthermore, candidates did not appreciate the interaction between internal complaints procedures and external schemes such as that operated by the Legal Ombudsman.

Procedure following a complaint being made

As noted above, a complaint should generally first be made using the firm's own procedure. Under Para 8.5, a solicitor must ensure that complaints are dealt with promptly, fairly and free of charge.

By Para 8.4, if a client has made a complaint to a solicitor, and if this has not been resolved to the client's satisfaction within eight weeks following the making of a complaint, the solicitor must ensure that the client is informed, in writing:

- of any right they have to complain to the Legal Ombudsman, the time frame for doing so and full details of how to contact the Legal Ombudsman, and
- if a complaint has been brought and the solicitor's complaints procedure has been exhausted:
  - that the solicitor cannot settle the complaint
  - of the name and website address of an alternative dispute resolution (ADR) approved body which would be competent to deal with the complaint, and
  - whether the solicitor agrees to use the scheme operated by that body.

PARAS 8.6–8.11: CLIENT INFORMATION AND PUBLICITY

Under Paras 8.6–8.11, a solicitor owes obligations regarding information given to the client and publicity of the solicitor and their firm (see also **Key term: publicity**, below). In addition to Paras 8.6–8.11, you are strongly advised to read in full the **SRA Transparency Rules**.

Key term: SRA Transparency Rules
The Transparency Rules set out the information that authorised firms should make available to clients and potential clients. The aims of these Rules are to ensure that people have accurate and relevant information about a solicitor or firm when they are considering purchasing legal services and that they will help members of the public and small businesses make informed choices, improving competition in the legal market.

The Transparency Rules require firms to include information on costs, complaints, publication and regulatory information.

Revision tip

The SRA Transparency Rules are quite detailed in respect of information that must be made available to the public on costs. Do take the opportunity to review which specified services these rules apply to and the information that must be included. The Transparency Rules can be obtained from the SRA's website.

Information to clients

Under Para 8.6, a solicitor must give clients information in a way they can understand. This includes ensuring that clients are in a position to make informed decisions about the services they need, how their matter will be handled and the options available to them. Following their first interview, it is common for a solicitor to send their client a **client care letter**.

Key term: client care letter

Although not expressly required by the Code of Conduct, it is advisable that solicitors provide their clients with the necessary legal and regulatory information in the form of a client care letter. The terms of business are usually attached to the client care letter also. This letter will provide an explanation of agreed work or scope of the retainer, funding method agreed, who will carry out the day-to-day work on the matter and who will have overall responsibility, a costs breakdown or estimate where a breakdown is not possible, the obligations on the solicitor and the client, the complaints procedure, if applicable the grades of fee-earner within the firm and the relevant hourly rates, timescales for the agreed work, actions required from the client and relevant contact details.

Importantly, therefore, any client care letter sent by a solicitor or firm must be written in a clear and accessible manner. It must be concise, written in plain English, and must prioritise information which is most relevant to the client. This will often require a balance to be struck by a solicitor between providing technical information and advice, and providing the information in a sufficiently client-friendly manner.

Information on costs

Para 8.7 requires solicitors to ensure that clients receive the best possible information about how their matter will be priced and, both at the time of engagement and when appropriate as their matter progresses, about the likely overall cost of the matter and any **costs** incurred.

Key term: costs

The SRA defines 'costs' as meaning a solicitor's fees and disbursements. 'Fees' means a solicitor's own charges or profit costs (including any VAT element). 'Disbursements' refer to money that has to be paid to third parties in connection with the matter that they are dealing with on behalf of the client, and include such things as court fees, fees to instruct a medical expert and barrister fees.

'Best possible information' is not defined by the SRA and requires a solicitor to use their own independent good judgement as to when the information they provide will be considered the 'best possible information'.

Exam warning

The duty to provide the best possible information on costs is a continuing duty. This means that a solicitor is under a continuous obligation to inform their clients about the costs which the client may be liable for. Do not think that the duty to provide the best possible information is satisfied and can be forgotten about after the first discussion between the solicitor and client.

To ensure that a solicitor complies with this obligation, the solicitor should explain clearly (in, for example, a client care letter):

- how their fees are calculated (including a costs breakdown)
- what the VAT implications are in any hourly rate or quote
- if their fees are liable to change, how and when this may happen
- whether the solicitor will require **money on account** from the client
- what additional fees or costs the client may be liable for (eg court and counsel fees).

Key term: money on account

At the start of the retainer, a solicitor may require a client to pay a sum of money on account for the costs and disbursements that will be incurred by the solicitor. This is particularly so when the client has agreed to pay on a private retainer (ie pay the costs personally) or a conditional fee arrangement where the disbursements are paid by the client.

It will rarely be possible to provide a client with a definite fee statement from the outset of a case. In this situation, a solicitor may consider it appropriate to stipulate a ceiling fee (ie a figure which the solicitor cannot go above without the permission of the client), or stipulate a review date when the solicitor will revisit their costs with the client.

Revision tip

Whilst a solicitor does not require prior approval for every item of expenditure, they should ask for a client's instructions for big expenses which mean that the original estimate is no longer accurate. For example, a solicitor who provides the client with an estimate of likely total costs will need to inform the client should that figure require amendment because of new features or changes (such as the need to instruct an expert witness). Look out for this in an MCQ.

Fee options

In providing a competent level of service, a solicitor must explain to the client the different ways in which their services may be paid for. **Table 2.8** provides some examples of ways to pay for a solicitor's fees. Any solicitor must be in a position to advise their client as to these options (bearing in mind Para 3.4 which requires a solicitor to consider and take account of their client's attributes, needs and circumstances).

Table 2.8: Fee options

Fee options	Explanation and examples
Hourly rate	The client is charged for the time spent on their case on an hourly basis.
Fixed fee	Most commonly seen in conveyancing cases, a solicitor may agree to act for a fixed fee (or fixed fee plus VAT and disbursements). If a solicitor charges by fixed fee, this fee cannot be changed without the client's consent.
Conditional Fee Agreements (CFAs)	An example of a CFA is to charge a client on a 'no win, no fee' basis. In essence, a CFA is an agreement between a client and their solicitor, whereby if the case is lost, the client will not have to pay their solicitor's fees. If the case is won, then the solicitor can charge an agreed 'uplift' on their fees (known as a 'success fee'), representing sometimes up to 100% of the solicitor's base fee. Any CFA must be in writing, signed by both the solicitor and the client, and specify the percentage of the success fee. CFAs cannot be entered into for any criminal work.
Damages-based Agreements (DBAs)	DBAs allow for a solicitor to recover their fees from a percentage of any damages obtained by the client. The maximum payment a solicitor may recover from the damages is capped at 25% of damages obtained (excluding future care and loss) in personal injury cases, and 50% of damages obtained in all other cases.
Legal expenses insurance	Some clients have the benefit of legal expenses insurance, which can include Before the Event Insurance (BTE) and After the Event Insurance (ATE). The client's costs may be met by the insurer, eg motor and home insurance policies. Such insurance methods are advisable alongside a CFA or DBA.

It is vital to remember that a solicitor must not take advantage of their clients and they have a duty to make clients aware of, and understand, the options for funding their claim and the terms of any fee agreement they enter into with their solicitor. For more detail on the different options available for funding legal services, including legal aid and variable fees, see ***Revise SQE: The Legal System and Services of England and Wales***.

Accurate publicity

By Para 8.8, a solicitor must ensure that any **publicity** in relation to their practice is accurate and not misleading.

Key term: publicity

The SRA defines 'publicity' as including all promotional material and activity, including the name or description of a solicitor's firm, stationery, advertisements, brochures, websites, directory entries, media appearances, promotional press releases and direct approaches to potential clients and other persons, whether conducted in person, in writing or in electronic form, but does not include press releases prepared on behalf of a client.

This is particularly relevant when a solicitor or their firm advertises the services available and offered. The duty within Para 8.8 includes information relating to a solicitor's charges and the circumstances in which interest is payable by or to clients.

This also includes any marketing material used by third parties that you work with.

The SRA's Warning Notice on *Marketing your services to members of the public* (2024) advises that any materials must not make misleading or inaccurate statements about such matters as:

- the prospects of success of any claim or within any areas of claim
- the level of any award likely to be made
- feedback provided by other claimants about the firm
- awards or other credentials held by the firm
- established ombudsman or compensation schemes that consumers can approach directly themselves for free.

The Warning Notice further advises solicitors that they must ensure that clients referred by a third party were not acquired by that third party through misleading publicity or promotional material.

Unsolicited approaches

By Para 8.9, a solicitor must not make unsolicited approaches to members of the public in order to advertise legal services provided by the solicitor, their business or employer.

Exam warning

Be aware that the rule against unsolicited approaches does not apply to current or former clients. This is to ensure that a firm can maintain its relations with current and former clients. Do not allow an MCQ to trick you into thinking that the restriction applies equally to former and current clients.

Table 2.9 identifies what this rule means for solicitors, with examples of permitted and not permitted approaches. For further information, see the SRA Guidance, *Unsolicited approaches (advertising) to members of the public* (2019).

Table 2.9: Unsolicited approaches

Permitted approaches	Not permitted approaches
Any advertisement done in a non-intrusive and non-targeted way. For example, advertisements in a newspaper, on the radio or on a social media platform would be permitted as they would not be considered a targeted approach.	Direct or specifically targeted approaches to members of the public in person, by phone or via any other means which targets them individually. For example, cold calling or door-to-door visits may be considered unsolicited and intrusive. This restriction applies even if the solicitor knows the members of the public personally (eg they are their neighbours).

What **Table 2.9** should show is that advertising to the public is permitted, so long as the solicitor complies with the Code of Conduct and any additional relevant law (such as data protection legislation). Use **Table 2.9** to help you understand **Practice example 2.13.**

Practice example 2.13

James is a sole practitioner specialising in personal injury law. James has identified a list of individuals who have recently been involved in a major road traffic accident. James sends each person on that list a letter stating that he can help them claim compensation.

What's your view on James' communication with the list of individuals?

The SRA's guidance *Unsolicited Approaches (Advertising) to Members of the Public* (December 2019) would treat James' conduct as a breach of Para 8.9. The SRA's Guidance suggests that James' communication involves a targeted approach to specific members of the public which may feel intrusive to those who receive it due to the particular circumstances that they find themselves in.

The SRA's Warning Notice on *Marketing your services to members of the public* (2024) clarifies that the prohibiton in Para 8.9 applies equally to any client referred to you by a third party, such as a lead generator business or a claims management company. A solicitor is under a duty to ensure that any client referred by a third party has not been acquired in a way that would breach the SRA's regulatory arrangements if the person acquiring the client were regulated by the SRA. Specifically, a solicitor/firm must be able to demonstrate that a client, referred to them by a third party, was not acquired through cold calling or door-knocking, or other targeted or unsolicited approaches. There should be arrangements in place to ensure this does not happen. The SRA is clear: 'It is not acceptable to say that the third party was not regulated by the SRA and so not subject to the prohibition on cold calling.'

Regulatory information

Under Paras 8.10 and 8.11, solicitors must provide clients with information on how solicitors are regulated, and what protection is available for clients. This will ordinarily be contained in a client care letter; however, a firm is obligated by the SRA Transparency Rules to display in a prominent place on its website (if it has one) its SRA number and the SRA's digital badge (an icon confirming that the firm is regulated by the SRA). Furthermore, on its letterheads and in emails, the firm must identify its SRA number and the words 'authorised and regulated by the Solicitors Regulation Authority'.

Particularly, Para 8.10 provides that a solicitor must ensure that clients understand whether and how the services they provide are regulated. This includes:

- explaining which activities will be carried out by the solicitor, as an authorised person
- explaining which services provided by the solicitor, their business or employer, and any separate business are regulated by an approved regulator, and
- ensuring that solicitors do not represent any business or employer which is not authorised by the SRA, including any separate business (see **Separate businesses** above), as being regulated by the SRA.

Furthermore, under Para 8.11, a solicitor must ensure that clients understand the regulatory protections available to them. For example, information on the SRA Compensation Fund and the firm's indemnity insurance will need to be provided.

CODE OF CONDUCT FOR FIRMS

The Code of Conduct for Firms describes the standards and business controls that the SRA, and the public, expect of firms (including sole practices) authorised by the SRA to provide legal services. As discussed above, the Code of Conduct for Firms largely mirrors that of the Code of Conduct for Solicitors, RELs, RFLs and RSLs. For that reason, we shall not repeat paragraphs of the Code that are identical and shall focus on the remit of the SQE1 Assessment.

Exam warning

The SQE1 Assessment Specification suggests that candidates are *only* required to understand:

- Para 8.1: Managers in authorised firms
- Paras 9.1 and 9.2: Compliance officers.

Despite this, you are strongly advised to read the Code of Conduct for Firms in full.

Para 8: managers in SRA authorised firms

Para 8.1 of the Code identifies that a firm's **manager** is responsible for a firm's compliance with the Code.

Key term: manager

For the purposes of the SRA Code of Conduct, a manager means the sole principal in a recognised sole practice; a member of a LLP; a director of a company; a partner in a partnership; or in relation to any other body, a member of its governing body.

This means that the managers must ensure the firm complies with all regulatory and legislative requirements, and must ensure that the firm has all the systems needed to achieve that objective. This responsibility can be both joint and several if there is more than one manager, and they share the management responsibility between them.

Para 9: compliance officers

Every firm must have a compliance officer for legal practice (COLP) and a compliance officer for finance and administration (COFA).

Table 2.10 identifies the responsibilities of both compliance officers.

Table 2.10: Responsibilities of compliance officers

Responsibilities of a COLP	Responsibilities of a COFA
A COLP must take *all reasonable steps* to: • ensure compliance with the terms and conditions of the firm's authorisation • ensure compliance by the firm and its managers, employees or interest holders with the regulatory arrangements which apply to them (except any obligations imposed under the SRA Accounts Rules) • ensure that the firm's managers and interest holders, and those they employ or contract with, do not cause or substantially contribute to a breach of the regulatory arrangements • ensure that a prompt report is made to the SRA of any serious breach of the terms and conditions of the firm's authorisation, or the regulatory arrangements which apply to the firm, managers or employees.	A COFA must take *all reasonable steps* to: • ensure that the firm and its managers and employees comply with any obligations imposed upon them under the SRA Accounts Rules • ensure that a prompt report is made to the SRA of any serious breach of the SRA Accounts Rules which apply to them.

Both the COLP and the COFA have a responsibility to ensure that the SRA is informed promptly of any facts or matters that the COLP and COFA reasonably believe should be brought to the SRA's attention in order that the SRA may investigate whether a serious breach of its regulatory arrangements has occurred, or otherwise exercise its regulatory powers.

The compliance officers should keep a record of all breaches that occur (see Para 2.2 of the Code of Conduct for Firms). These records are used to understand the risks of the business and implement any necessary processes to mitigate or remove this risk in future. As with solicitors, the compliance officer must make a judgement call as to whether any breach is considered 'serious' and should be reported to the SRA (see **Practice example 2.14**).

Practice example 2.14

Mark is a solicitor in a high-street law firm. Mark is concerned that one of his colleagues, Adam, is in breach of the SRA Code of Conduct and Accounts Rules. In particular, Mark discovered that Adam used client money in order to pay for a meal with Adam's family. Adam explained that he was merely borrowing the money and would repay it the next day.

What responsibilities exist for Mark and the compliance officers?

The misuse of client money is a breach of the regulatory requirements owed by Adam (see the Accounts Rules) and would likely be considered a 'serious breach' by the SRA. Mark has two options available to him: Mark may either report the matter directly to the SRA (in line with Para 7.7 of the Code for Individuals) or report the matter to the compliance officer (the COFA in particular, in line with Para 7.12 of the Code for Individuals).

If made aware, the COFA should first record the alleged breach. The COFA should then review the allegation and consider the nature of the alleged breach. In line with the SRA Enforcement Strategy, the SRA is concerned with 'serious breaches' of the Code and regulatory requirements. If the COFA does have reasonable grounds to believe that a serious breach has occurred, then the COFA should inform the SRA promptly of the matter so that the SRA may investigate it (Para 9.2 of the Code for Firms).

Exam warning

Remember that managers have ultimate responsibility for how the firm is run, and its compliance with the Code of Conduct, and not the COLP or COFA. Neither compliance officer is to be liable for the failings of the managers; the compliance officer will only be liable if they fail to meet the standard expected from their own responsibilities. Do not allow an MCQ to confuse these responsibilities.

THE REMAINDER OF THIS GUIDE

The remaining chapters will now focus your attention on how the SRA Principles and Code of Conduct apply to the various practice areas that are assessable on SQE1. These chapters will be structured according to the headings of the Code of Conduct and, throughout, will feature cross-references back to this chapter and **Chapter 1**.

KEY POINT CHECKLIST

This chapter has covered the following key knowledge points. You can use these to structure your revision, ensuring you recall the key details for each point, as covered in this chapter.

- The Code of Conduct includes both the Code for Solicitors, RELs and RFLs (the Code of Conduct for Individuals) and the Code for Firms. The two are largely identical and should be read together.
- Under Para 1, a solicitor must maintain trust and act fairly, which includes not unfairly discriminating against another.
- Under Para 2, a solicitor owes a number of obligations in respect of dispute resolution, including drawing the court's attention to relevant cases, statutory provisions and procedural irregularities which are likely to have a material effect on the outcome of proceedings.
- Under Para 3, a solicitor must ensure that the services provided and supervised are competent.
- Under Para 4, a solicitor must safeguard client money and must account for any financial benefit received as a result of their instructions (unless the client has agreed otherwise).
- Under Para 5, a solicitor owes obligations in respect of referrals, introductions and separate businesses.
- Under Para 6, a solicitor owes a number of duties in respect of confidentiality and disclosure. A solicitor also owes a number of duties in respect of conflicts of interest.
- Under Para 7, a solicitor must cooperate with the SRA and is accountable for their own conduct.
- Under Para 8, a solicitor owes a number of duties in respect of client identification, information on complaints, and client information and publicity.
- Under the Code of Conduct for Firms, candidates must be aware of the obligations imposed on managers of the firm and compliance officers of the firm.

KEY TERMS AND CONCEPTS

- Code of Conduct (**page 27**)
- Enforcement Strategy (**page 28**)
- retainer (**page 30**)
- litigant in person (**page 31**)
- non-disclosure agreements (**page 31**)
- Strategic Lawsuits against Public Participation (**page 33**)
- undertaking (**page 36**)
- financial benefit (**page 47**)
- introducers (**page 49**)
- reserved legal activity (**page 52**)
- own interest conflict (**page 53**)

- conflict of interest (**page 54**)
- notification requirements (**page 64**)
- reporting requirements (**page 64**)
- serious breach (**page 65**)
- Legal Ombudsman (**page 69**)
- SRA Transparency Rules (**page 70**)
- client care letter (**page 71**)
- costs (**page 71**)
- money on account (**page 72**)
- publicity (**page 74**)
- manager (**page 77**)

■ SQE1-STYLE QUESTIONS

QUESTION 1

A solicitor acts for a buyer in a conveyancing matter. The solicitor has been contacted by the seller of the property demanding receipt of the deposit money by 9 AM the following morning. Unable to make contact with the buyer, the solicitor telephones the seller and states that the firm will pay the deposit money by 9 AM tomorrow.

Which of the following best describes the ethical position of the solicitor and the firm?

A. Both the solicitor and their firm are bound by the undertaking and are personally liable to perform the undertaking as provided.

B. Neither the solicitor nor the firm are bound by the undertaking and are not personally liable to perform the undertaking as provided, but the buyer will be liable to perform the undertaking.

C. The solicitor, but not the firm, is bound by the undertaking and is personally liable to perform the undertaking as provided.

D. Neither the solicitor nor the firm are bound by the undertaking, nor are they personally liable to perform the undertaking as provided.

E. The firm, but not the solicitor, is bound by the undertaking and is personally liable to perform the undertaking as provided.

QUESTION 2

A solicitor acts on behalf of a woman who was involved in a road traffic accident. The woman is the defendant in a personal injury claim. The woman has no counter-claim against the claimant. The solicitor wishes to refer the woman to an insurance company in order to secure after the event (ATE) insurance to fund the solicitor's services. The insurance company offer the solicitor a referral fee of £200.

Will the solicitor be in breach of the Code of Conduct by accepting the referral fee?

A. Yes, the solicitor must not accept the referral fee in claims for damages following personal injury in any circumstances.
B. No, the solicitor can accept the referral fee in claims for damages following personal injury because they are acting for the defendant. The solicitor must account for the referral fee, unless agreed otherwise.
C. Yes, the solicitor must not accept the referral fee in claims for damages following personal injury given the potential for an own interest conflict.
D. No, the solicitor can accept the referral fee in claims for damages following personal injury because the fee is under £500. The solicitor must account for the referral fee, unless agreed otherwise.
E. Yes, the solicitor must not accept the referral fee in claims for damages without the consent of the woman.

QUESTION 3

A solicitor is arrested for assault following a house party. The police issue the solicitor with a caution but do not charge him with a criminal offence.

Is the solicitor obligated to notify the Solicitors Regulation Authority (SRA) of his caution?

A. No, the solicitor is only required to notify the SRA if he was convicted of an offence.
B. Yes, the solicitor must notify the SRA of his caution, but need not do it personally. The solicitor may notify the SRA via the firm's manager.
C. No, the solicitor is only required to notify the SRA if he was charged with, or convicted of, an offence.
D. Yes, the solicitor must notify the SRA of his caution personally or via the firm's compliance officer.
E. No, the solicitor is only required to notify the SRA of circumstances which involve serious misconduct, which the assault is not.

QUESTION 4

A solicitor is acting for a client whose mother has just died. The solicitor was instructed to deal with the probate. Based upon the initial instructions, the solicitor concluded the matter to be non-contentious and gave the client a likely quote of £1,000 plus VAT for costs. The solicitor has received correspondence from another firm of solicitors advising that they have been instructed to contest the will. Reviewing the documentation that forms part of the objections to the will, the solicitor considers the matter to be more complicated than originally thought.

Which of the following is the best course of action that should be taken by the solicitor?

A. The solicitor must give the client an update on the likely increase in costs if the matter becomes litigated.
B. The solicitor must give the client an updated quote to reflect the contested nature of the probate.
C. The solicitor is not permitted to alter the £1,000 fee as that is the original price quoted and agreed with the client.
D. The solicitor does not need to inform the client of the likely increase in costs given that the original quoted price was only an estimate.
E. The solicitor must charge the £1,000 fee plus VAT as agreed or cease to act.

QUESTION 5

A solicitor acts for a man who is buying a house. The solicitor is also later instructed to act for a mortgage company from whom the man has sought a loan in respect of the house. The man has recently been in touch with his solicitor, identifying that he is relieved that the survey of the property, sent to the mortgage company to value the house, omitted evidence which he considers would have prevented his loan from being approved. The solicitor did not identify a conflict of interest between the man and the mortgage provider when he accepted the instructions. However, the solicitor is now concerned that a conflict may exist and requires advice.

Which of the following is the best advice that should be given to the solicitor?

A. The solicitor can continue to act for the man but must cease to act for the mortgage company. The solicitor must not disclose the reason for ceasing to act to the mortgage company.
B. The solicitor can continue to act for both the man and the mortgage company. The solicitor must not disclose the information provided by the man to the mortgage company.
C. The solicitor must cease to act for both the man and the mortgage company. The solicitor must not disclose the reason for ceasing to act to both the man and the mortgage company.
D. The solicitor can continue to act for the man but must cease to act for the mortgage company. The solicitor must disclose the reason for ceasing to act to the mortgage company.
E. The solicitor can continue to act for the man but must cease to act for

the mortgage company. The solicitor must not disclose the reason for ceasing to act to the mortgage company unless the man consents to the disclosure.

ANSWERS TO QUESTIONS

Answers to 'What do you know already?' questions at the start of the chapter

1) False. Whilst Mark may have limited experience, the Code of Conduct applies to all individuals who conduct legal work regulated by the SRA. Mark's experience may be relevant to penalties imposed should a breach of the Code be found, but will not be relevant to the question of whether a breach actually occurred.
2) The notification requirement arises if:
   - the solicitor is subject to a criminal charge, conviction or caution
   - the solicitor is made bankrupt, enters an individual voluntary arrangement with their creditors or is subject to a debt relief order
   - the solicitor becomes aware of material change in information about them or their practice previously provided to the SRA
   - the solicitor becomes aware that information previously provided to the SRA about them or their practice is false, misleading, incomplete or inaccurate.
3) False. The duty of confidentiality survives the death of the client and passes to the personal representatives of the client. Decisions as to confidentiality will rest with the personal representatives.
4) A solicitor is not permitted to make unsolicited approaches to members of the public in order to advertise their legal services by Para 8.9 of the Code of Conduct. However, there is an exception in respect of current or former clients in order to advertise legal services provided by the firm or solicitor. Be aware, however, that former and current clients can opt out of receiving any unsolicited communications.

Answers to end-of-chapter SQE1-style questions

Question 1:

The correct answer was A. The solicitor, by providing an undertaking that the deposit will be paid by 9 AM the following morning, will be personally bound by that undertaking. However, given that the solicitor acts on behalf of their firm, the firm will also be bound by that undertaking. Therefore, all other options are incorrect.

Question 2:

The correct answer was B. The restriction on referral fees in personal injury cases applies only to claimant clients; it does not apply to defendant clients. Given that the defendant has no counter-claim, there is no restriction on the solicitor obtaining the referral fee (therefore options A, C, and E are wrong). However, the solicitor must account to the client for any financial benefit obtained, which includes referral fees. Option D is wrong because the level of referral fee is irrelevant to the Code of Conduct.

Question 3:

The correct answer was D. The Code of Conduct requires the solicitor to notify the SRA of any caution, charge, or conviction that they are subjected to. Because of this, it is irrelevant that the solicitor is not charged or convicted of the offence; the caution is sufficient (therefore options A and C are wrong). Option B is wrong in that notification through the firm's manager is not sufficient: the solicitor must either notify the SRA personally or through the firm's compliance officer. Option E is wrong on the basis that the seriousness of the misconduct is not relevant to the automatic notification procedure.

Question 4:

The correct answer was A. As the matter is now contested, the likelihood is that the costs will be of a higher amount than that expected by the solicitor, and of a higher amount initially communicated to the client. As the solicitor is unlikely to be able to give an accurate estimate at this point in time (therefore option B is wrong), the solicitor is better advised to update the client by advising on the likely increase in price. The solicitor is not obligated to maintain their original quote, therefore options C and E are wrong. Option D is incorrect because the solicitor is under a duty to provide the client with the best possible information in relation to costs when appropriate and as the matter progresses (ie they owe a continuing duty).

Question 5:

The correct answer was E. At first, there appeared to be no conflict between the man (as the borrower) and the mortgage company (as the lender). However, following the man's disclosure to the solicitor about the survey, the solicitor now holds material information which they would have to disclose to the mortgage company if they continued to act for them. As this material is adverse to the man, the solicitor is now faced with a conflict of interest. Unable to rely on any of the exceptions, the solicitor must cease to act for the mortgage company immediately and, given their duty of confidence to the man, must not disclose the reason for them ceasing to act. Option A is not the best answer because the solicitor can disclose the information to the mortgage company if the man consents (thus why option E is the best answer). Option B is wrong because the man and the mortgage company now have contrary interests and a conflict exists. Option C is incorrect because the solicitor can continue to act for the man in these circumstances as there does not appear to be any confidential information on the facts held by the solicitor in respect of the mortgage company. Option D is wrong because the solicitor is not permitted to disclose the reason for ceasing to act unless permitted by law (not evident here) or with the client's consent.

■ KEY CASES, RULES, STATUTES AND INSTRUMENTS

The SQE1 Assessment Specification has identified that candidates are required to understand the purpose, scope and content of the SRA Code of Conduct. Candidates will not be required to know specific paragraph numbers from the Code, but must be prepared to know the principles coming from those paragraph numbers.

The SQE1 Assessment Specification does not require you to know any case names, or statutory materials, for the topic of the SRA Code of Conduct.

3

Ethics and professional conduct in dispute resolution

David Sixsmith

■ MAKE SURE YOU KNOW

This chapter will cover the application of the Solicitors Regulation Authority (SRA) Principles and Code of Conduct to civil dispute resolution practice. This chapter will allow you to observe how ethical issues and professional conduct matters are likely to arise when practising in civil dispute resolution.

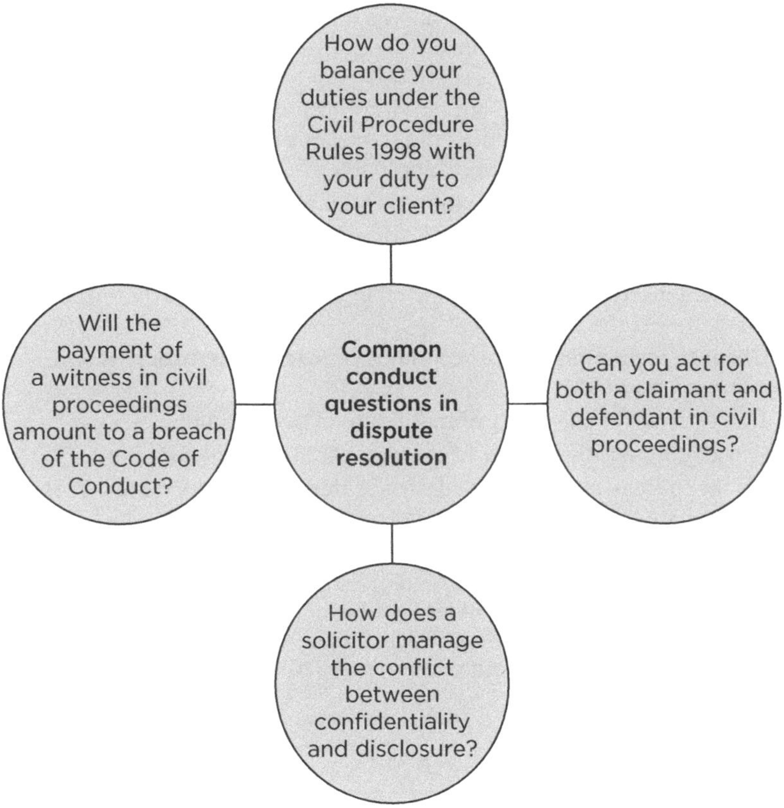

Dispute resolution features in the first of the SQE1 assessments (FLK1), and ethics and professional conduct relevant to civil dispute resolution will be assessed pervasively in that assessment.

SQE ASSESSMENT ADVICE

As you work through this chapter, remember to pay particular attention in your revision to:

- the conflict that exists between a solicitor's duty to the client and their duty to the court
- the way a solicitor should deal with witnesses in civil proceedings
- the conflict between the duty of confidentiality and the duty of disclosure
- the circumstances in which you can continue to act for two clients where a conflict of interest exists.

WHAT DO YOU KNOW ALREADY?

Have a go at these questions before reading this chapter. If you find some difficult or cannot remember the answers, make a note to look more closely at that area during your revision.

1) True or false? When dealing with a litigant in person on the opposing side of a dispute, you are entitled to put forward your client's legal position in the strongest possible terms, but not allowed to use your position to influence the opposing party.

   [You do not abuse your position by taking unfair advantage of clients or others (Para 1.2); page 90]

2) A client informs a solicitor that their witness statement contains a significant error which materially changes the nature of their evidence. What should the solicitor do?

   [Dispute resolution and proceedings before courts, tribunals and inquiries; page 92]

3) True or false? A solicitor's primary duty is to the court.

   [Misleading another party to the proceedings; page 91]

4) A solicitor fails to exchange witness statements by the deadline. The solicitor submits an application for relief from sanctions, which is unsuccessful. The client is already unhappy about the length of time the process is taking and has mentioned on more than one occasion that they are prepared to make a complaint. The solicitor is due to leave the practice the following week. What should the solicitor do?

   [Maintaining trust and acting fairly; page 106]

INTRODUCTION TO ETHICS AND PROFESSIONAL CONDUCT IN DISPUTE RESOLUTION

Civil litigation is a high-pressure environment in which to practice. That pressure can emanate from a variety of different sources, and there are times when the behaviour of clients who are desperate to be successful in their claim or defence can conflict with a solicitor's professional duty to the court. This can lead to a range of potential ethical issues arising for solicitors practising in the area of dispute resolution. This chapter will cover the nature of some of these issues, as well as providing guidance on how you could answer any questions relating to professional conduct in dispute resolution which might arise in your SQE1 assessment.

This chapter should be read in conjunction with ***Revise SQE: Dispute Resolution***. In that guide, you will find many **Key terms** and important substantive topics to assist you in furthering your understanding of your ethical and professional obligations.

In the present guide, **Chapters 1 and 2** set out the SRA Principles (the 'Principles') and Code of Conduct (the 'Code') respectively. This chapter will consider how relevant headings operate in the context of dispute resolution. The headings used reflect the headings of the Code of Conduct.

MAINTAINING TRUST AND ACTING FAIRLY

When dealing with civil disputes, you must maintain trust in your relationship with your client. The Code sets out ways in which you can achieve this. These are dealt with in turn.

You do not unfairly discriminate (Para 1.1)

Dispute resolution can be a particularly acrimonious arena. Parties to disputes can display behaviour towards each other outside the court room which you, as a legal representative, could find distasteful or inappropriate. They could belong to political parties or movements which do not align with your own views. It is important that you do not let any personal feelings you have towards the way in which your client may have behaved affect your professional conduct in any way. Examples can include:

- not allowing any difference in political viewpoints to affect the way in which a solicitor represents a client
- not allowing a client's sexual orientation to change the nature of the relationship between a solicitor and their client.

Practice example 3.1 demonstrates how this would operate in practice.

Practice example 3.1

Ron is a solicitor specialising in boundary disputes and is a member of a local group which campaigns for additional funding to support victims of domestic violence. He is representing Gary and Sheila, who are involved in a dispute with their neighbour about the position of the boundary fence between their respective properties. Sheila contacts Ron to tell him that Gary has just told her that he has a previous conviction for assaulting his former partner three years ago. She gives Ron written authority to receive instructions from Gary on her behalf, as the pressure of the litigation is getting to her, and she wants to concentrate on her relationship with Gary.

What should Ron do in this situation?

Ron should continue to act for Gary and Sheila and, if there is a written authority signed by Sheila authorising Ron to accept instructions from Gary on her behalf, he should do so. Whilst Gary's previous conviction clearly conflicts with Ron's personal views, this should not affect his conduct of the litigation or his professional relationship with Gary.

You do not abuse your position by taking unfair advantage of clients or others (Para 1.2)

As part of your practice in dispute resolution, you will inevitably encounter *litigants in person* (see **Chapter 2** for the **Key term**).

When you do, you must be careful to ensure that you do not use your position as a solicitor to threaten or pressurise them into agreeing to something on the basis that they do not know any better. For example, a solicitor cannot tell an unrepresented claimant that they will make as many procedural applications as possible to frustrate the litigation, run up costs, and delay trial if the claimant does not accept an undervalued settlement proposal.

Likewise, a solicitor cannot use their position to persuade their client to accept a settlement which is substantially lower than that to which they are entitled so that, for example, the file could be closed thus reducing that solicitor's workload.

You do not mislead clients, the court or others (Para 1.4)

A solicitor should not mislead or attempt to mislead their clients, the court, or others, either by their own acts or omissions, or by allowing or being complicit in the acts or omissions of others (including their client). Whilst this may seem obvious, there are many instances of solicitors breaching this part of the Code.

It is important to bear in mind that a solicitor does not need to act *intentionally* to be in breach of this professional requirement; it is an objective assessment as to whether they have done so. For example, let us look at a potential scenario where a solicitor is representing a claimant at trial. They did not draft the witness statements and, due to pressure of time in advance of the trial, only read them very briefly. In their summary, the judge referred to one of the claimant's witnesses as having stated something which they did not. The solicitor, as they did not read the statement properly, fails to correct the judge. This would be an instance of a solicitor misleading the court, albeit unintentionally, and therefore breaching the Code.

Here are some further examples which may assist you with understanding how a solicitor may mislead a client, the court, or the other party to the proceedings in the context of dispute resolution.

Misleading a client

Solicitors can mislead clients by, for example:

- informing them that their case is progressing well when, in fact, it has failed
- stating that a case is proceeding through court when it has not been issued
- backdating a letter sent to a client informing them that they have done something when they have not.

Misleading the court

Solicitors can mislead the court by, for example:

- signing a claim form, or particulars of claim, on behalf of a client when they know it contains a material fact which is untrue
- allowing counsel to make a misleading statement to the court when the solicitor knows that it is untrue
- making a false representation to the court about an opponent's conduct in their absence at a hearing.

Misleading another party to the proceedings

Solicitors can mislead another party to the proceedings by, for example:

- having instructions from their client that they will accept an offer of settlement from their opponent, but informing their opponent that their client will only accept a higher amount
- indicating that their client has instructed counsel to represent them at a mediation or hearing when this is not the case
- indicating that they have sought the opinion of an expert when this is not the case
- sending misleading or exaggerated legal claims intended to deter legitimate scrutiny (the conduct of which would amount to a SLAPP - see above).

DISPUTE RESOLUTION AND PROCEEDINGS BEFORE COURTS, TRIBUNALS AND INQUIRIES

As covered in **Chapter 2**, a solicitor's primary duty is to the court. Part 2 of the Code deals with the way in which a solicitor must behave in order to uphold their primary duty. SQE1 may ask you questions about how you would behave in response to certain scenarios which may arise during the course of practising in the area of dispute resolution. Examples of these are set out in this section.

You do not seek to influence the substance of evidence (Para 2.2)

A solicitor must not influence the substance of evidence, including generating false evidence or persuading witnesses to change their evidence. In civil proceedings, this can include:

- coaxing a witness into giving evidence which fits the nature of the claim or the defence, as opposed to it being a representation of what they witnessed. Whilst there is nothing which prevents a solicitor from drafting a witness statement on a witness's behalf, this must be an accurate representation of their own words rather than the solicitor's interpretation of what the witness experienced
- allowing a client to deliberately exclude evidence which is relevant to the case because it adversely affects their position in the litigation
- allowing a client to present evidence to the court which the solicitor knows is false or misleading.

Practice example 3.2 illustrates how this could work in practice.

Practice example 3.2

Nusrat is representing Jacob, defending a claim against his former partner, Gemma. Gemma is claiming an equitable interest in one of Jacob's properties on the basis that she paid cash for a substantial amount of the renovation work which was carried out to the property three years ago. Jacob's position is that Gemma made no such financial contribution and is therefore entitled to nothing. One month before the deadline for disclosure, Nusrat meets with Jacob to review the documentation he has in his possession. As Jacob looks through his folder of documents, Nusrat notices him removing pieces of paper and placing them to one side. Nusrat sees that one of the documents is a builder's receipt showing that £4,000 in cash was received from Gemma. When Nusrat raises this with Jacob, he says that he gave the cash to Gemma to pay the builder but he does not want to complicate things by including the document in the disclosure list.

What should Nusrat do in this situation?

The document in question is evidently relevant to the proceedings, and Jacob's attempt to conceal it is a clear attempt to influence the substance of evidence and mislead the court. Nusrat is aware of this and therefore cannot continue to act for Jacob if he maintains his refusal to disclose the document. Nusrat must inform Jacob that he must either disclose the document or she cannot continue to act for him. If he still refuses to disclose the document, Nusrat must remove herself from the court record and advise Jacob to seek alternative representation.

You do not provide or offer to provide any benefit to witnesses dependent upon the nature of their evidence or the outcome of the case (Para 2.3)

A solicitor must not offer any sort of benefit to influence what a witness says or, indeed, whether they appear at all. Examples of this can include the following situations:

- if a witness asks for financial remuneration which goes beyond compensation for expenses such as travel in exchange for giving evidence at court, the solicitor must refuse
- where a client asks their solicitor to offer payment to a witness in exchange for tailoring the content of their evidence to suit their client's case, the solicitor must refuse to do so.

You draw the court's attention to relevant cases and procedural irregularities (Para 2.7)

This duty can often be a difficult one to reconcile with the obligation to act in your client's best interests. Sometimes, a situation will arise where the other side's solicitor mistakenly concedes that a provision of the Civil Procedure Rules (CPR) 1998 operates in a way which benefits your client and is detrimental to theirs. What should a solicitor do in this situation? It is, of course, tempting to say nothing and allow the result to go in your client's favour, however this would not be compliant with a solicitor's obligations under this part of the Code. A solicitor must bring the court's attention to any mistakes which the other side may make in relation to the wording or operation of a particular provision.

Practice example 3.3 shows how this could arise in practice.

Practice example 3.3

Kirstie is representing Gavin, who is opposing an application under CPR 13 to set aside default judgment. The applicant is represented by a trainee solicitor. The applicant's argument is that they submitted a defence within the prescribed time limits and that the defence has a reasonable prospect of success, and as such the court has discretion to set aside the default judgment under CPR 13.2(b) and CPR 13.3(1)(a) respectively. During the hearing, the judge is satisfied that a defence was filed on time, however is not convinced that the applicant has a reasonable prospect of successfully defending the claim. Kirstie knows that, now that the applicant's representative has proved that the defence was filed on time, it is mandatory, not discretionary, for the court to make an order setting aside the judgment in default.

What should Kirstie do in this situation?

Kirstie must draw the court's attention to the wording of CPR 13.2, which clearly states that the court must set aside judgment in default where the applicant can prove that they submitted a defence within the prescribed time limits. This will, naturally, disadvantage Gavin as the litigation will now continue; however, Kirstie owes a duty to the court under Para 2.7 to draw their attention to the mistake made by the applicant's representative.

CONFLICT, CONFIDENTIALITY AND DISCLOSURE

Part 6 of the Code sets out a series of rules relating to when a solicitor should decline to act for particular clients. This section sets out how situations involving these rules may apply in the context of dispute resolution.

Conflict of interest (Para 6.2)

The SRA defines a conflict of interest as 'a situation where your separate duties to act in the best interests of two or more clients in the same or a related matter conflict'. Examples of how this might occur in the context of dispute resolution are as follows:

- representing opposing sides of a dispute
- acting for a client who wishes to make a claim against a company in which the solicitor has shares
- acting for a client defending an action taken by a company for whom the solicitor's spouse works
- recommending the appointment of an expert who has a pre-existing personal relationship with the solicitor.

The list above consists of perhaps the most obvious examples of a conflict of interest. However, there are other situations where a conflict may arise, for example, where a solicitor is consulted by two separate defendants to an action. At the time of instruction, it may appear that there is no direct conflict between the two defendants as they are defending the same action; however, the solicitor needs to consider whether there may be a potential conflict of interest at some point in the future.

If this type of scenario arises in an SQE1 question, consider the structure proffered in **Table 3.1**.

Table 3.1: Dealing with conflicts of interest in dispute resolution

<table>
<tr><th>Questions to ask</th><th>Actions to take</th></tr>
<tr><td>Is there a possibility that a conflict of interest will arise in the future? For example, is it possible that one defendant may blame the other in their defence at any point during the litigation?</td><td>A solicitor can ascertain this by taking full instructions from both clients at the outset of the matter to ascertain what defence(s) are going to be raised.</td></tr>
<tr><td>Is there anything that suggests that the solicitor will not be able to act in the best interests of both clients?</td><td>If the solicitor has to dilute or modify their approach to one client in order to account for the other, then this will be a conflict of interest and the solicitor must cease to act for at least one of the clients.</td></tr>
<tr><td colspan="2">In circumstances where the second client has already shared confidential information with the solicitor which is relevant to the first client, the solicitor must cease to act for both clients. This is to ensure that there is no conflict between the solicitor's duty of confidentiality to the second client and the duty to disclose all relevant information to the first client.

This is discussed in greater detail below (see Confidentiality and disclosure (Paras 6.3–6.5)).</td></tr>
</table>

If the solicitor decides that they can continue to act for both clients, they can potentially rely on the exception set out in Para 6.2(b), that the clients are competing for the same objective. If this is the case, the Code sets out that the following conditions also need to be met:

- that all of the clients have given informed written consent to the solicitor acting for both parties
- that there are effective safeguards in place to ensure that the solicitor's clients' confidential information is protected, and
- that the solicitor is satisfied that it is reasonable to act for both clients.

Revision tip

It is the solicitor who makes the decision concerning whether to continue to act, or cease to act, for a client in cases where there is a potential or actual conflict of interest. Remember this when answering an MCQ on this topic.

Confidentiality and disclosure (Paras 6.3–6.5)

Alongside a solicitor's primary duty to the court, they also need to balance their duty of confidentiality against their duty to disclose to their client any relevant information regarding their matter. This section will deal with both of these issues in the context of dispute resolution.

Confidentiality

Under Para 6.3, solicitors must keep the affairs of both current and former clients confidential unless disclosure is required or permitted by law or the client consents. Most obviously, this means that any information given to you by your client is to remain confidential unless one of those exceptions applies. However, there are circumstances in which a solicitor's duty of confidentiality to one client can conflict with their duty to act in the best interests of another, including the duty to disclose any information relevant to the client's case. Examples of this include:

- where a solicitor conducts an initial interview with a potential client about a litigated matter which does not lead to a retainer (see **Chapter 2** for the **Key term**) and the solicitor is then approached to act for the opposing party
- where a solicitor holds information relating to a former client which is material to a present client in their matter.

In both of these situations, the solicitor will be bound by their duty of confidentiality to their potential and former clients respectively, meaning they will not be able to act or continue to act for either the opposing party or the present party.

Disclosure

Para 6.4 requires a solicitor to make a client aware of all information material to their matter about which the solicitor has knowledge. The general rule is that a solicitor should not act for a new client where they have an adverse interest to that of a former client and they hold confidential information from the former client which relates to the new client.

However, there are situations which can arise where it comes to light that a solicitor is in possession of information from a client or former client which relates directly to another client's matter. What does a solicitor do in this situation?

Firstly, it is important to remember that *confidentiality trumps disclosure when the two conflict*. Therefore, the solicitor cannot breach confidentiality by disclosing the relevant information to their new client. However, the SRA set out two exceptions which would enable this to happen:

- where effective measures have been taken which result in there being no real risk of disclosure of the confidential information, or

- the current or former client whose information you or your business or employer holds has given informed consent, given or evidenced in writing, to you acting, including to any measures taken to protect their information.

Practice example 3.4 demonstrates how the duties of confidentiality and disclosure can conflict.

Practice example 3.4

Joshua has been consulted by Barry to defend an action against him for breach of contract. The action is being brought by Smart Fox Ltd, who contracted Barry to clean their offices. They are arguing that Barry failed to attend on four consecutive days, leading to a build-up of dirt in the office which, Smart Fox Ltd argue, cost them three valuable and lucrative clients. Five weeks prior, Joshua conducted an initial interview with Sally, the managing director of Smart Fox Ltd, about a potential sale of the business. As part of that meeting, Sally told Joshua that the business had just lost the same three clients as a result of their failure to provide quotes within the timescales they promised and because there had been a clash of personalities between the clients and Smart Fox's business development manager, Kevin.

What should Joshua do in this situation?

Joshua has a duty of confidentiality to Smart Fox Ltd, and therefore cannot disclose any information from his meeting with them to Barry. However, if Joshua agrees a retainer with Barry, he is under a duty to make him aware of all information he has which is material to Barry's matter. The information which Sally shared with Joshua is clearly material to the action which has been brought against Barry, and therefore Joshua must decline Barry's instruction.

FINAL ADVICE

The issues that may arise in dispute resolution are diverse and wide-ranging. This chapter has covered issues that are specific to this area of practice, but you must remain vigilant and aware of more general conduct issues that may occur. Using the revision guide ***Revise SQE: Dispute Resolution***, you should review the substantive law relating to dispute resolution and identify occasions when ethical and professional conduct issues may arise.

■ KEY POINT CHECKLIST

This chapter has covered the following key knowledge points. You can use these to structure your revision, ensuring you recall the key details for each point, as covered in this chapter.

- A solicitor cannot be in a position where they directly, or complicitly, mislead the court, their client or the opposing party.

- A solicitor is under a specific duty to draw the court's attention to any relevant cases, statutory provisions, or procedural irregularities of which the solicitor is aware, and which are likely to have a material effect on the outcome of the proceedings even if this comes at a detriment to the client.
- A solicitor may act on behalf of two or more clients who are involved in the same litigation, where there is no conflict of interest or significant risk of such.
- A solicitor can disclose information from a former client which is relevant to a current client's case, provided they obtain written consent from the former client to do so.

■ KEY TERMS AND CONCEPTS

There are no key terms for this specific chapter.

■ SQE1-STYLE QUESTIONS

QUESTION 1

A solicitor is acting for a client in a breach of contract claim. The solicitor, who is of Muslim faith, discovers that the client is a member of a far-right wing political party which has links to anti-Islamic protest groups. As a result, the solicitor ceases to act for the client.

Has the solicitor acted in accordance with the SRA Code of Conduct?

A. Yes. The solicitor can cease to act for the client on the basis of their affiliation with a political party where it would cause a direct conflict with their own race religion or sexual orientation.

B. Yes. The solicitor is the party who decides whether or not it is appropriate to represent or continue to represent a client.

C. No. The solicitor has a duty not to discriminate against a client on the basis of their political or ethical views.

D. No. Although the solicitor can cease to act for the client, they ought to have secured alternative representation for them first.

E. No. The solicitor is under a duty to act in the client's best interests, which are not served by them ceasing to act on the client's behalf.

QUESTION 2

A solicitor is acting for a client in a personal injury claim arising from a road traffic accident. The only witness to the accident is elderly, lives 40 miles away from the court at which the trial is taking place, and is in receipt of state benefits as her main form of income. The witness contacts the solicitor to say that she will not be prepared to attend trial unless the solicitor pays her to do so. The solicitor has already served the witness's statement on the defendant and, without her oral evidence, it weakens the client's case substantially.

Which of the following best describes how the solicitor should proceed?

A. The solicitor should agree to reimbursing the witness for any travel expenses and other associated losses she suffers as a result of attending court, but no more.

B. The solicitor should agree to reimbursing the witness for any travel expenses and other associated losses she suffers as a result of attending court, as well as paying her a small fee.

C. The solicitor should agree to reimbursing the witness for any travel expenses and other associated losses she suffers as a result of attending court, but no more. The solicitor can, however, arrange for the client to make a small payment to the witness in exchange for her attendance at court.

D. The solicitor should agree to reimbursing the witness for any travel expenses and other associated losses she suffers as a result of attending court, as well as paying her a fee. The witness's statement has already been filed, and so it could not be argued that the fee was dependant on the nature of the evidence.

E. The solicitor should refuse to pay the witness anything at all.

QUESTION 3

A solicitor is acting for a large company which has issued a claim against a small company for breach of contract. The defendant is represented by a trainee solicitor. The solicitor for the claimant makes an application for an interim payment order. During the course of discussions with the defendant's representative, the solicitor informs them that counsel will be representing the claimant at the scheduled hearing and that, as a result, the defendant is facing a significant interim payment order as well as a substantial costs order being made against them following the hearing. The solicitor has not, in fact, instructed counsel to represent the claimant at the hearing, although it is being considered by the claimant.

Has the solicitor acted in accordance with the SRA Code of Conduct?

A. Yes. Whilst the solicitor is not allowed to mislead the defendant's solicitor, the fact that their client is still considering the instruction of counsel is sufficient to mean that they have not breached the Code.

B. Yes. The solicitor has not misled the defendant's solicitor, they have merely set out a hypothetical scenario for the defendant's solicitor to consider.

C. No. There is a clear attempt to mislead the defendant's solicitor about the nature of the costs order which the court will make.
D. No. There is a clear attempt to mislead the defendant's solicitor about the attendance of counsel.
E. No. There is a clear attempt to mislead the defendant's solicitor about the nature and size of the interim payment order which the court is likely to make.

QUESTION 4

A solicitor is acting for a client (the respondent) in opposing an application to amend a statement of case which has already been served. During the course of the hearing, a legal executive acting for the applicant mistakenly states that, even with the permission of the court, the respondent still needs to provide written consent to the statement of case being amended. The solicitor knows this is not the case, however it assists the respondent's case significantly if the application is refused by the court. The solicitor therefore informs the court that the respondent refuses to provide written consent and the application therefore fails.

Has the solicitor acted in accordance with the SRA Code of Conduct?

A. No. The solicitor has deliberately misled the applicant by failing to identify their incorrect reading of the procedural rules.
B. No. The solicitor has deliberately misled the court by failing to identify the applicant's incorrect reading of the procedural rules.
C. No. Although the solicitor has not deliberately misled the court, by failing to correct the applicant's mistake they have been complicit in misleading the court.
D. Yes. The solicitor has acted in their client's best interests by simply taking advantage of a mistake made by the applicant.
E. Yes. Whilst the court has been misled, the solicitor was not directly responsible for this.

QUESTION 5

A solicitor is instructed to act on behalf of a client who is in dispute with their neighbour over the location of the boundary between their respective land. The solicitor's client argues that the neighbour has moved the boundary and that the client is, in fact, entitled to six inches more land than they currently have. The solicitor acted for the seller of their client's land 18 years ago and remembers being told by the seller that the boundary fence had been moved by agreement due to a mistake in the original title. The solicitor knows that sharing this information with their current client will save them a significant amount of money and stress in litigating the matter.

Which of the following is the best advice to give to the solicitor in line with the SRA Code of Conduct?

A. The solicitor's duty is to act in the best interests of their current client, rather than owing a duty to their former client. The solicitor is therefore entitled to share the information with their current client.

B. The solicitor owes a duty of confidentiality to their former client. They cannot therefore share the information with their current client under any circumstances.

C. The solicitor owes a duty of confidentiality to their former client. The only circumstance in which they could disclose the information is if they were required to do so by law.

D. The solicitor's duty to their current client is to make them aware of all information material to their matter about which the solicitor has knowledge. The information is relevant and the solicitor must therefore disclose it.

E. The solicitor owes a duty of confidentiality to their former client, however also owes a duty to their current client to make them aware of all information material to their matter about which the solicitor has knowledge. Unless consent to share the information can be obtained from the former client, the solicitor must cease to act in the matter.

■ ANSWERS TO QUESTIONS

Answers to 'What do you know already?' questions at the start of the chapter

1) True. Under Para 1.2, a solicitor must not abuse their position by taking advantage of their client or others.
2) The solicitor is under a duty not to mislead the court. If the witness statement was allowed to stand as drafted, the solicitor would be in breach of this duty. The solicitor should therefore try to persuade the client to amend their witness statement, failing which the solicitor should cease to act for the client.
3) True. Whilst the Code of Conduct places a solicitor under many other duties, their primary duty is to the court.
4) The solicitor should inform their client of the outcome of the application and its consequences immediately. Failing to do so would breach the solicitor's duty not to mislead their client.

Answers to end-of-chapter SQE1-style questions

Question 1:

The correct answer was C. Under Para 1.1, a solicitor is under a duty not to discriminate by allowing their personal views to affect professional relationships and the way in which they provide their services. The solicitor has ceased to act for the client on the basis of their political affiliation and is therefore in breach of Para 1.1, making options A and B incorrect. Option D is incorrect as the solicitor is not entitled to cease to act for the client in these circumstances and option E is wrong as, although a solicitor does have a duty to act in the client's best interests, there is no reason why this should not continue to be the case.

Question 2:

The correct answer was A. Under Para 2.3, a solicitor should not provide or offer to provide any benefit to a witness dependent on the nature of their evidence. Reimbursing the witness for travelling expenses would not be a benefit, as it puts them in the same position as they would have been in were it not for the need to attend court. If the solicitor pays the witness a fee, that would class as a benefit, rendering options B and D incorrect. Option C is incorrect as the solicitor would be responsible for arranging a benefit to be paid to the witness, breaching Para 2.3. Finally, option E is incorrect as reimbursement of losses is not in breach of the Code.

Question 3:

The correct answer was D. Under Para 1.4, a solicitor must not mislead their opponent. The solicitor has unambiguously confirmed to the defendant's solicitor that counsel has been instructed to conduct the hearing, which is clearly a misleading statement. This makes options A and B incorrect. Options C and E are incorrect as these statements are not misleading, they are just predictions about the outcome designed to put pressure on the defendant's representative. The statement that counsel is attending when the solicitor has no confirmation that this will be the case, however, is deliberately misleading.

Question 4:

The correct answer was B. Under Para 2.7, a solicitor must draw the court's attention to any procedural irregularities of which they are aware, and which are likely to have a material effect on the outcome of the proceedings. In this case, the solicitor knows that the applicant has accidentally misled the court on the wording of the test, and by failing to correct the mistake, the solicitor has deliberately misled the court themselves. This makes options D and E incorrect. Option A is incorrect as it is the court who has been misled, not the applicant, and option C is incorrect as the failure to correct the mistake was deliberate on the part of the solicitor.

Question 5:

The correct answer was E. Under Para 6.3, a solicitor is under a duty to keep confidential the affairs of all current and former clients unless disclosure is required by law or the client consents to the information being shared. This makes option C incorrect. In this case, this clashes with the duty under Para 6.4 to inform the client of all information of which the solicitor has knowledge which is material to their matter. The duty of confidentiality trumps the duty of disclosure, making options A and D incorrect. Option B is incorrect because it fails to take into account the duty of disclosure.

■ KEY CASES, RULES, STATUTES AND INSTRUMENTS

The SQE1 Assessment Specification has identified that candidates are required to understand the purpose, scope and content of the SRA Principles and Code of Conduct. Make sure that you understand the application of the SRA Principles and Code of Conduct to dispute resolution practice.

The SQE1 Assessment Specification does not require you to know any case names, or statutory materials, for the topic of ethics and professional conduct in dispute resolution.

4

Ethics and professional conduct in business law and practice

Benjamin Jones

■ MAKE SURE YOU KNOW

This chapter will cover the application of the Solicitors Regulation Authority (SRA) Principles and Code of Conduct to business law and practice (BLP). It will allow you to appreciate how ethical issues and professional conduct matters are likely to arise when practising in this area.

BLP features in the first of the SQE1 assessments (FLK1), and ethics and professional conduct relevant to BLP will be assessed pervasively in that assessment.

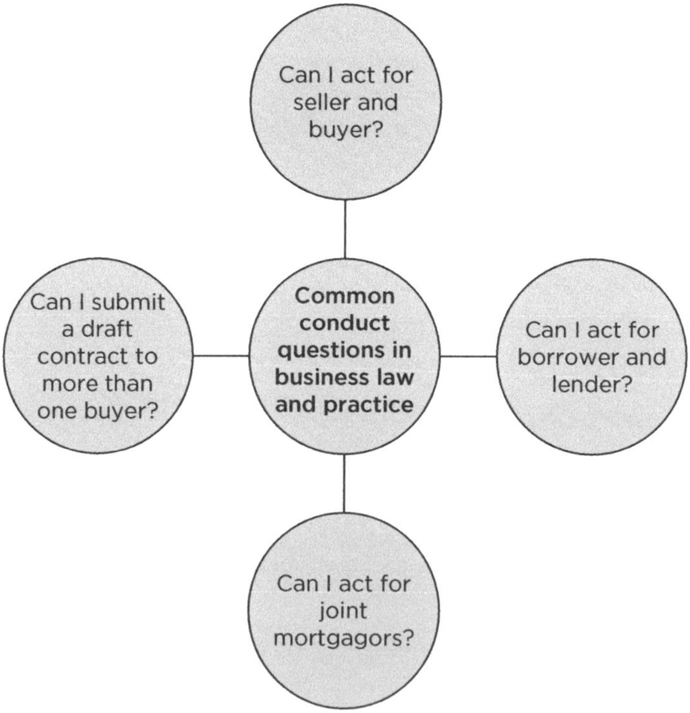

There are a number of cross-references to **Chapter 7** as many of the rules and principles mentioned there in relation to property practice are similarly applicable to transactional work in the area of BLP.

■ SQE ASSESSMENT ADVICE

As you work through this chapter, remember to pay particular attention in your revision to:

- the circumstances where a solicitor may act for seller and buyer in a business transaction
- issues that may arise when acting for joint buyers
- where a solicitor may act for borrower and lender
- issues that may arise when acting for guarantors.

■ WHAT DO YOU KNOW ALREADY?

Have a go at these questions before reading this chapter. If you find some difficult or cannot remember the answers, make a note to look more closely at that area during your revision.

1) A client has queried whether you may act for both parties in the negotiation of a commercial contract, at arm's length. What would you advise?

   [Conflict of interests; page 53]

2) True or false? You may be able to act for multiple individuals looking to form a partnership, or set up a limited company. However, you should not usually act for both the retiring partner and the continuing partners of a partnership in relation to the former's exit from the business.

   [Acting for seller and buyer; page 109]

3) A client has asked whether you may act for both the borrower and lender in the refinancing of their business. How would you advise?

   [Acting for borrower and lender; page 111]

4) True or false? You may always act for both the borrower and a third party guarantor.

   [Acting for guarantors; page 112]

INTRODUCTION TO ETHICS AND PROFESSIONAL CONDUCT IN BUSINESS LAW AND PRACTICE

BLP is a high-pressure area of practice. Clients will be very keen to achieve their commercial objectives and this can lead to a vast number of potential ethical and professional conduct issues for solicitors practising in the area. This chapter will cover the nature of some of these issues, as well as provide guidance on how you would answer questions relating to professional conduct in BLP, which may arise in your SQE1 assessment.

This chapter should be read in conjunction with ***Revise SQE: Business Law and Practice***. In that guide, you will find many **Key terms** and important substantive topics to assist you in furthering your understanding of your ethical and professional obligations.

In the present guide, **Chapters 1 and 2** set out the SRA Principles (the 'Principles') and Code of Conduct (the 'Code') respectively. This chapter will consider how relevant headings operate in the context of BLP. The headings used reflect the headings of the Code of Conduct.

MAINTAINING TRUST AND ACTING FAIRLY

When acting in BLP, you must maintain trust and act fairly in your relationship with your client and others. The Code sets out ways in which you may achieve this, and these are dealt with in turn.

You do not abuse your position by taking unfair advantage of clients or others (Para 1.2)

As part of your practice in BLP, you may encounter unrepresented parties and, in such circumstances, there is potential for this duty to be breached (see **Chapter 7**, **Unrepresented parties**, where this is dealt with more comprehensively). This may, for example, be in relation to an unrepresented seller, buyer or party to a commercial contract.

You perform all undertakings given by you, and do so within an agreed timescale, or if no timescale has been agreed, then within a reasonable amount of time (Para 1.3)

Undertakings are a key element of work in BLP (transactional work in particular). For example, you may be asked to provide an undertaking to hand over documents on completion, discharge pre-existing charges or procure registration of a charge at Companies House. You may also be required to provide an undertaking to pay a third party's costs.

You should refer to **Chapter 7**, **Maintaining trust and acting fairly** and **Undertakings**, where this is dealt with more comprehensively.

You do not mislead clients or others (Para 1.4)

A solicitor must not mislead or attempt to mislead clients or others, either by their own acts or omissions, or by allowing or being complicit in the acts or omissions of others (including their client) (Para 1.4). The rule is closely associated with Principles 2, 4, 5 and 7. Below are some examples, which may assist you in understanding this duty in the context of BLP.

Misleading a client

Solicitors may mislead a client by, for example, saying that a transaction is at a particular stage, when it is not. This could include confirming that draft documentation has been submitted to a potential buyer, or that a charge has been registered at Companies House.

Misleading others

Solicitors could mislead the other party to the proceedings by, for example, confirming that a finance offer is in place, when it is not, or that they are in possession of executed documents when they are not. You could also be misleading others by backdating documents.

CONFLICT, CONFIDENTIALITY AND DISCLOSURE

Part 6 of the Code provides a series of rules relating to when a solicitor should decline to act for particular clients. This section sets out how situations involving these rules may apply in the context of BLP.

Conflict of interest (Paras 6.1 and 6.2)

You must not act if you have an *own interest conflict* or a significant risk of such a conflict (Para 6.1). This is an absolute rule and there are no exceptions. To act in such circumstances would also be a breach of Principle 7 (to act in the best interests of each client).

The SRA guidance gives a specific example, within the context of BLP, of where a client asks you to carry out due diligence on a company in which you or your spouse own shares. There would be a clear conflict here as the solicitor, or a closely connected party to the solicitor, would have a personal financial interest in the company.

You must also 'not act in relation to a matter, or a particular aspect of it, if you have a *conflict of interest* or a significant risk of such a conflict in relation to that matter or aspect of it' (Para 6.2). The section applies equally to individuals and firms, and BLP can be a relatively high conflict area.

Revision tip

It is important to be able to distinguish between an *own interest conflict* and a *conflict of interest*. Make sure you understand their differences and that you could identify both in an MCQ. Return to **Chapter 2** to remind yourself of the relevant **Key terms**.

You should refer to **Chapter 7, Conflict of interests** where this is dealt with more comprehensively. However, some key examples of where a conflict of interest might occur in the context of BLP are the following:

- acting for seller and buyer in transactional work
- acting for one client seeking to lease an asset to another
- agreeing a commercial contract between two parties.

Of particular relevance to BLP is *competing for the same objective* exception, where a solicitor may act despite a conflict or a significant risk of one, where the clients are competing for the same objective (Para 6.2(b)). In this context, 'objective' is defined in **Chapter 2** and the exception is very specific (see **Practice example 4.1**). Otherwise, according to SRA guidance, acting for two clients seeking separately to purchase a particular asset could give rise to a conflict of interest or a significant risk of one arising.

Practice example 4.1

Two separate potential clients have instructed you to act on the acquisition of property being disposed of through a liquidation process.

Are you able to act for both clients?

The solicitor may be able to act here, under the competing for the same objective exception, but will need to adhere to the conditions in Para 6.2. The same would be the case if the property were being acquired through an auction or tender process.

A particular situation that can arise in the context of BLP is being instructed to set up a business (eg drafting a partnership agreement or incorporating a limited company). In such circumstances, a solicitor may act under the *substantially common interest* exception, provided that the key terms have been agreed (eg management, shareholdings and finance) (see **Practice example 4.2**).

Practice example 4.2

Two potential clients who wish to start up a business in partnership approach a solicitor. They have agreed all relevant commercial terms and the partnership will be based on equal ownership, participation, control and sharing of profits. They have asked whether the solicitor may act for them both.

Can the solicitor act for both clients in this case?

The solicitor may be able to act here, based on the substantially common interest exception, but will need to adhere to the conditions in Para 6.2. However, as the matter progresses, if it transpires that the parties no longer share the necessary common purpose and strong consensus regarding the matter, the solicitor will be required to cease to act for both clients. This is because the solicitor would possess confidential information, which would require disclosure.

According to SRA guidance, you may remove the risk of a conflict of interest or a potential conflict by restricting your retainer (see **Chapter 2** for the **Key term**). This involves only advising on aspects of a matter where a conflict is not likely to arise. **Practice example 4.3** is based on a specific example given by the SRA of where this is likely to apply in the context of BLP.

Practice example 4.3

Two commercial clients are keen for due diligence to be carried out in relation to a company they are considering purchasing. Ultimately, they may proceed with the purchase individually or collectively, but they have not yet decided upon this.

Are you able to act for both clients?

The solicitor may be able to act here on a retainer limited to due diligence, on the basis that all information will be shared. If the clients later decide to compete with each other, one or both of them would need to seek independent legal advice.

Acting for seller and buyer

Although, under the Code, there is no absolute prohibition on acting for both seller and buyer, the cases where this will be permissible are rare. You should refer to **Chapter 7, Acting for seller and buyer** where this is dealt with more comprehensively. The general principles are similarly applicable here in the context of transactional work within BLP, but the key points are reiterated in **Table 4.1**.

Table 4.1: Acting for seller and buyer

The general position
• SRA guidance specifically states that there is likely to be a conflict of interest or a significant risk of one arising where a client sells or leases an asset to another client. • A conflict is very likely to exist where assets are transferred for value, at **arm's length**, usually between unconnected parties. • The possibility of a conflict is also strongly linked to the need to negotiate between the parties. The more likely the need for negotiation, the more likely there will be a potential conflict.
The exceptions (see Chapter 2)
• The *substantially common interest* exception does not usually apply to a sale and purchase. • The *competing for the same objective* exception does not apply, as the parties are each working towards different objectives (disposal and acquisition).

Key term: arm's length

A transaction is at arm's length where both parties are not connected and are each acting in their own commercial self-interest.

A typical situation that may arise in the context of BLP is being asked to advise on what is effectively a sale or transfer between two connected parties (see **Practice examples 4.4** and **4.5**).

Practice example 4.4

Two of the three partners in a small business have approached you as one of them would like to retire (the 'retiring partner') and the other (the 'continuing partner') has agreed, in principle to buy the retiring partner's share.

Is there a conflict of interest or a risk of conflict of interest here?

On the facts, there is no immediate conflict of interest. However, the risk of one arising is significant. As the 'seller', the retiring partner will wish to dispose of their partnership share for the best possible price and minimise ongoing liability. However, the continuing partner as the 'buyer' may wish to negotiate the price down and may dispute the other's proposals as to ongoing liability. Therefore, there is a significant risk of conflict here.

Practice example 4.5

You act for a company in relation to the proposed transfer of assets to another company within the same group, as part of a solvent reorganisation.

Are you able to act for both companies in order to facilitate this?

Due to the connection between the parties, there is no immediate conflict of interest or risk of one arising. However, it would be advisable for key terms to be agreed first. Acting may also be justified under the substantially common interest exception, subject to compliance with the conditions under Para 6.2.

Acting for joint buyers

Subject to compliance with Para 6.2 of the Code, a solicitor may usually act for joint buyers in transactional work (eg a purchase as a joint venture or as partners), as they will usually have the same interest. In these circumstances, it is best practice to obtain instructions from all clients.

Acting for borrower and lender

Whilst it is usually possible to act for borrower and lender in straightforward residential property transactions, this is not usually possible within the context of commercial lending more generally. In many cases, a lender will insist on separate representation.

You should refer to **Chapter 7, Acting for borrower and lender** where this is considered more comprehensively. However, the key points in relation to BLP are:

- It is common for a solicitor engaged in BLP to be asked to act in relation to loan finance, such as general company borrowing, or company refinancing (effectively moving from one lender to another).
- In this context, it is likely that the terms of the loan facility (facility letter) will need to be negotiated.
- It is also possible that the security documentation (eg debenture and legal charge(s)) will be bespoke, and subject to negotiation. However, most institutional lenders use standard legal charges and debentures, particularly in straightforward and lower value transactions.
- Where negotiation of loan and security documentation is not required, it may be possible to act for both parties, under the *substantially common interest* exception (subject to compliance with the conditions in Para 6.2).

Accordingly, a solicitor should not usually act for both parties in commercial lending transactions where negotiations are required. However, in some circumstances separate representation may be limited to key areas of potential conflict (eg the negotiation of the facility letter and, possibly, the security documentation), with the borrower's solicitor acting for both parties on completion of the documentation (and/or investigation of title). In the case of such a limited retainer, a solicitor may rely on the *substantially common interest* exception (subject to compliance with the conditions in Para 6.2).

Practice example 4.6 provides an example of what to consider in practice in these situations.

Practice example 4.6

You have been instructed to act by a company in relation to refinancing. As part of the process, the lender will require negotiation of the facility letter, a debenture over the assets of the company and a legal charge over the company's freehold commercial property (see ***Revise SQE: Business Law and Practice*** for a full discussion of these substantive principles).

Are you able to act for both borrower and lender in this situation?

On the facts, this will not be possible. The Law Society guidance (see Chapter 7, page 179) does not apply here, as the property is commercial and the terms of the documentation will need to be negotiated (ie the

facility letter and possibly the security documentation). However, you may be able to act for both parties on a limited retainer (ie completion of the documentation and/or the investigation of title aspects only) under the substantially common interest exception, subject to compliance with the conditions in Para 6.2.

Acting for guarantors

A solicitor in BLP may be asked to act for a third party in relation to the guarantee of a client's business debts. For example, a wealthy parent may be asked to guarantee the business debts of their adult child, who is setting up in an unincorporated business, or the debts of the child's newly formed limited company. The guarantee may be personal and, in some cases, secured.

In these circumstances, there is a possibility of undue influence arising as, family connections aside, the guarantee will not strictly be in the third party's interests, as their personal assets will be at risk in the event of default. You should refer to **Chapter 7, Acting for joint mortgagors** as the same principles and similar concerns apply in these circumstances.

Exam warning

In the case of a guarantee, it is highly likely that there will be a conflict of interest or a significant risk of one. Look out for this in an MCQ. In this situation, it would be advisable for another fee earner within the firm to act in these circumstances, or that the guarantor receives separate representation from another firm. In any event, if acting for a third party guarantor, it is necessary to follow the *Etridge* guidelines (see **Chapter 7, page 180**).

It is also worth mentioning that a guarantee may be required between different companies within the same group, or between a director-shareholder and their 'own' company. In such circumstances, due to the connection between both parties and their sophisticated nature, it should be possible to act, either on the basis that there is no conflict of interest or significant risk of one, or under the *substantially common interest* exception (subject to compliance with the conditions in Para 6.2).

Confidentiality and Disclosure (Paras 6.3–6.5)

Paras 6.3–6.5 deal with the associated duties of confidentiality and disclosure. A solicitor is under a duty to act in the best interests of each client (Principle 7), and they must balance the two duties. In the event of conflict, the duty of confidentiality will usually prevail.

You should refer to **Chapter 7, Confidentiality and disclosure** as the same principles apply in these circumstances. Similar situations are likely to arise, particularly in transactional work.

FINAL ADVICE

The issues that may arise in BLP are diverse and wide ranging. This chapter has covered issues that are specific to this area of practice, but you must remain vigilant and aware of more general conduct issues that may occur (eg on costs and client care). Using ***Revise SQE: Business Law and Practice***, you should review the substantive law relating to business law and practice and identify occasions when ethical and professional conduct issues may arise.

■ KEY POINT CHECKLIST

This chapter has covered the following key knowledge points. You can use these to structure your revision, ensuring you recall the key details for each point, as covered in this chapter.

- A solicitor may not act where there is a conflict of interest or a significant risk of one. However, this is subject to two exceptions (with three preconditions), which may apply in the context of BLP.
- A solicitor may not usually act for seller and buyer in a business transaction (although there are some occasions where acting for transferor and transferee will be permissible).
- It is usually possible to act for joint buyers in transactional work.
- Acting for borrower and lender is not usually possible within the context of BLP, although there are limited exceptions.
- It may not always be possible to act for both borrower and a third party guarantor, due to the potential for conflict of interest. Where a third party guarantee is given, the *Etridge* guidelines must be adhered to.

■ KEY TERMS AND CONCEPTS

- arm's length **(page 110)**

■ SQE1-STYLE QUESTIONS

QUESTION 1

A solicitor acts for a private limited company, which has agreed in principle a new banking facility with a high street lender, subject to formal agreement of terms and bespoke security documentation. The bank will require completion of a debenture over the company's assets and a first legal charge over the company's business premises. The client has asked whether the solicitor may also act for the bank, in order to save costs.

Which of the following best describes the position?

A. The solicitor may act for the client and the bank here, provided that they follow current guidance from the Law Society.

B. The solicitor may act for the client and the bank here, as the parties are competing for the same objective.
C. The solicitor cannot act for the client and the bank here, as the loan and security documentation will need to be negotiated, and guidance from the Law Society in relation to residential transactions does not apply.
D. The solicitor could act for the client and the bank in relation to the investigation of title and/or completion, as the clients will most likely have a substantially common interest. The bank will need separate representation for negotiation of the terms of the documentation.
E. The solicitor may act for the client and the bank as the parties have a substantially common interest, subject to both the client and the bank giving informed consent, effective safeguards being in place and the solicitor being satisfied that it is reasonable so to act.

QUESTION 2

A client is a sole practitioner in an accountancy business and he has agreed to borrow a substantial sum from a high street lender. The loan will be used to expand the business, but to secure it, the lender will require a first legal charge over the matrimonial home that the client owns jointly with his wife. The client's wife has asked the client's solicitor to act for her in the transaction.

Which of the following best describes the position?

A. Provided the solicitor is satisfied there is no conflict of interest or a significant risk of one, they may act for both the client and the client's wife in relation to the proposed legal charge.
B. The solicitor may not act for the client and the client's wife in relation to the proposed legal charge in any circumstances.
C. The solicitor may act for the client only. The client's wife will require separate representation.
D. The solicitor may act for both the client and the client's wife, but will need to adhere to the guidelines from relevant case law in advising the wife.
E. Provided the solicitor is satisfied there is no conflict of interest, or a significant risk of one, they may act for both the client and the client's wife, with careful adherence to the guidelines from relevant case law.

QUESTION 3

A solicitor is approached to carry out due diligence on a private limited company. The solicitor's spouse is employed by the company as finance director and has a minority shareholding in the company.

Which of the following best describes the position?

A. The solicitor cannot act as there is an own interest conflict, due to the financial interest of the solicitor's spouse.
B. The solicitor cannot act as there is a conflict of interest.
C. The solicitor cannot act as there is an own interest conflict, unless the client gives informed consent to the solicitor acting.
D. The solicitor can act as there is no conflict of interest with an existing or former client.
E. The solicitor can act as they do not have a personal interest in the company, provided that they disclose the interest of their spouse.

QUESTION 4

A solicitor has been asked to act on the incorporation of a private limited company by the four proposed director-shareholders. The proposed director-shareholders have agreed finance terms with a high street lender and they agree as to the proposed management structure and shareholdings.

Which of the following best describes the position?

A. The solicitor may not act for all four proposed director-shareholders as although there is no immediate conflict of interest, there is a significant risk of one arising.
B. The solicitor may not act here under any circumstances.
C. The solicitor may act here, despite the potential risk of a conflict of interest arising, using the substantially common interest exception.
D. The solicitor may act here, despite the potential risk of a conflict of interest arising, as the proposed director-shareholders are competing for the same objective.
E. The solicitor may act here, despite the potential risk of a conflict of interest arising, using the substantially common interest exception, subject to the conditions of the exception.

QUESTION 5

A solicitor has been asked to act for both a retiring partner and a continuing partner on the retiring partner's exit from the business. Both partners have a good working relationship and they have agreed the basic terms.

Which of the following best describes the position?

A. The solicitor cannot act as there is a conflict of interest between the retiring partner and the continuing partner.
B. The solicitor cannot act, as there is a significant risk of a conflict of interest between the retiring partner and the continuing partner.

C. The solicitor could act, despite the significant risk of a conflict of interest, provided that both the retiring and continuing partner give informed consent.
D. The solicitor could act, as the retiring and continuing partners would be competing for the same objective. Both the retiring and continuing partners would need to give informed consent, effective safeguards would need to be put in place concerning protection of confidential information and the solicitor would need to be satisfied it is reasonable to do so.
E. The solicitor could act, despite the significant risk of a conflict of interest, provided that both the retiring and continuing partners give informed consent, effective safeguards are put in place concerning protection of confidential information and the solicitor is satisfied it is reasonable to do so.

ANSWERS TO QUESTIONS

Answers to 'What do you know already?' questions at the start of the chapter

1) This would not be advisable, due to the need to negotiate terms. It would be impossible to act in the best interests of each client and there would be significant risk of a conflict of interest arising.
2) True. You may usually act for all parties in the first instance, as there would be a substantially common interest between them. There is likely to be a significant risk of a conflict of interest in the second situation, due to the potential need for negotiation of commercial terms.
3) A solicitor should not usually act in these circumstances, due to the need to negotiate between the parties and the associated significant risk of a conflict of interest. Although, in some circumstances it may be possible to act under the substantially common interest exception (eg if a limited retainer is agreed and/or negotiation is not required).
4) False. You may not act if you consider there is a conflict of interest or a significant risk of one arising. This is highly likely in the circumstances. If you do act, you must adhere to the *Etridge* guidelines.

Answers to end-of-chapter SQE1-style questions

Question 1:

The correct answer was D. The solicitor cannot act under guidance from the Law Society as the conditions do not apply (this is not just a residential mortgage on standard terms). Therefore, option A is incorrect. The competing for the same objective exception does not apply here, so option B is incorrect. Option C is partially correct as, although separate representation will usually be required where commercial terms require negotiation, a solicitor may act in relation to the investigation of title and/or completion, under the substantially common interest exception (making option D correct). Option E is also incorrect, as it does not make this distinction, although it does outline the conditions attached to the exception, which option D does not.

Question 2:

The correct answer was E. The solicitor may act for both the client and the client's wife, but will need to adhere to guidance from case law (specifically, the *Etridge* guidelines). The solicitor must, however, first be satisfied that there is no conflict of interest and no significant risk of one arising in so acting. Option D is incorrect as it omits this additional detail, which is present in option E. Options A, B and C are incorrect as they do not make reference to the *Etridge* guidelines. Option B is also incorrect as it may be possible to act for both the client and the client's wife in some circumstances. Although the solicitor may ultimately decide that the client's wife may require separate representation (option C), they will need to consider first whether there is a conflict of interest or a significant risk of one arising.

Question 3:

The correct answer was A. This is an own interest conflict, rather than a conflict of interest, therefore, options B and D are incorrect. Options C and E are incorrect as the own interest conflict rule is strict and without exception. SRA guidance makes specific reference to the financial interests of connected parties to the solicitor; therefore, option E is also incorrect on this point.

Question 4:

The correct answer was E. The competing for the same objective exception does not apply on the facts, so option D is incorrect. Options A and B are incorrect, as the solicitor will need to consider whether there is a significant risk of conflict of interest arising and, if there is, they may still be able to act under the substantially common interest exception. Therefore, option C is partially correct, although option E is most correct as it refers to the relevant conditions.

Question 5:

The correct answer was B. Option A is incorrect as there is no immediate conflict of interest, because the basic terms are agreed. However, there is a significant risk of conflict arising, due to the potential for future disagreement and further negotiations as the deal progresses. Option D is incorrect, as the competing for the same objective exception does not apply on the facts. Despite the business connection and good relationship between the partners, the transaction is essentially a sale and purchase, for value, calling for negotiations of commercial terms at arm's length. Therefore, the substantially common interest exception will be unlikely to apply and option E (which mentions its conditions) is incorrect. Option C is also incorrect as informed consent only applies where either of the exceptions apply.

■ KEY CASES, RULES, STATUTES AND INSTRUMENTS

The SQE1 Assessment Specification has identified that candidates are required to understand the purpose, scope and content of the SRA Principles and Code of Conduct. Make sure that you understand the application of the SRA Principles and Code of Conduct to business law and practice.

The SQE1 Assessment Specification does not require you to know any case names, or statutory materials, for the topic of ethics and professional conduct in business law and practice. However, you should be aware of the *Etridge* guidelines and the principles therein due to their importance.

5

Ethics and professional conduct in criminal law and practice

James J Ball and Mark Thomas

■ MAKE SURE YOU KNOW

This chapter will cover the application of the Solicitors Regulation Authority (SRA) Principles and Code of Conduct to criminal law and practice. This chapter will allow you to observe how ethical issues and professional conduct matters are likely to arise when practising in criminal law.

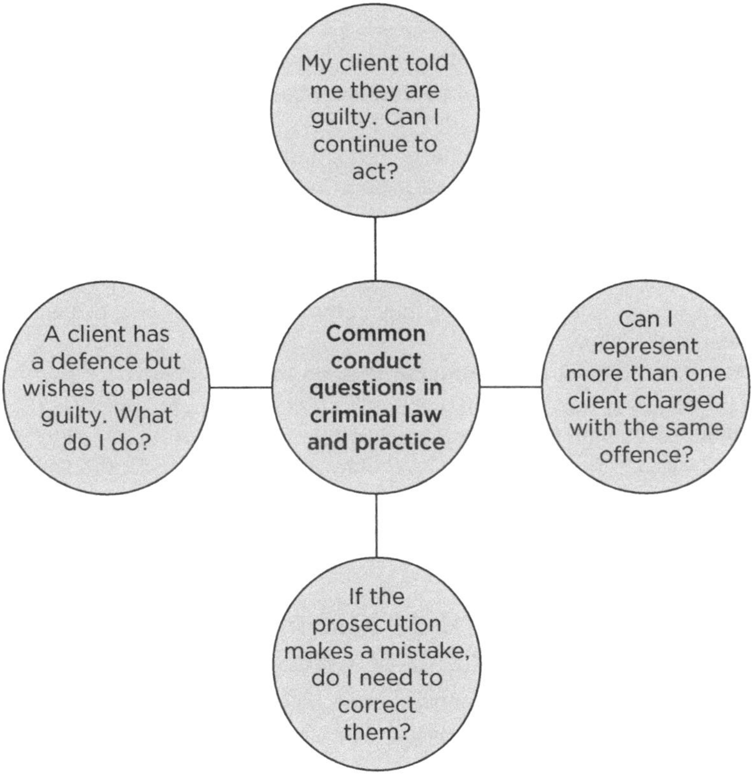

Criminal law and practice features in the second of the SQE1 assessments (FLK2), and ethics and professional conduct relevant to criminal practice will be covered pervasively in that assessment.

■ SQE ASSESSMENT ADVICE

As you work through this chapter, remember to pay particular attention in your revision to:

- the common conflict that exists between a solicitor's duty to the client and their duty to the court
- the circumstances in which a solicitor may continue to act where a client admits that they committed an offence, but wish to plead not guilty, and vice versa where an innocent client wishes to plead guilty
- the professional obligation owed where a solicitor intends to represent multiple clients accused of committing the same offence.

■ WHAT DO YOU KNOW ALREADY?

Have a go at these questions before reading this chapter. If you find some difficult or cannot remember the answers, make a note to look more closely at that area during your revision.

1) True or false? Given that a client in a criminal case is liable to lose their liberty, a solicitor's duty to that client outweighs all other duties.

   [Introduction to ethics and professional conduct in criminal law and practice; page 120]

2) A defendant to a criminal charge repeatedly changes their version of events. What should the solicitor do in this case?

   [Dispute resolution and proceedings before courts, tribunals and inquiries; page 129]

3) True or false? A solicitor must immediately cease to act where their client has informed them that they committed the offence, but wishes to plead not guilty.

   [Maintaining trust and acting fairly; page 147]

4) If a solicitor is the defence advocate at a sentencing hearing and the antecedents which the prosecution offers to the court are wrong, what must the defence solicitor do? Would your answer differ if the solicitor was explicitly asked to confirm the accuracy of the documents?

   [Mistakes or omissions made by a party; page 131]

INTRODUCTION TO ETHICS AND PROFESSIONAL CONDUCT IN CRIMINAL LAW AND PRACTICE

The adversarial nature of criminal practice will result in a multitude of ethical issues arising on a daily basis for a practising solicitor (see the **overview figure** for some examples).

This chapter should be read in conjunction with ***Revise SQE: Criminal Law*** and ***Revise SQE: Criminal Practice***. In those guides, you will find many **Key terms** and important substantive topics to assist you in furthering your understanding of your ethical and professional obligations.

In the present guide, **Chapters 1** and **2** set out the SRA Principles (the 'Principles') and Code of Conduct (the 'Code') respectively. This chapter will consider how relevant headings operate in the context of criminal practice. The headings used reflect the headings of the Code of Conduct.

Conflicting obligations

As discussed in **Chapter 1**, a solicitor will often be faced with conflicting obligations. For instance:

- Principle 7 states that the solicitor must act in the best interests of each client.
- Principle 1, on the other hand, states that the solicitor must act in a way that upholds the constitutional principle of the rule of law, and the proper administration of justice.

A natural conflict will often exist between these two principles, especially in the context of criminal practice where an individual's liberty may be at stake. However, from the outset, solicitors must remember that where a conflict exists between the Principles, those Principles which safeguard the wider public interest (such as the rule of law, and public confidence in a trustworthy solicitors' profession and a safe and effective market for regulated legal services) take precedence over an individual client's interests.

Revision tip

In this chapter, you will see a number of references to circumstances where a solicitor *must* cease to act for a client or withdraw from a case. In all circumstances, keep the following checklist in your mind:

1) Has the solicitor explained to the client why they can no longer represent them?
2) Has the solicitor informed the client that they are entitled to alternative legal advice/representation?
3) Has the solicitor explained that whilst they will cease to act on their behalf, the solicitor will maintain their duty of confidentiality?
4) Has the solicitor informed the police/court that they are unable to continue to act for 'professional reasons' and have not disclosed confidential information?

It is for the solicitor to decide whether there are compelling reasons to withdraw from a case. Such 'compelling reasons' refer to when the solicitor would be professionally embarrassed by continuing to act.

The effect of Procedural Rules on Professional Conduct

As discussed in **Chapter 1**, the Criminal Procedural Rules (CrimPR) 2025 impose duties on practitioners when dealing with a criminal case. The overriding objective in Rule 1.1 is that criminal cases be dealt with justly. By Rule 1.2, each participant in the conduct of each case must prepare and conduct the case in accordance with the overriding objective, and comply with these Rules, practice directions and directions made by the court. Rule 1.2 emphasises the need for openness and transparency in that all participants to a criminal case are required to 'at once inform the court and all parties of any significant failure (whether or not that participant is responsible for that failure)'. This accords with both the SRA Principles and the Code of Conduct in terms of making the court aware of any procedural irregularities.

Furthermore, Rule 3.3 provides that all parties to a case must actively assist the court in fulfilling its duty of actively managing the case to further the overriding objective 'Active assistance' in Rule 3.3 includes ensuring effective communication between the parties prior to the first hearing and throughout the course of the proceedings (and reporting to the court about such communications), alerting the court to any reason why the defendant could not effectively participate in the trial, etc.

The CrimPR 2025 are extensive in the obligations they impose on litigants and advocates in criminal proceedings. This includes, for example, the service of documents and timeframes applicable to the making of applications. A failure to comply with these obligations may run the risk of breaching one of the SRA Principles and/or the Code of Conduct.

Prosecution-focused guidance and rules

It is essential to remember that the SRA Principles and Code of Conduct apply equally to prosecutors (eg employees of the Crown Prosecution Service (CPS), Serious Fraud Office (SFO), Health and Safety Executive (HSE) etc), as they do to defence solicitors.

In addition to the Code of Conduct, prosecutors must also abide by certain prosecution-focused publications. This includes, for example, the Code for Crown Prosecutors (2018) and the Attorney General's Guideline on *The acceptance of pleas and the prosecutor's role in the sentencing exercise* (2012).

The Code for Crown Prosecutors prescribes a number of rules that prosecutors must abide by, many of which reflect the SRA Code of Conduct and, arguably, go beyond it. At the heart of the Code for Crown Prosecutors is the independence of a prosecutor. A prosecutor is independent from the police and other investigators; they are independent from the judiciary; they must be free to undertake their professional duties without political interference and must not be affected by improper or undue pressure or influence from any source.

Rule 1.1 of the Code of Conduct – that solicitors must not unfairly discriminate by allowing their personal views to affect their work – is reaffirmed in the Code for Crown Prosecutors which reminds prosecutors that when making decisions, they must be 'fair and objective' and they must not allow their personal views to influence their decisions. One particular passage (in para 2.7) bears relevance here: 'Prosecutors must always act in the interests of justice and not solely for the purpose of obtaining a conviction.'

It is worth keeping in mind the Code for Crown Prosecutors when considering ethical matters in criminal practice.

MAINTAINING TRUST AND ACTING FAIRLY

As with any area of practice, a solicitor must maintain trust and act fairly. There are a number of scenarios relevant to criminal practitioners under this heading.

You do not unfairly discriminate (Para 1.1)

A solicitor practising in criminal law will often come across unpleasant cases, for example sexual offences and offences involving the vulnerable (eg children or the elderly). Indeed, it is a common feature amongst lay people to ask the question 'how could you defend X?' It is paramount, therefore, that a solicitor does not allow their own personal views to affect the way that they provide their services. For example:

- a solicitor must not allow any personal or moral view on the client's culpability to affect their relationship with that client
- a solicitor must not allow the ethnicity or race of a client to affect the manner in which they represent them.

As discussed in full in **Chapter 2, Para 1: Maintaining trust and acting fairly**, a solicitor is never obliged to accept instructions. However, any refusal must not be for an unlawful or discriminatory reason, eg refusing instructions based on the client's gender or race. Equally, a prosecutor must not let any personal views about the ethnic or national origin, gender, disability, age, religion or belief, sexual orientation or gender identity of the suspect, defendant, victim or any witness influence their decisions in respect to charging the suspect with an offence.

You do not abuse your position by taking unfair advantage of clients or others (Para 1.2)

By Para 1.2, a solicitor must not abuse their position by taking unfair advantage of clients or others. In criminal cases, a client's liberty may be at risk. This means that a solicitor must be open and honest with them, even if the client will not like the advice or information they are given.

One particular example, which has caused concern for a number of years, involves the situation where a solicitor seeks to maximise the firm's financial returns at the expense of the client.

Practitioners will know that the later the proceedings continue, the greater the financial return. A guilty plea on the day of trial is more financially profitable than a guilty plea at the Plea and Trial Preparation Hearing (PTPH). Equally, a guilty plea during the course of the trial is more financially beneficial than a guilty plea at the PTPH (because the trial has been deemed 'effective' under the Litigator's Graduated Fee Scheme (LGFS).

As a result of that, a fear exists that a solicitor will intentionally take advantage of their client (and in doing so mislead them - see Para 1.4 below) to maximise their returns. Ethically, the answer to this issue is that a solictor must correctly advise their client on the strength and weaknesses of the case, and credit for a guilty plea as appropriate.

You do not mislead clients, the court or others (Para 1.4)

A solicitor must not mislead, or attempt to mislead, their clients, the court or others. Closely linked to Para 1.2 above, should a solicitor fail to advise their client as to the strength/weakness of the prosecution case in the hope that they could maximise the financial return for their firm, the solicitor would have breached Para 1.4. Three particular examples will benefit you in understanding the application of this duty to criminal practice.

A client provides false information that you know is false. What do you do?

It is unfortunately a high risk in criminal practice that a client will admit to you that they are lying about something. For example, a client may provide you with an alibi that you know to be false, or may give information to the court that you know to be false.

Suppose the client has provided false information to the court. What should you do? In this case, you should adopt the following approach:

- STEP 1: The solicitor should inform the client that they cannot mislead the court and must ask the client to correct the information.
- STEP 2: The solicitor should inform the client that if they will not correct the information, the solicitor will be forced to withdraw.
- STEP 3: The solicitor should remind the client that their conversations will remain confidential and that they will not reveal any information (unless obligated by law).
- STEP 4: If the client refuses to correct the information, the solicitor should then cease to act. The solicitor must not inform the court of the reasons for ceasing to act, nor should they disclose any confidential information

Revision tip

Should a solicitor have to withdraw from proceedings, it is common for them to explain that they are 'professionally embarrassed' or that their relationship with the client is no longer tenable. The court should not enquire further.

A client admits guilt but wishes to plead not guilty. What do you do?

This situation is capable of arising at both the police station and in court. The question to be answered here is: can the solicitor continue to act?

First, the solicitor should ascertain what the client means when they say that they are guilty. Often clients misunderstand the nature of the law and nature of guilty pleas. For example, there is a difference between the two statements:

- 'I am guilty. I killed him, and I am glad that I did'.
- 'I am guilty. I killed him because he was attacking me'.

In the latter example, a defence exists for the client. It is the duty of the solicitor to put this defence forward and require the prosecution to disprove the defence (though see, below, **A client has a defence but wishes to plead guilty. What do you do?**).

However, what is the case if a client has openly admitted that they committed the offence, no evident defence exists, and the client still wishes to plead not guilty?

- STEP 1: The solicitor should advise the client of the benefits of pleading guilty (eg reduction in sentence for an early guilty plea) and the limitations of a not guilty plea (see STEPS 2 and 3).
- STEP 2: The solicitor should advise the client that they may continue to represent the client, on a not guilty plea, and **put the prosecution to proof**.

Key term: put the prosecution to proof

Putting the prosecution to proof simply means that the defence requires the prosecution to prove its case and discharge its burden.

Remember from ***Revise SQE: Criminal Practice*** that the defendant is under no obligation to give evidence in their own defence; they can simply require the prosecution to prove their case. Examples of putting the prosecution to proof include:

- cross-examining a witness on the reliability of their evidence
- making a submission of no case to answer, that the prosecution has failed to put forward sufficient evidence that the magistrates or jury could reasonably convict on.

- STEP 3: However, the solicitor is not permitted to put any **positive case** forward on behalf of their client. The solicitor must not do anything which positively asserts the innocence of their client. The solicitor must be very careful, therefore, in how they conduct any cross-examination of prosecution witnesses.

Key term: positive case

Whilst not a legal term, a 'positive case' refers to the circumstances when a party to the proceedings goes beyond merely testing evidence, and puts forward evidence which seeks to demonstrate the defendant's innocence.

Revision tip

As you can appreciate, where a solicitor adopts the approach of not putting a positive case forward, other parties to the case (eg the judge and prosecution) are likely to identify that the defendant has informed their solicitor of their guilt. Indeed, a solicitor may be best advised to inform their client that the other parties will likely spot this. However, a solicitor *must not allow this to influence their conduct*. The solicitor must maintain confidentiality and must not disclose the reason for adopting an approach of not putting a positive case forward.

Examples of putting forward a positive case include:
- asking questions of a witness which suggest that someone other than the defendant committed the offence
- suggesting that a witness is lying (as opposed to merely being mistaken).

- STEP 4: The solicitor must consider whether they need to cease acting on behalf of the client. If the solicitor chooses to withdraw from a case, they must inform the client as to the reasons for this.
- STEP 5: In accordance with Para 6 of the Code of Conduct, the solicitor continues to owe a duty of confidentiality to the client and must not inform the court of the reason for their withdrawal. It is common for the solicitor to explain that they must withdraw 'for professional reasons'. See **Conflict, confidentiality and disclosure** for more detail.

See **Practice example 5.1** to apply your understanding.

Practice example 5.1

James is a criminal defence solicitor representing Mark in the Crown Court. Mark has informed James that he committed the offence but wishes to plead not guilty. The prosecution presents its case and James engages in very careful and cautious cross-examination of the prosecution witnesses, ensuring that his questions only test the prosecution evidence and nothing more. At the close of the prosecution's case, Mark demands that he is called to the witness stand to give evidence in his defence. Mark also demands that James calls witnesses who will allege that Mark did not commit the offence in question.

What should James do in this situation?

James should advise Mark that he is unable, by law, to present a positive case in his favour. Any evidence which positively represents Mark's innocence, whether through Mark's testimony, or that of Mark's witnesses, will breach James' duty to not mislead the court. This is because James is liable to breach the Code if he, by his own acts or omissions, misleads/attempts to mislead the court or allows/is complicit in others doing so. James should therefore seek for Mark to change his instructions. If Mark refuses to accept this position, James is advised to withdraw from the case, whilst continuing to maintain the confidentiality of Mark. James should inform the prosecution and the trial judge that he must withdraw for 'professional reasons' and advise Mark to seek alternative representation.

What is the approach if the client has informed their solicitor of their guilt at the police station (ie before proceedings have begun)? Under Para 1.4, the solicitor must also not mislead the police. We can observe two main scenarios where SQE1 may test the availability of the solicitor to be present in an interview:

- Where the client intends to deny having committed the offence or present a positive (fabricated) defence: The solicitor cannot be present in the interview and must decline to act/withdraw. The solicitor would continue to owe their duty of confidentiality and must not inform the police as to the reason for the withdrawal. The solicitor should inform the police that they are withdrawing for 'professional reasons'.
- Where the client intends to give a 'no comment' interview: The solicitor would be permitted under the Code to be present at the interview given that a 'no comment' interview *does not* involve the presentation of misleading information.

Revision tip

Remember that a solicitor should attempt to dissuade their client from lying to the police. An effective tool to do this is to explain to the client that the police are likely to uncover the lie and disprove what the client alleges. If the police do uncover the lie, the client may face serious consequences: such as being charged with perverting the course of justice. On the other hand, cooperating with the police is a matter which can be taken into account at sentencing as a form of mitigation - thus reducing any potential sentence imposed on a client. Allowing the client to weigh up the consequences of their conduct is vital to a solicitor's role.

A client has a defence but wishes to plead guilty. What do you do?

It is a common situation where a client has a valid defence available to them, but they wish to plead guilty. This may arise where the client believes that they have done wrong, and should be punished. Alternatively, the client may be too scared to deal with court proceedings.

What approach should the solicitor take, therefore, when a client has a defence but wishes to plead guilty? (See also **Practice example 5.2**.)

- STEP 1: The solicitor is under a duty to not mislead the client. The solicitor must inform the client of the available defence and its strength/limitations against the case for the prosecution. If the prosecution does not have a *prima facie* case against the client (ie there is no or little evidence of the defendant's guilt), the solicitor should advise the client of this.
- STEP 2: Should the client insist that they wish to plead guilty, the solicitor can continue to act for the client at any hearing, most importantly any sentencing hearing.
- STEP 3: The solicitor must inform the client that any plea in mitigation undertaken by the solicitor cannot feature any reference to the client's defence. More specifically, the solicitor cannot mention any factors, as part of mitigation, that would form a defence.
- STEP 4: The solicitor should keep a file note of the advice given and should ask the client to sign a written statement confirming their wish to plead guilty, despite the advice provided by the solicitor.

Practice example 5.2

Mark has been charged with the murder of his husband, Adam. Mark informs James, his solicitor, that Mark has been physically and mentally abused by Adam for many years. On the evening of the murder, Mark was violently attacked by Adam. Whilst Adam was sleeping, Mark grabbed a large carving knife and stabbed Adam to death. Mark informs James that he wishes to plead guilty because he killed Adam and should be punished for what he has done.

What advice would you give to James?

James should explain to Mark that he has a potential defence available to him (most likely loss of self-control or diminished responsibility (see *Revise SQE: Criminal Law*)). James should advise Mark that the defence is available and that, if successful, Mark would avoid the mandatory life sentence attached to a murder conviction. James should advise Mark as to the strength/limitations of the defence and explain that (with the exception of diminished responsibility), the burden would be on the prosecution to disprove the defence. If Mark persists in claiming that he is guilty, James should inform Mark of

the effect of this on his ability to act and to put forward mitigating evidence at the sentencing hearing. James should secure Mark's signature on a written statement as to the advice James has provided, and the decision that Mark has taken.

DISPUTE RESOLUTION AND PROCEEDINGS BEFORE COURTS, TRIBUNALS AND INQUIRIES

A solicitor's primary duty is to the court. The effect of this, under Para 2 of the Code, is that the solicitor must not act in a way that compromises their obligation to the court.

You do not seek to influence the substance of evidence (Para 2.2)

Under Para 2.2, the solicitor must not 'influence the substance of evidence, including generating false evidence or persuading witnesses to change their evidence'.

This provision has a number of consequences in criminal proceedings:

- A solicitor should never suggest a defence to fit the facts; the solicitor's duty is to identify potentially relevant defences that arise from the information they receive from the client.
- A solicitor should not put words into the client's mouth when it comes to the drafting of witness statements or defence statements, for example.

Exam warning

It is worth remembering that, if a solicitor tampers with evidence (Para 2.1) or otherwise influences evidence (Para 2.2), not only would they be in breach of the Code, but they could also be liable for an offence of perverting the course of public justice (the maximum sentence for which is life imprisonment).

Witness familiarisation and coaching

In addition, whilst a solicitor is permitted to engage in **witness familiarisation**, the solicitor must not engage in **witness coaching**.

Key term: witness familiarisation

Witness familiarisation refers to arrangements to familiarise witnesses with the layout of the court, the likely sequence of events when the witness is giving evidence and a balanced appraisal of the different responsibilities of the various participants. Witness familiarisation is not only permitted in criminal proceedings, but also promoted by the courts.

Key term: witness coaching

Witness coaching refers to the circumstances where the solicitor rehearses, practises or coaches a witness in relation to their evidence. Witness coaching is prohibited; a solicitor must not prepare a witness on what they should say, or how they should say it.

The distinction between witness familiarisation and witness coaching is often a difficult one to draw. For instance, it is permissible for a solicitor to advise a witness about the need to:

- listen to and answer the questions put to them
- speak clearly and slowly in order to ensure that the court hears what the witness is saying (this being consistent with the duty to not waste the court's time), and
- avoid irrelevant comments.

Solicitors should be cautious when engaging in witness familiarisation to ensure that they do not breach Para 2.2 of the Code. Witness familiarisation programmes are offered by various agencies and, if used, must be supervised by a solicitor or barrister.

Inconsistent statements

A common situation that arises in criminal practice is where a client repeatedly changes their version of events. Importantly, the presence of inconsistent statements from the client is not a reason that the solicitor should cease to act. However, the solicitor should always be wary of their duty not to mislead the court or others, and if they consider that the witness is lying, or fabricating their version of events, the solicitor must inform the client that they must cease to act if the client intends to present a false or misleading version of events to the police and/or court.

You only make assertions or put forward statements, representations or submissions to the court or others which are properly arguable (Para 2.4)

A common scenario that unfolds in the criminal courts is where a defendant instructs their solicitor to question a witness in a certain way. Common examples include calling them a liar, suggesting they are involved in illegal activities, or otherwise attacking their character. Para 2.4 applies equally to asking questions of witnesses. In essence, there must be an evidential basis for asking a particular question or set of questions. If there is no evidential basis for doing so, then the question will not be properly arguable. A suggestion of collusion amongst police officers, for example, would be contrary to Para 2.4 if there was no basis for it.

You draw the court's attention to relevant cases and procedural irregularities (Para 2.7)

In the criminal courts, it is possible that relevant cases and statutes may be omitted by the court, or the defence, or the prosecution may make a mistake in its documentation. What should the solicitor do in these situations?

Relevant cases or statutes

Where a party to the proceedings has failed to direct the court's attention to a relevant case or statute, which is likely to have a material effect on the outcome of the proceedings, the solicitor should bring this mistake or omission to the court's attention.

Mistakes or omissions made by a party

A common scenario that arises is where the solicitor is aware of a mistake or omission made on behalf of the other party, particularly the prosecution. Remember that Principles 7 and 1 require you to act in the best interests of the client whilst also upholding the rule of law and administration of justice.

When does a solicitor have a duty to correct an error or omission of the opponent?

The answer depends on whether the solicitor has been asked to confirm, approve or indicate a positive/negative reaction to a particular matter. Consider **Practice example 5.3** to assist you with this point.

Practice example 5.3

James has been charged with theft, contrary to s 1 Theft Act 1968. At trial, Mark, James' solicitor, is handed a list of previous convictions by the prosecution. The prosecuting solicitor asks Mark to check the list and confirm its accuracy. Mark, having reviewed the list, discovers that an error exists on the document. The document correctly lists all of James' previous convictions for theft, but misstates the value of those thefts. Mark knows that the value of those previous thefts may have relevance to any application to adduce bad character and to any plea in mitigation should James be convicted.

What advice would you give to Mark in this situation?

Given that Mark has been expressly asked by the prosecution to confirm the accuracy of the document, Mark is under a duty to not mislead the court and to draw the court's attention to procedural irregularities which are likely to have a material effect on the outcome of proceedings.

- **STEP 1: Mark should discuss the prosecution's error with James, explain his duty to the court and seek James' consent to correct the error.**

- **STEP 2: If James refuses to consent to correct the error, Mark must advise him that he will not be able to continue to act for James. If James persists in his refusal to consent, Mark must withdraw from the case.**

Would the advice in **Practice example 5.3** differ if Mark was not asked to confirm the accuracy of the list of previous convictions, but was merely handed the document? Guidance under a previous iteration of the Code of Conduct (2007) provided that:

> If you are acting for a defendant, you need not correct information given to the court by the prosecution or any other party which you know may allow the court to make incorrect assumptions about the client or the case, provided you do not indicate agreement with that information.

It is unknown whether this guidance would continue to apply under the current Code. It is possible, therefore, that by merely being handed the document, without an expectation to confirm its accuracy, Mark may not be under an obligation to correct the mistake of the prosecution. However, Mark would not be able to rely on the list of previous convictions and present them as an accurate record, as to do so would mislead the court. In summary, it is advisable that in any situation, the solicitor should cease to act if the defendant is unwilling to consent to the correction being made.

CONFLICT, CONFIDENTIALITY AND DISCLOSURE

A solicitor's primary duty is to the court. The effect of this, under Para 2 of the Code, is that the solicitor must not act in a way that compromises their obligation to the court.

Conflict of interest (Para 6.2)

In criminal cases, it is common for a solicitor to be called to the police station to represent two or more clients (for our purposes, let us call them C1 and C2) alleged to have committed the same offence. In this situation, the solicitor must ensure that they comply with Para 6.2 (see **Chapter 2, page 54** for a full discussion, including the exception to the Code). Please note, however, that the exceptions in Para 6.2(a) and (b) do *not* apply in criminal proceedings.

Table 5.1 outlines some examples of where solicitors may identify a conflict of interest. In identifying the conflict, bear in mind the best interests of the client.

Table 5.1: Identifying conflicts of interest

A conflict will arise where it is in the best interests of C1:
to give evidence against C2

Table 5.1: (continued)

to make a statement incriminating C2
to provide prejudicial information regarding C2 to an investigator
to rely on confidential information given by C2 without their consent

Revision tip

The Law Society has produced a practice note entitled *Conflicts of interest in criminal cases* (2019). This practice note provides useful guidance and application of the duty to avoid conflicts of interest in criminal cases. You can access the practice note on lawsociety.org.uk.

What should you do when confronted with a potential conflict between two or more clients?

- STEP 1: Stay alert! From the outset, a solicitor may know little about the clients for whom they have been informed to represent. Until a solicitor has received disclosure from the police, they are unlikely to know whether any conflict exists, or could exist.
- STEP 2: The solicitor should interview the clients separately. The solicitor should interview C1, and gain instructions as far as possible from them, before they interview, or have any contact with, C2. As part of the interview, the solicitor should ascertain whether the clients consider there to be any actual or potential conflict between them. If, for example, C1 denies committing the offence and blames C2, it is evident that the solicitor cannot and should not act for C2.
- STEP 3: The decision as to whether there is a conflict of interest, and whether the solicitor is able to act for both clients, is one for the solicitor. It is often the case that the police will suggest that a conflict exists, and the solicitor may speak to the custody officer/investigating officer to ascertain why they believe such a conflict exists. However, this is a matter to be determined by the solicitor.
- STEP 4: The starting point for determining whether a conflict exists is to ask whether the solicitor is able to act in the best interests of each client if they represent both clients. The more likely the solicitor will feel constrained in the advice they would give, or the actions they would take, the more likely a conflict of interest exists.
- STEP 5: If a solicitor considers that a conflict does exist, or there is a significant risk of such a conflict (such as any of those examples in **Table 5.1**), the solicitor should cease to act immediately for at least one of the clients. At the police station, the solicitor should inform the police that C1 or C2 requires separate legal advice.
- STEP 6: If the solicitor ceases to act for C1, for example, they must maintain their duty of confidentiality to C1. If it becomes apparent that the solicitor will hold confidential information of C1, which is relevant to C2, the solicitor must cease to act for C2 also. This is because of their duty under Para 6.4 - to disclose all relevant information to the client. As a

result of this, it is common for the solicitor to cease to act for both clients from the outset.

Revision tip

Keep in your mind that when a solicitor ceases to act on behalf of one client, they must question whether their duty of continuing confidentiality prevents them from acting for the second client. In the majority of cases, the solicitor will hold confidential information and is unlikely to be able to act for either client.

Exam warning

The solicitor must focus their attention on the question of conflicts of interest and should not allow external pressures to affect their decision as to whether they can act. For example, the law requires one solicitor to be appointed to act for all co-defendants in a legal aid case unless there is, or is likely to be, a conflict of interest. The fact that both clients may be in receipt of legal aid to pay for a solicitor's fees should not, therefore, override the solicitor's determination as to whether they can act for both clients or not. Should the courts question why a solicitor cannot act for both defendants, the solicitor should respond that it would be 'unprofessional' for them to continue to act.

As a case progresses, a solicitor may realise that a conflict exists between C1 and C2. A solicitor must always remain vigilant to such conflicts or potential conflicts. A common example where conflicts arise later in the proceedings is where both C1 and C2 admit guilt and, in preparation of the sentencing hearing, C1 (for example) identifies mitigation which works against that of C2 (see **Practice example 5.4**).

Practice example 5.4

Tina has been instructed to represent David and Ben at the police station. Both David and Ben intend to plead guilty to the offences alleged against them. In interview, Tina does not identify any conflict of interest between David and Ben and is satisfied that she is able to represent them both. At the sentencing hearing, Tina learns that David's mitigation is that he only played a minor role in committing the offence and the more significant role was played by Ben. Ben disputes this and claims that David played the major role in this offence.

What advice would you give Tina?

Whilst Tina may not have identified a conflict of interest at the beginning of her interactions with David and Ben, it is now evident that a conflict exists between the pair regarding their mitigation to sentencing. Tina ought to have been aware that such conflict may arise and, with more focused questioning, may have considered that there

was a 'significant risk' of such conflict from the outset. Tina should clarify the position of David and Ben and, if they maintain their disputed accounts, Tina must cease to act for both of them to ensure she complies with her duties under the Code.

Confidentiality (Para 6.3)

Given that the liberty of a particular client may be at risk, maintaining their confidentiality is of vital importance to the client's interests. Under Para 6.3 of the Code, the solicitor must keep the affairs of current and former clients confidential unless disclosure is required or permitted by law or the client consents. **Chapter 2, Paras 6.3–6.5: confidentiality and disclosure** discussed this obligation, and its exceptions, in full. In this section, we shall consider some examples particularly pertinent to criminal practice.

Extent of the client's 'affairs'

Para 6.3 refers to keeping the 'affairs' of the clients confidential. Importantly, confidentiality only attaches to information given to a solicitor, by their client or a third party, *in connection with* the retainer (see **Chapter 2** for the **Key term**) in which the solicitor or their firm is instructed. Should a solicitor have information unrelated to the retainer, this may not be covered by their duty. To demonstrate this point, the SRA give the following example in their *Confidentiality of client information* (2019) guidance:

> An example of this would be where you are attending the client at the police station and whilst there, the client steals another's phone. In these circumstances to give a statement to the police would not breach your duty of confidentiality as it is unrelated to the matter on which you are advising.

Revision tip

Alongside the obligation of confidentiality in the Code, a client also has the benefit of legal professional privilege. Such privilege protects any communication between the client and their solicitor which is connected with the actual, or contemplated, litigation (ie the criminal case). These communications extend to third parties, such as barristers and expert witnesses.

It is important to remember this additional protection of confidentiality available to the client; only they can waive privilege.

What if another solicitor requests disclosure?

A common situation that arises is where one solicitor (representing C1, for example) is requested to disclose information to a second solicitor (representing C2). The second solicitor may request information relating to the offence with which both C1 and C2 are charged. To put it simply, the solicitor representing C1 should not respond to this request for disclosure. If, for example, the solicitor considers that it would be in the best interests of C1 to make such disclosure, they should explain this to C1 and seek their written informed consent to make the disclosure. This will, however, be a rare occurrence in criminal practice.

Disclosure (Paras 6.4–6.5)

Para 6.4 provides that where a solicitor acts for a client on a matter, they must 'make the client aware of all information material to the matter of which [they] have knowledge'. In a criminal case, this means that the client must have all information relevant to the charge against them disclosed to them. However, Para 6.4 is subject to a number of exceptions which have particular bearing in criminal proceedings. The full list of exceptions is contained in **Chapter 2, Duty of disclosure (Para 6.4)**; we shall consider two particular exceptions relevant to criminal practice (see **Table 5.2**).

Table 5.2: Exceptions to disclosure

Exception	Explanation and example
Where the disclosure of the information is prohibited by legal restrictions imposed in the interests of national security or the prevention of crime.	If the solicitor is in possession of information that may result in a criminal offence being committed, the solicitor may withhold this information from the client. For example, if the solicitor is aware that the police are planning a raid of the client's business, and the solicitor suspects that the client (if made aware) would attempt to interfere with that raid, the solicitor may withhold the information.
Where the solicitor has reason to believe that serious physical or mental injury will be caused to their client or another if the information is disclosed.	If the solicitor is in possession of information which the solicitor has reason to believe will cause harm or injury to the client or another, they can withhold the information. For example, if the solicitor is concerned that their client may cause harm to a witness who has been questioned by the police if the solicitor discloses this information.

Observe **Practice example 5.5** for a common scenario arising in the police station.

Practice example 5.5

James is a solicitor representing Mark at the police station. Whilst at the police station, James speaks with the investigating officer. The officer informs James that he has information relevant to the case, but identifies that the information is sensitive and cannot be disclosed further.

What should James do in this situation?

James has a duty to disclose all relevant information to Mark. James should inform the police officer of this duty. In order to act in the best interests of Mark, James should request that the officer disclose the information and should remind them of the limited exceptions that exist where James would be able to withhold the information from Mark.

Legal aid and information (Para 8.7)

Para 8.7 of the Code of Conduct requires a solicitor to ensure that clients receive the best possible information about how their matter will be priced and, both at the time of engagement and when appropriate as their matter progresses, about the likely overall cost of the matter and any costs incurred.

For the majority of defendants, their case will be funded by legal aid. This provision in the Code may seem somewhat redundant then. However, Para 7.1 still requires a solicitor to advise their client:

- whether legal aid is available in their case
- whether a contribution is required
- what cost implications there are to proceedings (eg costs upon conviction or following unsuccessful appeals).

As discussed in **Chapter 2**, this requirement will generally be covered in the client care letter, though a reminder of cost implications especially will be relevant during conferences at court.

FINAL ADVICE

The issues that may arise in criminal practice are diverse and wide ranging. This chapter has covered issues that are specific to this area of practice, but you must remain vigilant and aware of more general conduct issues that may occur in criminal proceedings. Using ***Revise SQE: Criminal Law*** and ***Revise SQE: Criminal Practice***, we advise that you review the substantive law relating to criminal law and litigation and identify occasions when ethical and professional conduct issues may arise.

■ KEY POINT CHECKLIST

This chapter has covered the following key knowledge points. You can use these to structure your revision, ensuring you recall the key details for each point, as covered in this chapter.

- The solicitor owes divided loyalty between the court and the client. In criminal proceedings, the solicitor must not allow the adversarial nature of proceedings, or the potential loss of liberty of the client, to interfere with their duty to the court.
- A solicitor may continue to act for a client who has informed them that they committed the criminal offence but wish to plead not guilty, where the client does not present a positive case of innocence.
- A solicitor may act on behalf of two or more clients accused of the same offence where there is no conflict of interest or significant risk of such.
- A solicitor must maintain the confidentiality of current and former clients at all times, even in circumstances where they have withdrawn for professional reasons.

KEY TERMS AND CONCEPTS

- put the prosecution to proof (**page 125**)
- positive case (**page 126**)
- witness familiarisation (**page 129**)
- witness coaching (**page 130**)

SQE1-STYLE QUESTIONS

QUESTION 1

A man is charged with burglary, contrary to s 9 Theft Act 1968. The prosecution's evidence largely rests on the visual identification of a witness to the offence. The witness claims to have seen the man enter and exit the building at the time the alleged offence was committed. The witness' view was obstructed, and it was night-time when the identification was made. The man informs his solicitor that he committed the offence in question but wishes to plead not guilty.

Which of the following best describes the ethical position of the solicitor?

A. The solicitor must cease to act for the man immediately and must inform the court they are ceasing to act for professional reasons.

B. The solicitor may continue to represent the man. The solicitor is able to cross-examine prosecution witnesses, make a submission of no case to answer, and examine-in-chief defence witnesses, including the man.

C. The solicitor may continue to represent the man. The solicitor is able to cross-examine prosecution witnesses and make a submission of no case to answer. However, the solicitor is not permitted to put forward a positive case for the defence.

D. The solicitor must cease to act for the man immediately and must inform the court as to the reasons for ceasing to act.

E. The solicitor may continue to represent the man. The solicitor is unable to cross-examine prosecution witnesses, make a submission of no case to answer, or put forward a positive case for the defence.

QUESTION 2

A woman is charged with theft, contrary to s 1 Theft Act 1968, and pleads guilty. At present, the facts of the case indicate that a custodial sentence cannot be imposed. Immediately before the sentencing hearing starts, the prosecutor hands the defence solicitor the antecedents and asks if they are agreed. In confidence, the defence solicitor speaks with the woman. The woman explains that she has previous convictions for theft and that, as these are currently missing from the paperwork, the antecedents are therefore inaccurate. The defence solicitor now believes that these convictions will impact the sentence, making custody a strong possibility.

Which of the following best describes what action the solicitor should take to ensure that they comply with their ethical obligations?

A. The solicitor must firstly explain to the woman that they now have a duty to disclose these previous convictions to the court, and ask whether she consents to doing so. The solicitor must explain that if the woman does not consent, then the solicitor must cease to act. The solicitor must disclose the reason for ceasing to act to the court.

B. The solicitor may continue to act for the woman but must not disclose the previous convictions to the court or the prosecutor.

C. The solicitor must firstly explain to the woman that they now have a duty to disclose these previous convictions to the court, and ask whether she consents to doing so. The solicitor must explain that if the woman does not consent, then the solicitor must cease to act. The solicitor must only disclose the reason for ceasing to act to the court if asked by the judge.

D. The solicitor must cease to act immediately and has a duty to disclose the previous convictions to the court or the prosecutor.

E. The solicitor must firstly explain to the woman that they now have a duty to disclose these previous convictions to the court, and ask whether she consents to doing so. The solicitor must explain that if the woman does not consent, then the solicitor must cease to act. The solicitor must not, however, disclose the reason for ceasing to act to the court, even if asked by the judge.

QUESTION 3

A solicitor advocate appears on behalf of a woman charged with assault. The woman maintains that she did not commit the offence. However, in a meeting with the solicitor, the woman discloses that she is distraught with the stress of proceedings, and tells the solicitor that she has 'had enough' and that she wishes to plead guilty to the offence despite the fact that she is innocent. The solicitor's attempts to dissuade the woman from entering such a plea are unsuccessful.

Which of the following correctly identifies the appropriate conduct of the solicitor?

A. If the woman insists on entering a guilty plea, despite maintaining her innocence, the solicitor can continue to represent her and there are no restrictions on the mitigation the solicitor can put forward at any sentencing hearing.

B. If the woman insists on entering a guilty plea, despite maintaining her innocence, the solicitor must withdraw immediately from the case, as to continue to represent the woman would mean they would be knowingly misleading the court.

C. If the woman insists on entering a guilty plea, despite maintaining her innocence, the solicitor can continue to represent the woman, but the solicitor must inform the court that the woman is pleading guilty against the solicitor's advice.

D. If the woman insists on entering a guilty plea, despite maintaining her innocence, the solicitor must withdraw immediately from the case, as to continue to represent the woman would mean they would be knowingly misleading the court. The solicitor must also inform the court as to the reason that they are ceasing to act.

E. If the woman insists on entering a guilty plea, despite maintaining her innocence, the solicitor can continue to represent her, but there are restrictions on what the solicitor can say at any sentencing hearing in terms of mitigation.

QUESTION 4

A man is charged with assault. The man is a member of a far-right extremist group with previous convictions for racially aggravated assault. The man has extreme views on immigration and has previously expressed a hatred towards non-white communities. The man seeks to instruct a solicitor to act on his behalf. The solicitor finds the man's views and beliefs abhorrent as they are in conflict with their own.

Which of the following best describes the position of the solicitor?

A. The solicitor would be entitled to refuse the man's instructions as the conflict between their political views and opinions and that of the man would mean that they would be professionally embarrassed.
B. The solicitor would be obliged to accept the instruction, despite finding the conduct, opinions and beliefs of the man unacceptable, and must act in the best interests of the man in representing him.
C. The solicitor would not be entitled to refuse the man's instruction on the basis that they find the conduct, opinions and beliefs of the man unacceptable. To do so would be discriminatory.
D. The solicitor would be entitled to refuse the man's instruction on the basis that they find the conduct, opinions and beliefs of the man unacceptable, as such refusal would not be discriminatory.
E. The solicitor would be obliged to accept the instruction but could apply to the court to be released from their professional obligations to the man, as to represent him would not be in his best interests.

QUESTION 5

A solicitor works in a criminal practice and is instructed to act on behalf of a man charged with burglary. Following a meeting, the solicitor overhears the man on his mobile phone negotiating to buy firearms for a planned burglary of a commercial premises.

Which of the following best describes the solicitor's duty in this case?

A. The solicitor should contact the police immediately. Disclosure to the police is permitted by law in this circumstance and will not amount to a breach of confidence.
B. The solicitor should confront the man and advise him that he should not engage in criminal conduct. If the man refuses to cease in his conduct, the solicitor should contact the police.
C. The solicitor is not permitted to contact the police, as to do so would breach the solicitor's duty to maintain client confidentiality, unless the man consents to the disclosure.
D. The solicitor should contact the police immediately. Whilst disclosure to the police is permitted by law in this circumstance, disclosure will still amount to a breach of confidence.
E. The solicitor is not permitted to contact the police, as to do so would breach the solicitor's duty to maintain client confidentiality.

ANSWERS TO QUESTIONS

Answers to 'What do you know already?' questions at the start of the chapter

1) False. Whilst the likely loss of liberty will be a factor only relevant in criminal proceedings, this does not mean that the potential loss of liberty outweighs the solicitor's other duties and interests.
2) The solicitor should be wary of ensuring that they are not misleading the court. The solicitor should seek to ascertain exactly what the client's version of events is and, in the circumstances where they believe that the client may present a false case to the court, the solicitor should cease to act.
3) False. A solicitor may continue to act for the client so long as they do not present a positive defence for the client. The solicitor is permitted to test the prosecution evidence, but must not call any evidence suggesting the innocence of the client.
4) The solicitor must request consent from the client to disclose the inaccuracy to the prosecutor. If the client refuses, the solicitor can continue to act but must not make any positive reference to the inaccuracy. In the alternative circumstance where the prosecution explicitly requests confirmation of accuracy, the solicitor must cease to act in order to avoid misleading the court if the client refuses to consent to the solicitor correcting the record. The solicitor should explain this clearly to the client.

Answers to end-of-chapter SQE1-style questions

Question 1:

The correct answer was C. This is because the solicitor is not obliged to withdraw from the case (options A and D are therefore wrong). The solicitor is able to continue to act for the man, and is permitted to put the prosecution to proof. This means that the solicitor is able to cross-examine prosecution witnesses and make a submission of no case to answer (therefore option E is wrong). However, the solicitor is not permitted to put forward any positive defence for the man which they know to be false or misleading (therefore option B is incorrect). The solicitor is not permitted to allow the man to give evidence that he did not, for example, commit the offence in question. Given that the prosecution's case is relatively weak in this instance due to the difficulties of the eyewitness testimony, the solicitor will likely be able to test the prosecution's case without putting forward a positive (and false) case for the defence.

Question 2:

The correct answer was E. In line with Para 1.4, the solicitor must not mislead the court. To continue to act without correcting the inaccuracies of the antecedents, after having been explicitly asked to check them by the prosecution, would mislead the court and breach the duty under Para 1.4 (therefore option B is wrong). However, Para 6.3 also requires the solicitor to maintain client confidentiality: a solicitor must not disclose client information without the client's consent. Option E represents the best answer here given that the solicitor must seek the consent of the client to continue to act, and if the client is unwilling to disclose the material, at that point the solicitor must cease to act. Option A is wrong because the solicitor would be in breach of their duty of confidence if they were to disclose the reasons for ceasing to act. Option C is wrong because the solicitor is not permitted to disclose client information, even if asked by the judge. Option D is wrong because the necessity to cease to act only arises where the client refuses to consent to the disclosure, meaning that the solicitor would be in breach of their duty to not mislead the court.

Question 3:

The correct answer was E. The solicitor is still permitted to represent the woman; however, the solicitor would be restricted as to what they could say in mitigation (therefore option A is wrong) (for example that she was remorseful for her conduct, as she had maintained to the solicitor that she is innocent and this would therefore be actively misleading the court). Options B and D are wrong because the solicitor can continue to represent the woman without misleading the court, as long as they observe the restrictions on mitigation. Options C and D are equally wrong because they would involve a breach of confidentiality by disclosing the reason for withdrawing to the court.

Question 4:

The correct answer was D. A solicitor is never obligated to accept instructions so long as such refusal is not as a result of any discrimination. Whilst it is arguable that the solicitor has discriminated against the man because of his extremist views, it is unlikely that this will amount to discriminatory conduct within Para 1.1 of the Code (therefore option C is wrong). Option A is unlikely to be the best answer because professional embarrassment would not be in issue. Options B and E are wrong because a solicitor is never obligated to accept instructions.

Question 5:

The correct answer was A. The solicitor is able to make a disclosure of the affairs of the client where the disclosure is permitted by law (Para 6.3). Potential commission, or attempted commission, of a criminal offence would be a matter to be disclosed. There is no breach of confidence as the disclosure would be permitted by law (therefore options C, D, and E are wrong). Option B is wrong because the solicitor is not obligated under the Code to dissuade the man from committing or attempting to commit an offence.

■ KEY CASES, RULES, STATUTES AND INSTRUMENTS

The SQE1 Assessment Specification has identified that candidates are required to understand the purpose, scope and content of the SRA Principles and Code of Conduct. Make sure that you understand the application of the SRA Principles and Code of Conduct to criminal law and practice.

The SQE1 Assessment Specification does not require you to know any case names, or statutory materials, for the topic of ethics and professional conduct in criminal law and practice.

6

Ethics and professional conduct in wills and the administration of estates

Richard Clements and Mark Thomas

■ MAKE SURE YOU KNOW

This chapter will cover the application of the Solicitors Regulation Authority (SRA) Principles and Code of Conduct to wills and the administration of estates.

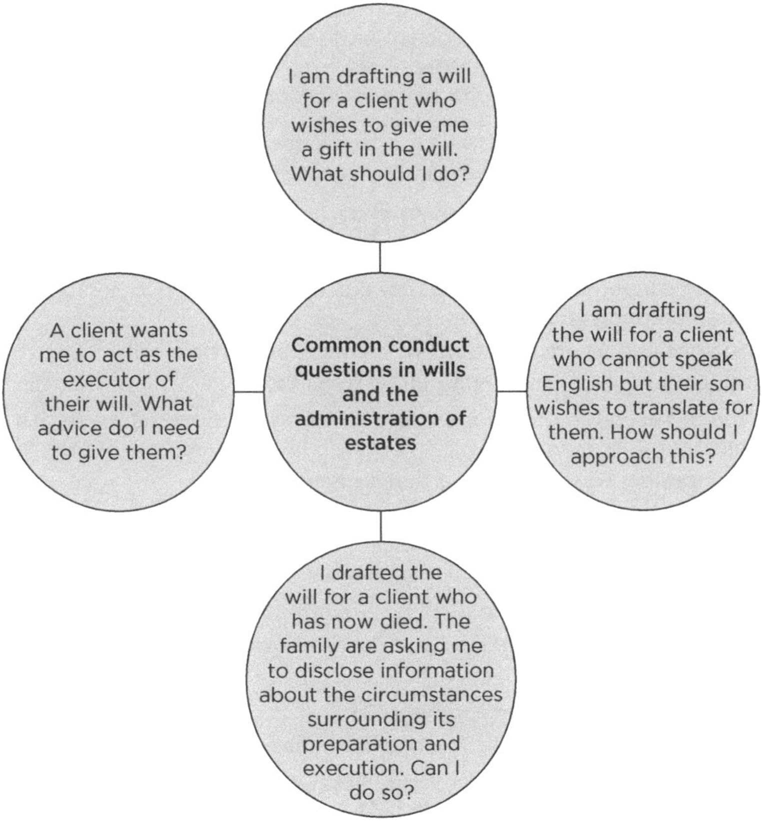

The chapter will allow you to observe how ethical issues and professional conduct matters are likely to arise when clients make wills, apply for probate, and personal representatives administer the estate of the deceased.

Wills and the administration of estates feature in the second of the SQE1 assessments (FLK2), and ethics and professional conduct relevant to wills and the administration of estates will be assessed pervasively in that assessment.

SQE ASSESSMENT ADVICE

As you work through this chapter, remember to pay particular attention in your revision to:

- whether a solicitor is permitted to draft a will for a client in circumstances when the client wishes to make a gift in their will to the solicitor
- the role of a solicitor when a client wishes them to act as executor for their will
- the need to identify your client in circumstances where family members, friends or other individuals make contact with the solicitor
- the alteration of communication to suit the needs of the client, including deaf, blind and illiterate testators
- the duty to maintain the confidence of a client who has died and how that conflicts with duties to current clients relevant to the will.

WHAT DO YOU KNOW ALREADY?

Have a go at these questions before reading this chapter. If you find some difficult or cannot remember the answers, make a note to look more closely at that area during your revision.

1) True or false? There is a standard fee for drawing up a will.

   [Maintaining trust and acting fairly; page 147]

2) True or false? The provisions of the SRA Code of Conduct mean that the solicitors who draw up a will cannot also be the executors of that will.

   [Maintaining trust and acting fairly; page 147]

3) When should a solicitor check that the client's instructions truly represent the wishes of that client?

   (a) If the client is elderly

   (b) If the client is accompanied by a relative

   (c) If the client seems to have mental health problems

   (d) All of the above.

   [Service and competence; page 149]

4) True or false? Once the testator/testatrix has died, the executors of the will are free to distribute the assets in the will to the beneficiaries.

   [Client money and assets; page 153]

INTRODUCTION TO ETHICS AND PROFESSIONAL CONDUCT IN WILLS AND THE ADMINISTRATION OF ESTATES

Everyone dies, and so advising on the administration of the estates of the deceased is a major area of work for solicitors.

This chapter should be read in conjunction with ***Revise SQE: Trusts Law*** and ***Revise SQE: Wills and the Administration of Estates***. In those guides, you will find many **Key terms** and important substantive topics to assist you in furthering your understanding of your ethical and professional obligations.

There are an increasing number of disputes about wills and inheritance and although there are many laws that govern this area, many ethical considerations are also raised by disputes between members of warring families.

This chapter considers some of these ethical issues and provides guidance on how you might answer questions in your SQE1 assessment on the appropriate professional conduct relating to wills and the administration of estates.

Revision tip

Throughout this chapter, we will be making numerous references to the *STEP Code for Will Preparation in England and Wales* (STEP 2016). The *STEP Code* is a set of ethical principles that demonstrate the standard of transparency and service expected when a will is drafted. Make sure you read the *STEP Code* in full to understand best ethical practice in will drafting. You can view the *STEP Code* here: www.step.org/public/step-will-code.

In the present guide, **Chapters 1** and **2** set out the SRA Principles (the 'Principles') and Code of Conduct (the 'Code') respectively. This chapter will consider how relevant headings operate in the context of wills and the administration of estates. The headings used reflect the headings of the Code of Conduct.

MAINTAINING TRUST AND ACTING FAIRLY

When dealing with wills and the administration of estates, you must maintain trust and treat your clients fairly. The Code requires that:

- you do not unfairly discriminate
- you do not mislead your client or others
- you do not abuse your position by taking unfair advantage of clients
- you perform all undertakings within an agreed or reasonable time.

For the purposes of this chapter we shall focus on the duty to not mislead or to abuse your position. For examples of unfair discrimination and the provision of undertakings, see the other chapters in this guide.

You do not abuse your position by taking unfair advantage of clients or others (Para 1.2)

The SRA in its guidance *Drafting and Preparation of Wills* (2019) advises that a solicitor 'must not exploit a client's lack of knowledge by leading them to believe that appointing a solicitor as an executor is essential or that it is the default position for someone making a will'. This statement reflects Principle 7, which requires the solicitor to act in the best interests of the client, meaning that a solicitor must not encourage a client to appoint them, or their firm, as their executor unless it is clearly in the client's best interests to do so. This obligation is especially important given that a solicitor would wish to charge for their services (see **client information and publicity** below). It is for this reason that the *STEP Code* stipulates that 'the preparation of a will must not be conditional on the will drafter being appointed executor and/or trustee'.

However, it is common for solicitors to act as executors for an individual's will. In some professionally drafted wills, the executors will also be identified as trustees where the circumstances require a trustee. This means that they have statutory powers and duties as defined by statute and common law. We shall consider some of these issues now.

Duty of care and exclusion clauses

By s 1 Trustee Act (TA) 2000, a solicitor who acts as trustee under a will must act with such care and skills as is reasonable in the circumstances. Should a solicitor fall below this standard, they will be in breach of trust (see ***Revise SQE: Trusts Law*** for more detail on this). It is common, therefore, for a professionally drafted will to exclude liability to the client or intended beneficiaries for loss arising out of the work, or lack thereof, of the solicitor drafting the will. Importantly, liability cannot be excluded in all circumstances (eg one cannot exclude liability for their own fraud). It is important that a solicitor does not attempt, therefore, to exclude all liability.

Exclusion clauses for negligence are permissible, however. The *STEP Code* advises that 'any limited exclusions of duty or liability must be clearly drawn to the attention of the client, explained and then agreed with the client'. This advice is closely linked with Principle 4 (acting with honesty) and Principle 7 (acting in the best interests of each client).

Revision tip

SQE1 assesses not just your knowledge of the law, but also how ethical considerations from the SRA's Code of Conduct intertwine with the law. We have just read how the law allows the exclusion of liability, but that it would not be ethical to do this without informing the client. In some MCQs, you will need to carefully assess whether you are being asked about the law or about ethics.

Payment for services

As with exclusion clauses, a solicitor who has been asked to act as an executor will likely want to insert a clause in the will allowing them to be paid for their services. The TA 2000 allows trustees to charge for 'reasonable remuneration', though many will precedents will often not refer to 'reasonable' in their charging clause (see ***Revise SQE: Wills and the Administration of Estates***).

Again, a solicitor drawing up the will must make this clear to the client and must advise them of the other options available in selecting an executor. In practice, a solicitor would draw the client's attention to such a clause by going through the will with them. By doing so, the solicitor can identify the clause and explain the basis of charges (this being in addition to the client being sent the will in draft with explanations prior to signing).

You do not mislead or attempt to mislead your clients (Para 1.4)

A client (testator/testatrix) may draw up their own will. However, a solicitor would likely advise that it would be better for them (or another solicitor) to draft the will to avoid unforeseen legal problems. The solicitor must clearly specify what they will charge for preparing the will and warn that the cost will increase depending on the complexity of the will, eg number of beneficiaries, nature of bequests, whether the client wants to set up a trust in their will etc.

SERVICE AND COMPETENCE

A solicitor acts on the instructions of their client and must deliver the service requested in a timely and competent manner based on an up-to-date knowledge of the law. Wills are quite often disputed, so the solicitor must ensure that they have understood and upheld the wishes of the testator/testatrix.

You only act for clients on instructions from the client (Para 3.1)

When acting for a client in will drafting, a solicitor must ensure that the client has the capacity to make a will and is not subject to any undue influence.

Mental capacity

A testator/testatrix must have mental capacity (also known as 'testamentary capacity') to make a will. If the testator/testatrix lacks mental capacity, the will can be challenged and declared invalid. Please refer to ***Revise SQE: Wills and the Administration of Estates*** for a discussion of the *Banks v Goodfellow* test for mental capacity to create a will. The issue here is: How should a solicitor deal with a concern regarding the capacity of a client? This issue is explored in **Practice example 6.1**.

Practice example 6.1

Frances is 80 years of age and wishes to change her will. Her former will divided her property equally between her daughter and her son. She now wishes to make a new will, leaving all her property to her daughter, who has been living with her and caring for her. Her son claims that Frances is suffering from Alzheimer's disease and lacks the capacity to change her will.

How should Frances' solicitor deal with this problem?

The following details the process that is recommended in the *STEP Code*:

- **STEP 1: The solicitor must not prepare a will if they know, or have reasonable grounds for concluding, that Frances lacks the necessary mental capacity.**
- **STEP 2: The solicitor must endeavour to ascertain if, with their assistance, Frances would be capable of making a valid will.**
- **STEP 3: Where there is doubt as to capacity, the solicitor should seek expert advice to help them make their decision on Frances' capacity (referred to as the 'golden rule'). The solicitor should ask a medical practitioner to undertake a capacity assessment and to be present when Frances makes her new will. The medical practitioner must satisfy themselves that Frances understands the nature and effect of the new will.**
- **STEP 4: Most importantly, a solicitor should keep a written record of the steps taken, their conclusions as to capacity (including their reasons for reaching those conclusions) and a written record from the medical practitioner. These would be important evidence if the will is challenged.**

Undue influence

A solicitor must also try to ensure that a will really does represent the wishes of their client. If the client has been subject to force or fear in order to make or change their will, that will is invalid. A solicitor should be on their guard if a relative or other person has persuaded the testator/testatrix to alter the will. This issue has become especially prominent following the COVID-19 pandemic and the use of remote witnessing of wills. According to Para 3.1, the solicitor must satisfy themselves that the client's instructions represent the client's wishes. This may prove more difficult with remote meetings and witnessing.

To ensure that the risk of undue influence is removed/mitigated, the *STEP Code* prescribes that when taking instructions from a client, the solicitor must endeavour to ensure that 'no member of the testator's family, or an intended beneficiary under the will, is present during the meeting'. The *STEP Code* goes on to say that:

> It is understood that in some circumstances this may not be possible, and if the solicitor feels able to proceed with the interview they must:
> a. provide a careful explanation of the potential for challenge to the terms of the will, and
> b. take careful note of the third party's participation in the meeting in order to assist with any later dispute.

You ensure that the service you provide to clients is competent and delivered in a timely manner (Para 3.2)

By Para 3.2, a solicitor must ensure that the service they provide to clients is competent and delivered in a timely manner. One question that arises here is: How long should a solicitor take to draft a will?

The Law Society, in their publication *Wills and Inheritance Protocol* (Law Society 2013) provide the following guidance:

- When a solicitor receives instructions from the client, they should agree a date for the preparation of the will that is acceptable to the client, and reflects any need for urgency (for example, to take into account the health condition of the client).
- Unless otherwise agreed, once the client has provided all the information needed to complete the agreed instructions, the solicitor should:
  - send the draft will to the client within seven working days, and
  - send the final version to the client for execution within seven working days of receiving approval of the draft, or if a draft is not supplied, send the will to the client for execution within ten working days.

Revision tip

There is no legal regulation of wills in England and Wales. Practitioners rely on guidance from the Law Society and other organisations such as STEP. It is advised that you follow this guidance carefully. For instance, STEP do not dictate a timeframe to be followed for the drafting of a will, but do advise that the task must be undertaken 'expeditiously'. Make sure you use this guidance as part of your revision for SQE1.

You consider and take account of your client's attributes, needs and circumstances (Para 3.4)

The will that is prepared must be appropriate for the client's circumstances. This means that the will must be drafted in such a way that is clear and understandable. Inappropriately complex wills must be avoided.

Particular circumstances of clients

A solicitor specialising in private client law will undoubtedly come into contact with clients who require a greater level of assistance than their average client. For example, a client may be blind, illiterate or English may not be their first language. In these circumstances, the solicitor must ensure that they tailor their services to suit the needs of the client (this also ensures that a firm avoids claims for unlawful discrimination in respect of their provision of services to clients with a disability). **Table 6.1** provides some examples of what measures could be taken.

Table 6.1: Measures to assist clients

Client attributes, needs or circumstances	Necessary adjustments
Clients who are blind or illiterate	A client who is blind will require the will to be read out loud to them. A solicitor may seek to have the will transcribed into Braille (if the client can read such); however, such transcription must be done professionally (and independently of the client/their family).
Deaf clients and clients whose first language is not English	A client who is deaf may require a sign-language interpreter when engaging with their solicitor. This individual must be independent of the client/their family. Likewise, where English is not their first language, or the client struggles with English, an interpreter may be required (but, once more, they must be independent to avoid any risk of undue influence).

Clients who do not see the value of a will

Many clients, including those who are not particularly wealthy, think that they do not need to make a will, because their property will automatically go to their closest relatives when they die. This is true up to a point, but clients need to be warned that, under the intestacy rules, property may not pass to their intended recipients. For instance, a client must be advised that property *cannot* pass via the intestacy rules to:

- a cohabitant upon death
- stepchildren, or
- children who have not been formally adopted.

Should a client wish for any of the above individuals to benefit from their estate, they should be advised to make a will.

CLIENT MONEY AND ASSETS

Executors derive their authority from the will itself. In the majority of cases, once the testator/testatrix has died, the executors will apply to the court for a grant of probate. Depending on the assets in question, a grant of probate may not be required, but in the majority of cases it is. The grant of probate confirms their authority to collect the assets of the deceased and then distribute them to the beneficiaries named in the will. The executors may be solicitors or lay people, but often lay executors will employ solicitors to apply for probate. Probate is usually obtained within a year of the date of death.

You safeguard money and assets entrusted to you by clients and others (Para 4.2)

The executors' first duty is to collect and secure the assets of the deceased. They then have powers to administer that property and even to sell, mortgage or lease it, which may be necessary to pay debts or taxes, and distribute the property to the beneficiaries.

A solicitor may have to advise an individual as to how the estate will be distributed and the timeframe for this. An illustration of how this might work in practice can be seen in **Practice example 6.2**.

Practice example 6.2

Mark has just died and your firm of solicitors are the executors of his will. His widow consults you in great distress because she claims to have no money. She is sure that Mark left all his property to her and asks whether the executors can let her have some of the money now.

What advice would you give her?

You would have to tell Mark's widow that she might have access to property that is not governed by the will, such as a joint bank account with Mark or rights under a pension. If her home with Mark was held as a joint tenancy, irrespective of the will, it now belongs to her under the right of survivorship.

CONFLICT, CONFIDENTIALITY AND DISCLOSURE

Part 6 of the Code of Conduct sets out a series of rules relating to when a solicitor should decline to act for particular clients. This section sets out how situations involving these rules may apply in the context of wills and the administration of estates.

Own interest conflict (Para 6.1)

In line with the Code of Conduct, a solicitor must not act for a client where there is a significant risk of a conflict of interest, either an *own interest conflict* or a *conflict of interest* (return to **Chapter 2** for a full discussion and to remind yourself of these **Key term** definitions). Solicitors must be aware of the potential risks involved in acting for a private client.

Gifts made to solicitors in the will

It is common, especially when a solicitor who is a family friend of the testator is involved, for a will to make a gift of significant value to the solicitor, a member of their family, another employee of the firm, or their family member. What should a solicitor do in this situation?

- STEP 1: The solicitor must satisfy themselves that the client has first taken independent legal advice with regard to making the gift.
- STEP 2: The solicitor should make a record of the advice provided and seek written confirmation from the client that they have obtained such independent legal advice.
- STEP 3: If the client refuses to take independent legal advice, the solicitor should cease to act for the client where the client still wishes to include the gift in their will.

In a similar situation, where benefit under the will is to pass to a body, such as a charity, with which the solicitor has substantial involvement, the *STEP Code* provides that best practice is for the solicitor to decline to draft the will, and to arrange for another suitably qualified individual to assist the client.

Exam warning

The rule on ceasing to act is not absolute. Whether a solicitor ceases to act is a decision for them and it will depend on the specific circumstances within which they find themselves. For example, a solicitor who is drafting a will for their parents, where the parents intend to leave their estate equally to the solicitor and their siblings may consider it acceptable that they continue to act. However, these circumstances will be limited, and the *STEP Code* strongly advises against solicitors acting in this situation.

Rule against self-dealing

Executors hold the legal title to all the assets of the deceased and so are in a good position to know the value of those assets, which may not be obvious to the beneficiaries. For that reason, executors are not permitted to buy or otherwise acquire any of those assets. This is known as the rule against 'self-dealing'. The rule is strict, and any transaction entered into by a solicitor, acting as executor, is voidable (ie the beneficiaries can request the transaction to be set aside). See ***Revise SQE: Trusts Law*** for a greater insight into the rule against self-dealing.

Conflict of interest (Para 6.2)

A solicitor is not permitted to act if they have a conflict of interest or a significant risk of such a conflict. The SRA defines a conflict of interest as 'a situation where your separate duties to act in the best interests of two or more clients in the same or a related matter conflict'. This can be a particular problem in wills and the administration of estates, where family members quite often dispute the provisions of a will.

Common examples of conflicts arising include:

- If a solicitor receives instructions from more than one client, in a meeting regarding more than one will, a conflict may arise where the wills come into conflict.
- If a solicitor drafted the will, or is the executor, or is acting for the executors, the solicitor should not act for potential clients disputing the will.
- If a solicitor acts for a client disputing the will, they cannot act for a client with a different claim about the same will. A solicitor would, however, be able to act for a group of clients if they had the same claim about the will and they consented.

Confidentiality and disclosure (Paras 6.3–6.5)

A solicitor must keep the affairs of the client confidential unless the client consents.

Confidentiality generally

In line with Para 6.3, a solicitor must not inform anyone else of the contents of a will unless the client consents. This duty continues after death, as the right to confidentiality passes to the personal representatives of the client. After probate has been granted, however, a will becomes a public document, available from the Probate Registry to anyone. However, the duty of confidentiality continues in respect of any matter covered by the retainer (see **Chapter 2** for the **Key term**) (eg communications between the client and solicitor when drafting the will).

Exam warning

Whilst the contents of the will become a public document upon the grant of probate, solicitors must maintain the confidentiality of their client for any other matters connected to the retainer. Do not allow the publication of the will to confuse your understanding of a solicitor's obligation of confidence in respect of any information obtained from the client and advice given to the client.

Some information might still be private. Wills may contain discretionary trusts to give flexibility as to how the estate is to be distributed, eg the trustees, often the same people as the executors, have discretion to distribute property amongst the deceased's children and grandchildren. These beneficiaries have no right to know what others in their category are receiving. Family members often want to know about wills and their contents. **Practice example 6.3** illustrates how the Code applies.

Practice example 6.3

Richard and David are two brothers. The pair are concerned that their elderly parents, Bert and Molly, might have changed their wills. They know that you are Bert and Molly's usual solicitor and ask you to tell them what is in their parents' wills.

What should you do?

Unless Bert and Molly give their permission, you cannot inform the brothers of the contents of the will. In fact, you cannot even inform them that you were the individual who drafted the will (if you did). If you did draft the will, you may consider speaking to Bert and Molly to make them aware of the request and seek instructions accordingly. Further, you should have already ensured that you were satisfied that Bert and Molly had the mental capacity to make wills when you first drafted the will. See *Mental capacity* above.

Confidentiality and disputed wills

A solicitor may be faced with a situation where a will that they have prepared is disputed. In these circumstances, a solicitor may be asked to disclose information about the circumstances surrounding its preparation and execution (known as a *Larke v Nugus* request (taken from a case of the same name)). The issue becomes: under what circumstances can, and should, a solicitor do so?

- STEP 1: A solicitor is not obligated to comply with a *Larke v Nugus* request, but it is considered best practice in order to avoid potentially costly litigation.
- STEP 2A: If a solicitor chooses not to respond to a *Larke v Nugus* request, they should consider that they may be compelled to do so by the court (which is not only inconvenient, but also costly).
- STEP 2B: If a solicitor chooses to respond to a *Larke v Nugus* request, their conduct depends on whether the solicitor is named as an executor in that will:
  - If the solicitor is named as the executor, they should provide the requested statement and relevant documents, so long as no other person has a sustainable claim to legal privilege (ie there is not another person who can claim privilege/confidentiality) in the material.
  - If the solicitor is not named as the executor, they should obtain the consent of the executors before making any disclosure. If the executors

do not wish to give consent, the solicitor must advise them of the potential for the court to subpoena them to produce some or all of the documents requested.

- STEP 3: The SRA Code of Conduct does not prohibit charging for the preparation of a *Larke v Nugus* statement. However, those charges should be reasonable, in accordance with a solicitor's duty to treat others fairly under Paras 1.1 to 1.4 of the Code.

Disclosure

When a solicitor acts for a client, Para 6.4 of the Code obliges them to 'make the client aware of all information material to the matter of which you have knowledge'. That leads to a conflict of interests where that information comes from another client or former client and is confidential. If the 'new' client has an adverse interest to the other client, and there is a risk that the confidential information could be disclosed, the solicitor must not act for the new client, unless the solicitor obtains written permission from the former or other client.

Therefore, a solicitor should carefully check the provisions of the Code if they are asked to act in a family dispute about a will or inheritance. The solicitor might well have confidential information from one member of a family which they cannot disclose to other members of the family. See **Conflict of interest** above.

Revision tip

Conflicts of interest are common in wills and the administration of estates, but as we have explained, they are not always as straightforward as they might seem. It is quite likely that this sort of MCQ will occur in the SQE1 assessment.

WHEN YOU ARE PROVIDING SERVICES TO THE PUBLIC OR A SECTION OF THE PUBLIC

A number of issues can be identified as relevant to wills and the administration of estates under this heading of the Code.

Client identification (Para 8.1)

Para 8.1 obligates a solicitor to identify who they are acting for in relation to any matter. In the context of will drafting, the solicitor must take all reasonable steps to identify the client in order to prevent fraud by impersonation of a client. See ***Revise SQE: The Legal System and Services of England and Wales*** for more detail on the Money Laundering Regulations 2007.

Complaints handling (Paras 8.2–8.5)

Paras 8.2–8.5 detail the obligations imposed on solicitors in respect of the handling of complaints. Particularly, solicitors providing service to the public must have a complaints system and inform clients, in writing, of how it works at the time of engagement. If the client is not satisfied within eight weeks, they must be informed, in writing, of their right to appeal to the Legal Ombudsman (see **Key term** in **Chapter 2**).

CLIENT INFORMATION AND PUBLICITY

Under paras 8.6–8.11, a solicitor owes a number of obligations to their client. This includes an obligation to provide information to clients on their case and costs.

You give clients information in a way they can understand (Para 8.6)

Will drafting, and the administration of estates, is a complex business. A solicitor must be in a position to provide information to their clients clearly and effectively. Below are some examples of the type of information relevant to a client seeking advice on wills and the administration of their estate.

Appointment of executors

A will should have executors, usually with a minimum of two people and a maximum of four (you can technically have more than four executors; however this is unworkable and only four may go on the grant of probate). Most testators/testatrices appoint two people or alternatively a professional body (such as a trust corporation or a partnership of solicitors). A solicitor must advise a client to choose trusted and competent friends or relatives as executors, as discussed above (see **You do not abuse your position by taking unfair advantage of clients or others**).

Before a solicitor drafts a will which appoints them, or their firm, as the executor, the solicitor must satisfy themselves that the client has made this decision on a fully informed basis. This means that the solicitor should:

- STEP 1: Explain the options available to the client regarding their choice of executor.
- STEP 2: Ensure the client understands that an executor does not have to be a professional person or a business. The solicitor should explain that the executor could instead be a family member or a beneficiary under the will.
- STEP 3: Reassure a client that lay executors can subsequently instruct a solicitor to act for them if this proves necessary (and can be indemnified out of the estate for the solicitors' fees).
- STEP 4: Record any advice that is given concerning the appointment of executors, including a recording of the client's decision.

Storage of wills

Before a will is admitted into probate, it is a private document; it is not readily available for public sight. Indeed, many wills remain hidden until a client dies. In light of this, clients are best advised to consider the use of an official storage of their original will. His Majesty's Courts and Tribunals Service (HMCTS) offers a low-cost wills storage service which clients should be informed about.

Many solicitors' firms charge clients for the safe storage of their original will, whilst others will not. In any regard, a solicitor must properly advise their client as to the options available for the storage of their will. Storage in a central official service, such as with the Probate Registry, may make it convenient for executors to access the will. Alternatively, storage with the solicitor may be more appropriate, allowing for easy access by executors and by the creator of the will.

Regardless of whether the will is officially stored or not, the SRA, in their guidance *Drafting and preparation of wills*, state that a solicitor should advise their client to:

- make sure that all their executors know where to find the original version of the will
- keep a copy of the will at their home with the relevant details
- keep the solicitor informed of any changes to their address or contact details, and
- review their will regularly to make sure it still reflects their wishes and circumstances.

Extending or limiting the general law through a will

Various statutory provisions provide trustees (and as a result, executors) with a raft of duties and powers at their disposal. For example, a trustee may:

- make any kind of investment as if they were absolutely entitled to the assets of the estate (Trustee Act (TA) 2000, s 3)
- invest in land within the UK for the purpose of investment, occupation by a beneficiary, or any other reason (TA 2000, s 8)
- maintain an infant beneficiary, or advance capital to beneficiaries entitled to capital (TA 1925, ss 31 and 32).

A solicitor must be in a position to advise a client, when drafting a will, that the will has the ability to restrict and extend the operation of the law. For example, a testator may wish to restrict investments to family businesses only (therefore curtailing the general power of investment in s 3 above). Alternatively, they may wish to extend the trustee's power of investment in land to include property outside of the UK. The solicitor must explain the effect of these statutory provisions and modify them in the will as instructed.

You ensure that clients receive the best possible information about how their matter will be priced (Para 8.7)

As can be seen in **Chapter 2, Paras 8.6–8.11: client information and publicity**, Para 8.7 of the Code requires a solicitor to ensure that their client receives the 'best possible' information about the price of their service and the likely overall costs. This provision is particularly important in will drafting when 'standard fees' are often given by solicitors for work done.

Revision tip

You may want to look at the pricing information which now has to be published by each firm on their websites. Firms are required to publish an estimated price for estate work. This will help you put Para 8.7 into practice.

The *STEP Code* requires that the basis of charging must be reasonable for the work being undertaken and the client's requirements. STEP advises that it is reasonable for charges to 'reflect complexity, time spent, risk and the qualification of the will drafter'.

If the client chooses the solicitors' firm to be the executor, the solicitor must warn the client of the fees that they will charge for applying for probate on the death of the client and for administering the will. This could be a fixed fee or, more likely, the fee will depend upon the amount of work required. An illustration of this can be seen in **Practice example 6.4**.

Practice example 6.4

Harry has just died, and your firm of solicitors are the executor of his will. You advise his son, Ken, who is the only beneficiary of the will, that it will cost him £3,000 plus VAT and disbursements for your firm to apply for probate and administer the will. However, Sarah, who claims to have been a cohabitant of Ken, informs your firm that she is going to make a claim under the Inheritance (Provision for Family and Dependants) Act 1975 (a statute that you are required to know for SQE1, see ***Revise SQE: Wills and the Administration of Estates***).

What advice should you give to Ken?

You must advise Ken that this claim by Sarah makes the matter contentious and could result in the case going to court. This will be more expensive, and you should provide an update on your fees and advise on the likely cost (remember that your duty to provide the 'best possible information' is a continuing duty). As your firm was only appointed as executor, you should also advise Ken that he is free to employ a different solicitor to deal with this matter.

FINAL ADVICE

The issues that may arise in wills and the administration of estates are diverse and wide ranging. This chapter has covered issues that are specific to this area of practice, but you must remain vigilant and aware of more general conduct issues that may occur (eg on costs and client care). Using ***Revise SQE: Wills and the Administration of Estates***, you should review the substantive law relating to wills and the administration of estates and identify occasions when ethical and professional conduct issues may arise.

■ KEY POINT CHECKLIST

This chapter has covered the following key knowledge points. You can use these to structure your revision, ensuring you recall the key details for each point, as covered in this chapter.

- A solicitor must fully inform their client about the effects of the provisions of the client's will.
- A solicitor must provide their services on time and at the price agreed, which will vary according to the complexity of the will and the instructions.
- A solicitor must ensure that their instructions truly represent the wishes of their client.
- A solicitor has a duty to protect the assets of their client.
- A solicitor must keep the affairs of their client confidential, even where their client is dead, and avoid any conflict with their own interests or the interests of others.

■ KEY TERMS AND CONCEPTS

There are no key terms for this specific chapter.

■ SQE1-STYLE QUESTIONS

QUESTION 1

A solicitors' firm was appointed as executor of the deceased's will. The firm inserted a clause in the will that they would not be liable for any loss or damage unless it was caused by their actual fraud. The firm did not tell the testator that they had done this. The beneficiaries of the will consider that the solicitors' firm has taken an excessive time to administer the will and lost them money. The beneficiaries complain to the firm, but the firm dismiss the complaint.

Which of the following is the best course of action for the beneficiaries?

A. The beneficiaries should sue the solicitors' firm.

B. The beneficiaries should complain to the Legal Ombudsman.

C. The beneficiaries have no remedy as such clauses are legal.
D. The beneficiaries have no claim as their complaint has gone through the correct procedure and been dismissed.
E. The beneficiaries should ask the solicitors' firm to reconsider their complaint.

QUESTION 2

A solicitor is engaged by a son, who brings his mother to the solicitor's practice and explains that his mother wants to change her will. The solicitor is told by the son that his mother's previous will divided her property equally between her three children, but now she wants to leave all her property to her son. The solicitor also learns that the mother has recently been discharged from a care home, at the request of her son, and entrusted to his care.

Which of the following best describes how the solicitor should proceed?

A. The solicitor should accept the son's request as any will may be revoked.
B. The solicitor should accept the son's request if they are satisfied that the mother has the mental capacity to make a will.
C. The solicitor should accept the son's request as there is no legal obligation to leave money to all children.
D. The solicitor should accept the son's request if a doctor certifies that the mother has the legal capacity to make a will.
E. The solicitor should accept the son's request if they have confirmed with the mother that they represent her instructions.

QUESTION 3

The executors of a will have instructed a solicitor to apply for the grant of probate on their behalf. The executors are going to undertake the estate administration themselves upon receiving the grant of probate. After 18 months, probate has still not been granted, but the solicitor will not explain why. The executors are concerned about the delay and increasing expense and wish to make a complaint.

Which of the following most accurately represents the solicitor's conduct in this case?

A. The solicitor has misled the executors.
B. The solicitor has taken unfair advantage of the executors.
C. The solicitor has not established an effective complaints procedure.
D. The solicitor has not progressed the matter within an agreed or reasonable time.
E. The solicitor has not given proper information to the executors about the likely cost.

QUESTION 4

The executors of a will ask a solicitor to make an application for probate on their behalf. The solicitor accepts the instruction, but upon reading the will discovers that the testatrix has left land to the testatrix's daughter. That land adjoins land owned by the solicitor, and the solicitor wishes to buy that land.

Which of the following is the best advice to give the solicitor in line with the SRA Code of Conduct?

A. The solicitor should inform the executors of the possible conflict of interest and gain their consent to proceed.
B. The solicitor should inform the beneficiaries of the possible conflict of interest and gain their consent to proceed.
C. The solicitor should not accept the instruction as there is a conflict of interest.
D. The solicitor may accept the instruction and offer to buy the land after probate has been granted.
E. The solicitor should not accept the instruction because they would be taking unfair advantage of the client.

QUESTION 5

A solicitor drew up a will for an elderly man ten years ago. The solicitor had some concerns about the man's mental state and requested a capacity assessment by a medical practitioner. The man was content for the assessment to be made but insisted that he did not want his family to know. The medical practitioner certified that the man had sufficient mental capacity to make a will, making a full report confirming this, and the will was executed in the presence of the medical practitioner. The man has recently died and his son, who is unhappy about the terms of the will, seeks the solicitor's advice.

Which of the following best describes how the solicitor should proceed?

A. The solicitor may accept the instruction, as the man was a former and not a current client.
B. The solicitor may accept the instruction if the former client consents to the disclosure of the confidential information.
C. The solicitor may not accept the instruction because the confidential information is material to the son's claim.
D. The solicitor may accept the instruction but must not disclose the confidential information about mental capacity.
E. The solicitor may not accept the instruction because there are always conflicts of interest in disputes between family members.

■ ANSWERS TO QUESTIONS

Answers to 'What do you know already?' questions at the start of the chapter

1) False. The fee will depend upon the complexity of the will. The Code requires that the fee must be made clear to the client and that the provisions of the will must be properly explained to the client.
2) False. It is common for the solicitors who drew up the will to also be named as executors. However, the solicitors must explain to the client that this is not compulsory and that the client might prefer to appoint relatives or friends. The solicitors must also advise on their charges and the services that they will perform.
3) The correct answer was (d). In every circumstance, the solicitor has to ensure that they are properly acting on the wishes and instructions of the client. In all three circumstances, an issue may arise which brings doubt as to the wishes/instructions of the client.
4) False. The executors should wait for probate to be granted. Solicitors/executors have a duty to safeguard the client's money.

Answers to end-of-chapter SQE1-style questions

Question 1:

The correct answer was B. Clauses excluding liability are legal, but solicitors are obliged to warn clients that they propose to include such a clause and explain what its effect would be. Paras 8.2–8.5 of the Code require solicitors to have a complaints procedure and inform clients in writing of its provisions. If a complaint is not resolved to the client's satisfaction, they must be informed in writing of their right to complain to the Legal Ombudsman. As the firm has dismissed the claim, the next step in the process is to complain to the Legal Ombudsman. Therefore all other options are incorrect.

Question 2:

The correct answer was E. Legally, it is correct that a person can revoke their existing will, simply by making a new will, and there is no obligation in English law to leave money to children or any other relative. However, there is a suspicion here that the son might have undue influence over his mother. We are not given any information in the question that the mother might lack mental capacity, so the better answer is E. The primary duty under Para 3.1 of the Code is that the solicitor must satisfy themselves that the son's instructions represent the wishes of the mother, which covers both mental capacity and duress. All other options are therefore incorrect.

Question 3:

The correct answer was D. The executors could probably base the complaint on all five of the possible answers, but you are asked to select the best answer. The question does not tell us very much about what the solicitor has done, so we do not know whether they have misled the executors or taken advantage of them or what kind of complaints procedure they have or whether they have agreed the cost of the application or agreed a timescale. But the grant of probate should usually be obtained well within a year of making the application, so 18 months, without explanation, is not a reasonable time (Para 1.3). Therefore, option D is the best answer.

Question 4:

The correct answer was C. This is a clear example of an own interest conflict (Para 6.1). An executor cannot purchase property from the estate as a result of the self-dealing rule, nor should someone acting for them (therefore option D is wrong). There is no provision in Part 6 of the Code for clients or anyone else to consent where such a conflict exists (therefore options A and B are incorrect). As to option E, we have no information in the question that the solicitor would be taking unfair advantage, by, for example, obtaining a low price for the land.

Question 5:

The correct answer was C. If the solicitor accepts the son as his client, he must disclose 'information material to the matter of which [the solicitor] has knowledge' (Para 6.4.(a)). Knowledge about the testator's mental capacity is clearly material, but it is confidential, so as there is no way of taking 'effective measures' to prevent disclosure (therefore option D is wrong) and as it is now impossible to obtain the consent of the former client (therefore option B is wrong), the solicitor must decline to act for the son (Para 6.5). Obligations of confidence are owed to former clients, even from ten years ago, so option A is incorrect. Option E is too wide a principle; there is not always a conflict of interests for a solicitor dealing with family disputes.

■ KEY CASES, RULES, STATUTES AND INSTRUMENTS

The SQE1 Assessment Specification has identified that candidates are required to understand the purpose, scope and content of the SRA Principles and Code of Conduct. Make sure that you understand the application of the SRA Principles and Code of Conduct to wills and the administration of estates.

The SQE1 Assessment Specification does not require you to know any case names, or statutory materials, for the topic of ethics and professional conduct in wills and the administration of estates.

7

Ethics and professional conduct in property practice

Benjamin Jones

■ MAKE SURE YOU KNOW

This chapter will cover the application of the Solicitors Regulation Authority (SRA) Principles and Code of Conduct to property transactions. It will allow you to appreciate how ethical issues and professional conduct matters are likely to arise when practising in property law.

Property practice features in the second of the SQE1 assessments (FLK2), and ethics and professional conduct relevant to property law will be assessed pervasively in that assessment.

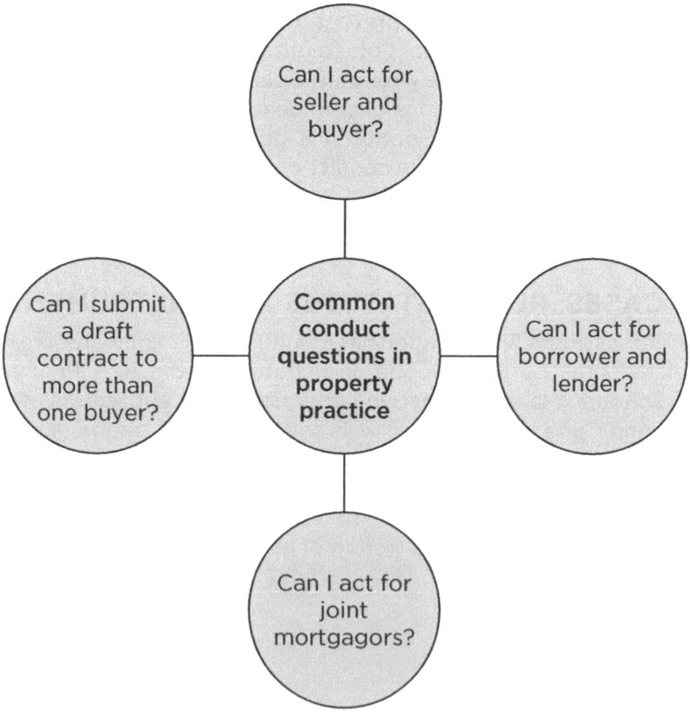

■ SQE ASSESSMENT ADVICE

As you work through this chapter, remember to pay particular attention in your revision to:

- the duty to maintain trust and act fairly (including dealing with unrepresented parties and conduct relating to contract races and undertakings)
- circumstances where a solicitor may act for seller and buyer
- issues that may arise when acting for joint buyers
- where a solicitor may act for borrower and lender
- issues that may arise where acting for joint mortgagors.

■ WHAT DO YOU KNOW ALREADY?

Have a go at these questions before reading this chapter. If you find some difficult or cannot remember the answers, make a note to look more closely at that area during your revision.

1) Where there is a potential contract race, what must you do if your seller client refuses to allow you to disclose the position to all prospective buyers?

   [Contract races; page 172]

2) In what circumstances may you act for both seller and buyer in a property transaction?

   [Acting for seller and buyer; page 175]

3) True or false? It is always possible to act for both borrower and lender in a property transaction.

   [Acting for borrower and lender; page 178]

4) What is the name of the key House of Lords case dealing with acting for joint mortgagors, to secure the business borrowing of only one mortgagor?

   [Acting for joint mortgagors; page 180]

INTRODUCTION TO ETHICS AND PROFESSIONAL CONDUCT IN PROPERTY PRACTICE

Property practice is a fast-moving and high-pressure area of practice. Clients in a property transaction will be very keen to achieve their ultimate goal of completion. Particularly in the residential context, they are likely to be highly emotionally involved, and commercial clients are likely to be subject to commercial pressures. This can lead to a vast number of potential ethical and professional conduct issues for solicitors practising in the area. This chapter will cover the nature of some of these issues, as well as provide guidance on how you would answer questions relating to professional conduct in property practice, which may arise in your SQE1 assessment.

This chapter should be read in conjunction with ***Revise SQE: Property Practice***. In that guide, you will find many **Key terms** and important substantive topics to assist you in furthering your understanding of your ethical and professional obligations.

In the present guide, **Chapters 1** and **2** set out the SRA Principles (the 'Principles') and Code of Conduct (the 'Code') respectively. This chapter will consider how relevant headings operate in the context of property law and practice. The headings used reflect the headings of the Code of Conduct.

MAINTAINING TRUST AND ACTING FAIRLY

When acting in property law, you must maintain trust and act fairly in your relationship with your client and others. The Code sets out ways in which you may achieve this, and these are dealt with in turn.

You do not abuse your position by taking unfair advantage of clients or others (Para 1.2)

As part of your practice in property law, you may encounter **unrepresented parties** and, in such circumstances, there is potential for this duty to be breached.

Key term: unrepresented parties

An unrepresented party is someone who does not have legal representation (eg a seller or buyer, or landlord or tenant who has not appointed a solicitor to act on their behalf). The party could be an individual, a company or an organisation.

Unrepresented parties

When you encounter unrepresented parties you must be careful to ensure that you do not use your position as a solicitor to take unfair advantage of them. You will have a duty to act in your own client's best interests (Principle 7), but you must also act with integrity (Principle 5). In the event of conflict, the duty to uphold trust and confidence in the profession (Principle 2) will prevail (see **Practice example 7.1**).

Practice example 7.1

You act for the tenant on the taking of a commercial lease. The landlord, who is unrepresented, produces a draft lease that is clearly defective, as it contains neither a forfeiture clause, nor a number of standard tenant covenants for a lease of its type.

How would you approach this situation?

In the circumstances, you must advise the landlord to take independent legal advice concerning the terms of the proposed lease. You must avoid giving actual advice, which could suggest that you are acting for the landlord and would give rise to a conflict of interest (Para 6.2). You must balance acting in the best interests of your client (by not highlighting the specific errors or remedying them) with not taking unfair advantage of the landlord (achieved by pointing out the need to take independent advice).

Revision tip

When submitting certain applications to HM Land Registry, evidence of the identity of unrepresented parties must be provided (see HM Land Registry Practice Guide 67). This is an additional safeguard to prevent fraud in these circumstances.

You must also avoid breaching this principle in the context of a **contract race** (see **Contract races, page 172**).

Key term: contract race

A contract race arises where a client who is selling property instructs their solicitor to submit draft contract documentation to more than one potential buyer. The first to exchange contracts 'wins' the 'race' to buy the property.

You perform all undertakings given by you and do so within an agreed timescale, or if no timescale has been agreed, then within a reasonable amount of time (Para 1.3)

Undertakings (see **Chapter 2** for the **Key term**) are an important element of property transactions.

Undertakings

You will be required to give routine undertakings at various stages in a property transaction. These include undertakings to send part contract over to the seller/buyer on exchange of contracts, and to discharge your client's mortgage(s) when acting on a sale.

You may also be asked to give a more bespoke undertaking, as required in particular circumstances (eg to pay the landlord's legal costs, either on the grant of a lease, or on an application for a consent or licence under a lease). Undertakings assist in the smooth running of matters and are an essential element of most of a solicitor's transactional work.

At the heart of undertakings are the duties to uphold public trust and confidence in the profession (Principle 2) and to act with honesty, integrity and in the best interests of the client (Principles 4, 5 and 7).

An undertaking does not need to be in writing and, once given, it may only be withdrawn by agreement (see **Practice example 7.2**).

Practice example 7.2

Your client, the seller of a residential property, leaves an old and broken freestanding fridge freezer in the kitchen of the property, on completion. You subsequently receive a telephone call from the buyer's solicitor and you say, without authority, that your client will remove the offending item by 10 AM the next day.

Have you given an undertaking in this situation?

Yes, you have given an undertaking. It was an oral statement that a third party (your client) will remove the fridge freezer or cause it to be removed by the required time. It did not need to be in writing and you did not need to use the word 'undertake' or 'undertaking'. It is reasonable for the buyer's solicitor and their client to rely upon this. You will be personally bound by the undertaking, even though you had no authority to give it and performance of it is beyond your control.

Accordingly, when making your decision whether or not to give an undertaking (there is no obligation to give or receive one) the key question is that of *control*. You must be clear about precisely what you are promising to do and when you are promising to do it. If anything within the required undertaking is outside of your control, you must either not give the undertaking, or qualify it suitably (eg through pre-conditions).

From a practical perspective, you should always obtain the client's consent to give an undertaking, particularly a non-routine one. Although it is possible to give an oral undertaking, it is best practice to confirm undertakings in writing, as you must keep and maintain appropriate records to demonstrate the existence, compliance with, and discharge of undertakings (see Para 2.2 of the Code of Conduct for Firms). It is necessary to ensure that an undertaking is appropriately and carefully worded as any ambiguity is likely to be interpreted in favour of the recipient.

It is also important to be aware of some transaction-specific practical points for common undertakings in property transactions (see **Table 7.1**).

Table 7.1: Transaction-specific points on undertakings

Particular undertaking	Action to be taken
To pay a sum from the net proceeds of sale (eg a bridging loan)	Ascertain the net proceeds first (after payment of costs, disbursements, discharge of mortgage, agent's fees etc). Obtain a redemption statement from any mortgagee to assist with this.
To pay costs	Limit the wording to a precise amount/ maximum limit (including any VAT properly payable). Do not give an undertaking without being in receipt of cleared funds on account. Although at common law, such an undertaking will be limited to proper costs,* you should limit this further, to proper and reasonable costs and set an upward limit.
*Proper costs are those properly incurred in relation to the transaction (they do not have to be reasonable), whereas proper and reasonable costs must also be reasonable. For example, if costs of £1000 were incurred in a matter, when reasonable costs would be £500, the proper and reasonable costs would be limited to £500.	

Practice example 7.3 brings these points together and provides an example of a non-routine undertaking in practice.

Practice example 7.3

Your client, who needs to raise some capital as a matter of urgency, has decided to sell her house and move into rented accommodation. The property is subject to a mortgage in favour of a high street bank and your firm has been instructed on the sale and discharge of the mortgage. The client owes £30,000 by way of an unsecured loan from a third party and the third party's solicitors have asked for an undertaking to repay the loan amount, plus interest, within the next three months, from the sale proceeds of the house.

How would you approach this situation?

You should not give an undertaking in the requested terms as actual completion of the sale is beyond your control (the matter may not proceed and completion may not occur). Any undertaking will need to be conditional on your firm completing the transaction and receiving the sale proceeds (whenever that may be). You should seek to limit

the obligation to pay interest to that properly payable under the agreement and you should also ascertain that the net proceeds of sale would be sufficient to repay. You should obtain your client's written consent to the proposed undertaking and provide the undertaking in writing. You are under no obligation to give the undertaking, but you should not act in the completion of the transaction unless you are able to fulfil it.

Revision tip

When approaching questions on undertakings, always consider the question of *control*. If the promise is not entirely within your control, then you will need to qualify the undertaking, or refuse to give it.

You do not mislead clients or others (Para 1.4)

A solicitor must not mislead or attempt to mislead clients or others, either by their own acts or omissions, or by allowing or being complicit in the acts or omissions of others (including their client). The rule is closely associated with Principles 2, 4, 5 and 7. Below are some examples, which may assist you in understanding this duty in the context of property law.

Misleading a client

Solicitors may mislead clients by, for example, saying that a transaction is at a particular stage, when it is not. This could include confirming that draft contract documentation has been submitted to the buyer's solicitor, or that the property has been registered at HM Land Registry.

Misleading others

Solicitors could mislead the other party to the proceedings by, for example, confirming that a mortgage offer has been received when it has not, or that the transaction is not part of a chain of transactions, when it is. Contract races may also give rise to a potential breach of this duty (see immediately below).

Contract races

A seller, with more than one offer to buy a property, may be tempted to instruct you to submit draft contract documents to more than one party, thereby creating a contract race (see **Key term**, above). The main aim will be to accelerate exchange of contracts by creating pressure, due to the competition to proceed. This can give rise to two potential breaches of the Code:

- the duty not to abuse your position by taking unfair advantage of others (Para 1.2); and
- the duty not to mislead or attempt to mislead others (Para 1.4).

Contract races are permissible, provided that all prospective buyers are aware of the situation. Accordingly, the following steps must be taken by a seller's solicitor to avoid a breach of the Code:

- STEP 1: The solicitor should obtain their client's consent to disclose the proposed contract race to all potential buyers immediately. It is best practice for this to be confirmed in writing. There is no obligation to set out the 'rules' of the race; it is the disclosure of the proposed circumstances that is important, to avoid taking unfair advantage of third parties, or misleading them.
- STEP 2: If the client's consent is not forthcoming, the solicitor must immediately cease to act. They will not be able to disclose the reason, due to the duty of confidentiality owed to their client (Para 6.3, see **Confidentiality and disclosure**, below). To continue would be a breach of Principle 2 (the duty to uphold public trust and confidence in the profession).

The seller should also be informed of the risks associated with a contract race. They may lose one or more buyers, who may be concerned about the unpredictability involved in the 'race' and the potential for wasted time and expense, should they not 'win'.

Exam warning

Due to the potential for conflict of interest, you should not act for seller and buyer in a contract race (see Para 6.2 and **Conflict, confidentiality and disclosure**, below). However, acting for more than one buyer may be possible, if the solicitor can satisfy the requirements of Para 6.2(b) of the Code, as the clients would arguably be competing for the same objective (again, see **Conflict, confidentiality and disclosure**, below). Do not let an MCQ trick you into thinking this is not possible.

Practice example 7.4 provides an example of a contract race in practice.

Practice example 7.4

You act for a small developer in the sale of the last remaining plot on a residential development. They have received three asking price offers, subject to contract, and they are very keen to sell the plot to move on to another project. Accordingly, they would like you to submit draft contract documentation to the solicitors for all three parties, with the first to exchange contracts being bound to complete.

How would you approach this situation?

This is a potential contract race. You must seek your client's consent to disclose the situation to all prospective buyers immediately. If this is not forthcoming, you must cease to act, but you will be unable to disclose your reasons, due to the duty of confidentiality owed to your client. You should also advise your client of the potential risks associated with contract races.

CONFLICT, CONFIDENTIALITY AND DISCLOSURE

Part 6 of the Code provides a series of rules relating to when a solicitor should decline to act for particular clients. This section sets out how situations involving these rules may apply in the context of property law.

Conflict of interest (Paras 6.1 and 6.2)

You must not act if you have an *own interest conflict* or a significant risk of such a conflict (see **Chapter 4, Conflict of interest**). For example, a solicitor acting on a purchase of property where they or those close to them hold shares in the seller company, or are employed by the seller, would be in breach of this duty.

You also 'must not act in relation to a matter, or a particular aspect of it, if you have a *conflict of interest* or a significant risk of such a conflict in relation to that matter or aspect of it' (Para 6.2) - return to **Chapter 2** for a full discussion and to remind yourself of the **Key term** definitions. The section applies equally to individuals and firms (Para 6.2, SRA Code of Conduct for Firms).

Property law is a high conflict area and acting where there is a conflict or a significant risk of one could also be a breach of the duties to act with integrity (Principle 5) and to act in the best interests of each client (Principle 7).

A key example of where this might occur in the context of property law is where a solicitor is asked to act for both seller and buyer (see **Acting for seller and buyer**, below).

The general duty is subject to two exceptions (see **Chapter 2, page 52**). The *substantially common interest* exception is discussed below, in the context of specific types of transaction. It will usually be possible, under the *competing for the same objective* exception, to act for two or more prospective buyers in relation to a proposed purchase at auction, or through an insolvency, bid or tender process. The exception is very specific and could clearly apply in the context of commercial property work and business law and practice (see **Chapter 4, page 94**). Otherwise, according to SRA guidance, acting for two clients seeking separately to purchase a particular asset could give rise to a conflict of interest or a significant risk of one arising.

Exam warning

Do not forget that if *either* of the exceptions apply, there are three *additional* conditions in Para 6.2 that must also be satisfied for the solicitor to act or continue to act. These additional conditions are detailed in **Chapter 2, page 55**. Do not forget these conditions or allow an MCQ to make you believe that they are not required.

Accordingly, it is necessary to consider both whether a conflict exists, and whether one is likely to exist or arise in the future. In the case of the former, you will be *unable to act* (unless an exception applies) and in the case of the latter, you *must cease to act* (unless an exception applies).

Exam warning

Remember that the exceptions *only* apply to cases involving a conflict of interest. There are *no* exceptions where there is an own interest conflict. Return to **Chapter 2** to remind yourself of these key rules.

Figure 7.1 provides a systematic approach to questions on this topic.

Application of these rules within the context of different scenarios is considered below.

Acting for seller and buyer

When a client approaches a solicitor to act in relation to a property transaction, they will usually be keen to progress as quickly and as inexpensively as possible. From their perspective, the key terms will have been agreed (subject to contract) and they will want the formalities to be completed without unnecessary delay. The seller and buyer may also have instructed the same solicitor or firm to act on previous transactions, so they may each have a loyalty to them. Therefore, it is not uncommon for a solicitor to be approached to act for both parties in a property transaction, due to the perceived saving of time and costs and possibly pre-existing or former client relationships.

Revision tip

Although, under the Code, there is no absolute prohibition on acting for buyer and seller, property law is a high conflict area and cases where this will be permissible will be rare. SRA guidance specifically states that there is likely to be a conflict of interest or a significant risk of one arising where a client sells or leases an asset to another client. In most circumstances, it will simply not be possible, or at best inadvisable, to act, so it is necessary to consider the rules carefully.

A conflict is very likely to exist where property is transferred for value, as buyer and seller at *arm's length* (see **Chapter 4** for the **Key term**) are likely to have different interests. Sellers will want to protect themselves from ongoing liability and buyers will be concerned with obtaining good and marketable title. Accordingly, a solicitor may not be able to give the best independent advice to both parties. If there is an inequality of bargaining power, or if one party is particularly vulnerable, the potential for conflict will be increased (eg a layperson selling land to an experienced developer). These factors should therefore be considered.

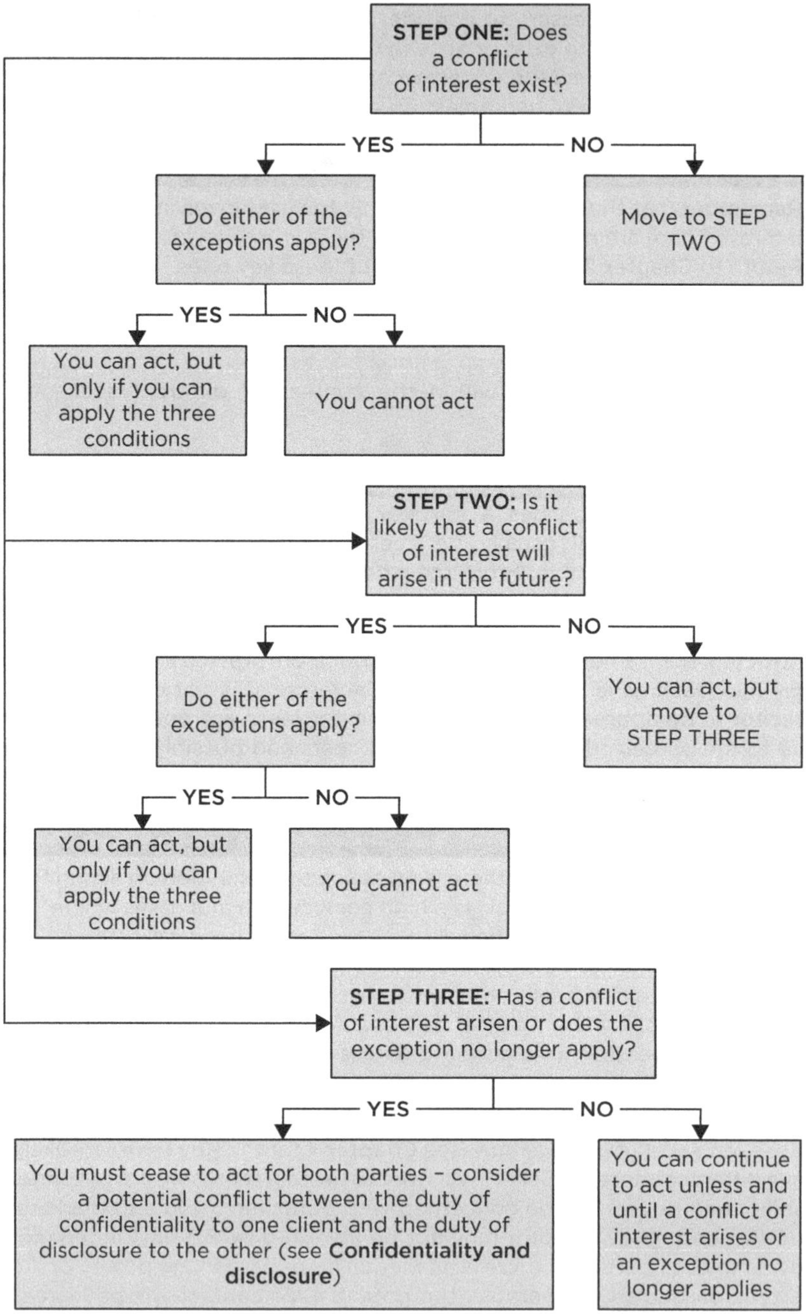

Figure 7.1: Conflict of interest

The possibility of a conflict is also strongly linked to the need to negotiate between the parties. In more complex transactions, particularly those involving high value commercial property, or the grant of commercial leases, there will be a real need to negotiate terms (eg VAT on a freehold transaction and tenant covenants on the grant of a lease). Acting for both parties would be highly inadvisable in these circumstances, as you could not give them both independent advice. Even in more straightforward arm's length residential transactions, negotiations may arise because of adverse matters uncovered by the results of searches and enquiries, title investigation or survey.

It is also necessary to consider the two exceptions in this context. The substantially common interest exception does not usually apply here, as buyer and seller at arm's length clearly have different interests and not a common purpose. The competing for the same objective exception does not apply in the case of transfer of land more generally, as the parties are each working towards different objectives (disposal and acquisition).

Therefore, for typical sales, where usually unconnected parties transfer land for value at arm's length, and the grant of leases, the risk is particularly high. It would therefore be particularly unwise to act for both parties in these circumstances.

However, acting for both parties where land is gifted or transferred between connected parties will be more likely to be permissible (eg transfers between companies in the same group, or a gratuitous transfer from spouse to spouse, or from parent to adult child). In these circumstances, it is arguable that no conflict of interest arises or is likely to arise and that the transaction could also come within the substantially common interest exception.

Exam warning

When considering whether you can act for both parties in the transfer of land, the circumstances are particularly important. You should therefore read any MCQ carefully. It may be possible to act where land is gifted, or transferred between connected parties.

The key risk in deciding whether to act for both seller and buyer is that if a conflict arises at a later date, the solicitor would need to decline to act, possibly even for both parties if they hold relevant confidential information. This is because the duty of confidentiality usually takes precedence over the duty of disclosure (see **Confidentiality and disclosure**, below). Having to cease to act part way through a transaction can be professionally embarrassing and also lead to disappointment, disruption and inconvenience to clients, ultimately resulting in loss of business and, potentially, damage to professional reputation.

If you are satisfied that there is no conflict or significant risk of conflict, it would be advisable to record the reasons for the decision and obtain the clients' informed consent. It may also be advisable for each party to be represented by a different fee earner within the firm.

If you are satisfied that the transaction comes within the substantially common interest exception, you would also need to comply with the three conditions in Para 6.2 of the Code.

Acting for joint buyers

Subject to compliance with Para 6.2 of the Code, a solicitor may usually act for joint buyers (including joint tenants), as they usually have the same interest in acquiring good and marketable title to the property. In these circumstances, it is best practice to obtain instructions from all clients, due to the risk of duress or undue influence between the parties (particularly if one is more vulnerable).

In residential cases, the parties will need to receive separate advice on how the equitable interest should be held.

Acting for borrower and lender

Subject to compliance with Para 6.2 of the Code, it may be possible to act for both borrower and lender in the case of a straightforward residential property transaction. It is important to realise that, in these circumstances, the solicitor will have two clients (the borrower and the lender).

Although acting for borrower and lender is very common in straightforward residential property transactions, there is the potential for conflict to arise more generally in the following circumstances:

- where the lender seeks to impose unusually onerous, non-standard terms on the borrower
- where you are aware of the borrower being unable to comply with, or likely to breach a condition of the proposed mortgage (eg a condition as to drawdown of funds, or an ongoing obligation under the mortgage). An example of the latter would be where the proposed mortgage provides that the lender's consent will be required to any proposed lease or third party occupancy of the property, and you are aware of such a proposed arrangement, but the borrower has asked you not to inform the lender
- the proposed mortgage will not be on standard terms and you are required to negotiate the terms of the loan facility and/or mortgage/security documentation. This is more typical in complex and/or high value commercial transactions, where the lender will usually insist on separate legal representation in any event.

Law Society guidance provides that acting for borrower and lender is permissible in the following circumstances:

- where there is a *standard mortgage* (ie the terms are not individually negotiated) of a *private residence*
- by an *institutional lender*, which has lending as a significant part of its business activities
- using the Law Society/UK Finance (formerly the Council of Mortgage Lenders) *approved certificate of title*, and
- you are satisfied that it is *reasonable* and in the clients' best interests for you to act.

All of the conditions must be satisfied and are nearly always satisfied in straightforward residential transactions where the mortgage deed will usually be provided on a 'take it or leave it' basis, with no room for individual negotiation.

Revision tip

Although you do not need to know the Law Society guidance by name, you should be aware of the principles behind it, as it is widely known and commonly referred to.

Acting for borrower and lender in such circumstances is also highly likely to fall within the substantially common interest exception, as both parties will be keen to obtain good and marketable title. In such circumstances, the solicitor would also need to comply with the conditions in Para 6.2.

In the event of a conflict of interest arising or a substantially common interest no longer applying where a solicitor had previously decided to act for both borrower and lender, there will be potential for a conflict between the allied duties of confidentiality and disclosure (Paras 6.3–6.5). The duty of confidentiality will prevail and the solicitor must cease to act for both parties, unless they obtain the other's consent (see **Confidentiality and disclosure**, below).

Acting for borrower and lender is much less common in commercial transactions (particularly high value ones) and the lender will usually instruct its own solicitors, to protect its own interests (see **Chapter 4, page 111**). The loan and sometimes, in more complex transactions, the security documents will need to be negotiated and the certificate of title may not be in a standard form. Therefore, the standard Law Society guidance will not apply. However, in some circumstances separate representation may be limited to key areas of potential conflict (eg the negotiation of the facility letter and, if required, the security documentation), with the borrower's solicitor acting for both parties on investigation of title and, possibly, completion of the documentation (ie a more limited retainer). In such circumstances, the solicitor may rely on the substantially common interest exception, particularly on a purchase, as both parties will require the property to have good and marketable title.

Practice example 7.5 provides an example of what to consider in practice in these situations.

Practice example 7.5

You have been instructed to act by a first-time buyer in relation to the purchase of a residential property. She will be borrowing from a high street bank in order to fund the purchase, and the bank will receive a mortgage over the property.

Are you able to act for both buyer and lender in this situation?

On the facts, this should certainly be possible. It is highly likely that the Law Society guidance will apply here and all of the conditions will be satisfied.

Acting for joint mortgagors

Subject to compliance with Para 6.2 of the Code, a solicitor may often act for joint borrowers/mortgagors, as no conflict of interest usually arises in doing so.

However, there is a possibility of undue influence arising where the proposed mortgage of a property is to secure the borrowing or debts of a business of only one of the owners/proposed mortgagors of the property, rather than personal debts. Similar concerns arise in any situation where a third-party guarantee is required (secured or unsecured) and this can occur in the context of business law and practice (see **Chapter 4, page 112**).

The typical scenario involves a family home co-owned by two spouses, one of whom is in business. As legal owners, the two co-owners will need to be party to the proposed mortgage as *mortgagors*, even though the *borrower* will effectively be the business (ie either the individual as sole trader, or partner in a partnership or as guarantor of a company in which they have an interest).

In such circumstances, there is a strong possibility of the mortgage being set aside on the grounds of duress or undue influence. This is because it is not strictly in the interests of the disinterested spouse to mortgage their personal interest, for what is essentially a third party debt. If the business is unsuccessful, the property may be repossessed and sold to recover the debt. Therefore, consideration should be given, on a case-by-case basis, as to whether the solicitor would be in breach of Para 6.2 by agreeing to act in the first place.

Whilst it is possible for the same solicitor to act for borrower and spouse under the ***Etridge* guidelines**, many firms, quite understandably, insist on another fee earner within the firm advising in these circumstances, or that the disinterested spouse receives separate representation from another firm. The risk will be heightened if the spouse is particularly vulnerable and/or has no involvement with the business in any capacity. However, the spouse may have good reason to sign in any event, to support the borrower's business as a source of income.

If a solicitor does decide to act, they must follow the *Etridge* guidelines.

Key term: *Etridge* guidelines

The guidelines set out in the case of *Royal Bank of Scotland v Etridge (No 2) and others* [2001] UKHL 44 to give proper advice to the borrower's spouse in these circumstances. The key points are summarised in **Table 7.2**.

Table 7.2: Etridge *guidelines*

Decide whether you can act
• Be sure you have the necessary expertise to interpret the financial information to be provided • Decide whether there is a conflict of interest
Prior to giving advice
• Obtain full information about the borrowing (ie application, purpose, amount, terms and current debt of the business). The borrower must, of course, consent to this disclosure
Give the advice at a separate face to face meeting
• Explain (in non-technical language) the full legal and serious practical implications of entering into the mortgage • Make it clear that they have a choice whether or not to proceed and, if they do choose to proceed, the lender will rely on what the solicitor has done • Require them to countersign confirmation of the advice • Obtain authorisation to provide the lender with written confirmation (see below)
Provide written confirmation of the following to the lender
• The solicitor was duly instructed by the individual • They understood the solicitor's role and the bank's reliance on it • The solicitor had received the information needed to give the advice • They appreciated the full implications of the proposed mortgage and consent to it

Revision tip

Although you do not usually need to be aware of specific authorities, you should have knowledge of the *Etridge* case, as it is the seminal decision concerning the law and practice in this area.

It is important to emphasise that the *Etridge* guidelines are there to protect the lender in advancing the loan, and it is the solicitor who should first decide whether they may be able to act, without breaching Para 6.2 of the Code. It may be that the risk of potential liability to the firm outweighs the immediate financial benefit of the instructions. It may also be decided, on the facts, that despite the conflict, the parties have a substantially common interest in proceeding and, if so, the conditions in Para 6.2 must be complied with.

Practice example 7.6 provides an example of what to consider in practice in these situations.

Practice example 7.6

You act for a client who is the sole director and shareholder of a private limited company. The company was incorporated earlier this year and the company's bank has asked her to provide a personal guarantee for the company's debts. The guarantee is to be secured by way of a first legal charge over the family home, which is jointly owned by the client and her wife. The wife, whilst supportive of her spouse's business activities, has no personal interest in, or other connection with, the company. The bank has sought to instruct your firm to act in advising the wife on the proposed mortgage.

How would you approach this situation?

You may act for the wife if you are confident there is no conflict of interest or significant risk of one arising. You should consider the facts carefully (including the wife's lack of personal interest in the company). The *Etridge* case provides that you may act for both parties, but you must take great care to adhere to the guidelines within the case. Whilst not a requirement, it may be advisable for another solicitor within the firm to act for the wife, or for you to suggest that she receives independent legal representation from outside of the firm.

Confidentiality and disclosure (Paras 6.3–6.5)

Paras 6.3–6.5 deal with the associated duties of confidentiality and disclosure. A solicitor is under a duty to act in the best interests of each client (Principle 7) and they must balance the two duties. In the event of conflict, the duty of confidentiality will usually prevail. This section will deal with both of these issues in the context of property law.

Confidentiality

Solicitors must keep the affairs of current and former clients confidential, unless disclosure is required or permitted by law (eg in the case of suspected mortgage fraud, or a report to the relevant authorities of suspected money laundering – see ***Revise SQE: The Legal System and Services of England and Wales***) or the client consents (Para 6.3).

However, there are circumstances in which a solicitor's duty of confidentiality to one client may conflict with their duty to act in the best interests of another, and to disclose information to them.

Disclosure

Where you are acting for a client on a matter, the general rule (subject to limited exceptions in Para 6.4) is that you must make the client aware of all information material to the matter of which you have knowledge (Para 6.4). However, if there is conflict between the allied duties of confidentiality and disclosure, the duty of confidentiality will prevail.

Practice example 7.7 provides an illustration of these principles in action.

Practice example 7.7

You act for a borrower and their lender in the acquisition and mortgage of a freehold commercial property. The lender's standard mortgage terms require that lender's consent be obtained to any lease or sharing of occupation or possession, and the mortgage offer has been made on the understanding that the property will be for owner-occupation by the borrower. However, you are aware of the borrower's plans to sublet part of the property.

How would you approach this situation?

You must bring this to the attention of the borrower and seek consent to disclose this to the lender as there is a clear conflict of interest on the facts. If consent is not forthcoming, you must cease to act. However, you must not disclose your reasons to the lender, as you owe a duty of confidentiality to the borrower, which trumps the duty of disclosure owed to the lender.

There are circumstances in which a solicitor's duty of confidentiality to one client may conflict with their duty to act in the best interests of another. This could include where a solicitor holds information relating to a former client, which is material to a present client in their matter.

Under Para 6.5, you must 'not act for a client in a matter where that client has an interest adverse to the interest of another current or former client of you or your business or employer, for whom you or your business or employer holds confidential information, which is material to that matter'. However, this is subject to two exceptions:

(1) Where 'effective measures have been taken which result in there being no real risk of disclosure of the confidential information', or
(2) 'The current or former client whose information you or your business or employer holds has given informed consent, given or evidenced in writing, to you acting, including any measures taken to protect their information.'

Therefore, the general rule (subject to the two exceptions) is that you should not act for a client where you hold confidential information from an existing or former client, which is relevant to the client. If such confidential information becomes known to the solicitor, whilst acting, the duty of confidentiality will take priority over the duty of disclosure, subject to compliance with the two exceptions.

Practice example 7.8 provides an illustration of these principles in action.

Practice example 7.8

A potential client approaches you in relation to the acquisition of a freehold development site. You are aware of a number of title issues with the site, having acted on the previous sale to the current seller. You suspect these title issues have led to the proposed sale (which is below market value).

How would you approach this situation?

Your duty of confidentiality to the former client trumps the duty of disclosure to the potential client. Although you would carry out a thorough investigation of title to reveal issues with the title, you should not act in these circumstances, unless informed consent can be obtained from the former client. If the former client is approached, you must take care not to breach the duty of confidentiality owed to the potential client.

FINAL ADVICE

The issues that may arise in property practice are diverse and wide ranging. This chapter has covered issues that are specific to this area of practice, but you must remain vigilant and aware of more general conduct issues that may occur (eg costs information and client care). Using ***Revise SQE: Property Practice***, you should review the substantive law relating to property practice and identify occasions when ethical and professional conduct issues may arise.

■ KEY POINT CHECKLIST

This chapter has covered the following key knowledge points. You can use these to structure your revision, ensuring you recall the key details for each point, as covered in this chapter.

- Great care must be taken to avoid taking unfair advantage of unrepresented parties in property transactions.
- It is possible to act for a seller in a contract race, provided that the relevant procedure is carefully adhered to.

- A solicitor may not usually act for seller and buyer in a property transaction (although there are some occasions where acting for transferor and transferee will be permissible).
- It is usually possible to act for joint buyers in a property transaction.
- Acting for borrower and lender may be possible in the case of straightforward residential property transactions.
- It may not always be possible to act for joint mortgagors to secure the business borrowing of only one of them or their business, due to the potential for conflict of interest. Where a solicitor does decide to act, the *Etridge* guidelines must be adhered to.

■ KEY TERMS AND CONCEPTS

- unrepresented parties (**page 168**)
- contract race (**page 169**)
- *Etridge* guidelines (**page 181**)

■ SQE1-STYLE QUESTIONS

QUESTION 1

A solicitor acts for the proposed tenant of a lease of commercial property and the heads of terms provide that the tenant will pay the landlord's legal costs in relation to the preparation, negotiation and completion of the lease. The landlord's solicitors have requested an undertaking from the tenant solicitor's firm to meet these costs before they will issue draft documentation. The tenant is a long-established, regular and reliable client of the tenant solicitor's firm and they are keen to proceed without delay. Accordingly, to expedite the process, the tenant's solicitor confirms in a telephone conversation with the landlord's solicitor that the tenant solicitor's firm will meet these costs.

Which of the following best describes who is liable for the costs?

A. The solicitor and the firm are liable as an undertaking has been given.

B. The solicitor is liable as undertakings are personally binding.

C. An undertaking has not been given, as the word 'undertake' or 'undertaking' was not used and it was neither given, nor confirmed in writing.

D. The firm is liable as the undertaking was clearly given on behalf of the firm.

E. The client is liable as the undertaking was given on their behalf.

QUESTION 2

A property developer client has instructed a solicitor in relation to the proposed gift of one of the properties from their portfolio, to their adult daughter. The daughter has asked if the solicitor can also act for her on the transfer.

Which of the following best describes the position?

A. In no circumstances can the solicitor act here, as it is never possible to act for transferor and transferee in a property transaction, due to the potential for conflict of interest.

B. The solicitor should be able to act in this matter on the facts. Due to the connection between the parties and the fact that the transaction involves a gift, there is unlikely to be a conflict of interest or a significant risk of one arising.

C. The solicitor can act in this matter as the parties are competing for the same objective.

D. The solicitor can act in this matter as the parties have a substantially common interest.

E. The solicitor should not act in this matter, as the daughter will be the one to benefit from the transaction and there is an imbalance of power between them.

QUESTION 3

The seller of a residential property, who is keen to proceed as soon as possible, instructs their solicitor to submit draft contract documentation to three interested parties.

Which of the following best describes the position?

A. The solicitor will be unable to do this under the Code of Conduct and must immediately cease to act. They will owe a duty of confidentiality to the seller and so must not disclose their reasons for ceasing to act.

B. Provided that the solicitor informs all three prospective buyers of the situation, there will be no breach of the Code of Conduct. They will owe a duty of confidentiality to the seller.

C. The solicitor must obtain the seller's consent to disclose the position to the prospective buyers and, if this is not forthcoming, they must cease to act immediately. If it is forthcoming, disclosure must be made immediately.

D. The solicitor must obtain the seller's consent to disclose the position to the prospective buyers and, if this is not forthcoming, they must cease to act immediately. They will owe a duty of confidentiality to the seller.

E. The solicitor must obtain the seller's consent to disclose the position to the prospective buyers and, if this is not forthcoming, they must cease to act immediately. They will owe a duty of confidentiality to the seller. If the seller's consent is forthcoming, disclosure must be made.

QUESTION 4

A solicitor is instructed to act in relation to the acquisition of a leasehold flat and is aware that their firm acted for the previous owner of the property in long, protracted and unsuccessful litigation concerning liability for repairs under the lease. The freehold owner and management company denied liability and a settlement was never reached. The main reason that the litigation was unsuccessful was because the lease was defective as originally drafted. The value, marketability and security for lending purposes were adversely affected and the former client sold to the current seller for a cash sum significantly below their original acquisition cost. The current purchase is in excess of the market value for a similar flat without a seriously defective lease and the lease is unlikely to be acceptable to the buyer's lender.

Which of the following best describes the position?

A. The duty of confidentiality to the former client takes precedence over the duty of disclosure to the new client in these circumstances.

B. There is a conflict between the duty of confidentiality to the former client and the duty of disclosure to the new client. Unless the former client provides consent to share the information, the solicitor must cease to act in the matter.

C. The solicitor is under a duty to their new client to disclose all information material to their matter about which the solicitor has knowledge. This clearly includes this information and therefore the solicitor must disclose it.

D. The duty of confidentiality to the former client will always take precedence.

E. The solicitor should act in the best interests of current, rather than former, clients and should therefore disclose the information.

QUESTION 5

A solicitor has been instructed to act on the purchase of a freehold residential property, for owner-occupation and their client has asked whether the firm may also act for the lender, a high street bank, in the same matter.

Which of the following best describes the position?

A. The solicitor may act provided that the proposed mortgage is a standard document that does not need to be negotiated, the Law Society/UK Finance standard certificate of title is used and it is otherwise reasonable to act.

B. The solicitor may act despite the risk of conflict of interest, under the substantially common interest exception. Both parties would need to give informed consent, effective safeguards would need to be put in place concerning protection of confidential information, and the solicitor would need to be satisfied it is reasonable to do so.

C. The solicitor may act despite the risk of conflict of interest, under the competing for the same objective exception. Both parties would need to give informed consent, effective safeguards would need to be put in place concerning protection of confidential information, and the solicitor would need to be satisfied it is reasonable to do so.

D. The solicitor may not act due to the substantial risk of a conflict of interest arising. However, if both parties gave informed consent, effective safeguards were put in place concerning protection of confidential information and the solicitor was satisfied it was reasonable to do so, acting for both parties may be possible.

E. The solicitor may act provided that the proposed mortgage is a standard document that does not need to be negotiated, the Law Society/UK Finance standard certificate of title is used and it is otherwise reasonable to act. Both parties would need to give informed consent, effective safeguards would need to be put in place concerning protection of confidential information and the solicitor would need to be satisfied it is reasonable to do so.

■ ANSWERS TO QUESTIONS

Answers to 'What do you know already?' questions at the start of the chapter

1) You must refuse to act, although you will owe a duty of confidentiality to your client, so you should not disclose the reasons for doing so.
2) A solicitor may act for the seller and buyer if there is no conflict of interest or significant risk of one arising. This is highly unlikely in the field of property law, as it is a high conflict area. However, it may be possible where a gift, or undervalue with gift element is involved, or both parties are connected and arm's length negotiation will not be required.
3) False. It is usually possible in straightforward residential transactions, where standard documentation is used and there is an institutional lender. It is not usually possible where negotiation of terms and security documentation is involved, or in more complex, commercial transactions.
4) The decision is *Royal Bank of Scotland v Etridge (No 2) and others* [2001] UKHL 44.

Answers to end-of-chapter SQE1-style questions

Question 1:

The correct answer was A. The undertaking will be personally binding on the solicitor, and as it was made on behalf of the firm, the firm will be liable too. Therefore, options B and D are partially correct. An undertaking was given, even though the word ‘undertake’ or ‘undertaking’ was not used. There is clearly an enforceable promise and there is no need for an undertaking to be made, or confirmed in writing. Therefore, option C is incorrect. Option E is incorrect, as it does not reflect the terms of the undertaking and the solicitor did not clearly and expressly disclaim personal liability. The undertaking should have been given in writing, with careful attention to its terms. The solicitor should also have obtained cleared funds on account before giving it.

Question 2:

The correct answer was B. The transaction is not at arm’s length as it is a gift and there is a connection between the parties, so the solicitor should be able to act here, as it is unlikely there will be a conflict of interest or a significant risk of one arising. There is no evidence on the facts of inequality of bargaining power or vulnerability, which makes option E incorrect. Option A is incorrect in that there is no absolute prohibition on acting for transferor and transferee, but it is highly unlikely that there will not be a conflict of interest or a significant risk of one arising, where there is a sale at arm’s length (typically for value) usually between unconnected parties. The risk increases the more complex a transaction is, as there is likely to be more need for negotiation between the parties. Option C is incorrect as parties to a conveyancing transaction have different objectives (disposal and acquisition respectively). Option D is also possibly correct. Due to the nature of the transaction, it could be argued that the parties have a substantially common interest (in which case the three conditions in Para 6.2 would need to be complied with). However, option B is most correct and straightforward here.

Question 3:

The correct answer was E. Option E outlines all of the key requirements. Option A is incorrect as there is no requirement immediately to cease to act just because a potential contract race arises. Consent to disclose must be obtained and, if received, disclosure must be made immediately. If it is not forthcoming, the solicitor must cease to act immediately, but will owe a duty of confidentiality to the seller. Option B is incorrect as it omits the need to obtain client consent to the disclosure before making it. Option C is only partially correct as it fails to mention the duty of confidentiality. Option D is also only partially correct as it omits the need to disclose, should consent be forthcoming.

Question 4:

The correct answer was B. The duty of confidentiality will trump the duty of disclosure unless informed consent is given. Options A and D are partially correct, as the duty of confidentiality usually takes precedence; however, this is subject to permitted exceptions (including where informed consent has been obtained from the former client, as provided for in option B). Options C and E are incorrect, as they do not acknowledge the duty of confidentiality owed to previous clients.

Question 5:

The correct answer was A. The exception under the Law Society guidance will most probably apply here. Option B is incorrect as although the substantially common interest exception may also apply on the facts, and the pre-conditions are correctly set out, it would be more straightforward to rely on the Law Society guidance. For the same reason, option D is also incorrect and it does not specifically refer to the substantially common interest exception. Option C is incorrect, as the competing for the same objective exception does not apply on the facts. Option E is incorrect as it conflates the Law Society guidance with the conditions attached to the exceptions to the general rule.

■ KEY CASES, RULES, STATUTES AND INSTRUMENTS

The SQE1 Assessment Specification has identified that candidates are required to understand the purpose, scope and content of the SRA Principles and Code of Conduct. Make sure that you understand the application of the SRA Principles and Code of Conduct to property practice.

The SQE1 Assessment Specification does not require you to know any case names, or statutory materials, for the topic of ethics and professional conduct in property practice. However, you should be aware of the *Etridge* guidelines and the principles therein due to their importance.

8

Ethics and professional conduct in solicitors' accounts

Tina McKee

■ MAKE SURE YOU KNOW

This chapter will cover the application of the Solicitors Regulation Authority (SRA) Principles and Code of Conduct in the context of solicitors' accounts. This chapter will allow you to observe how ethical issues and professional conduct matters often overlap with solicitors' obligations under the SRA Accounts Rules 2019.

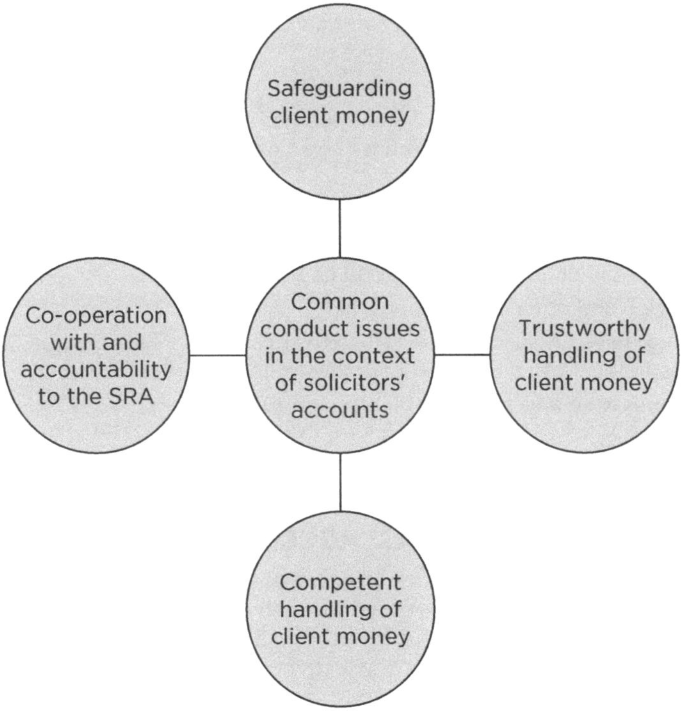

Issues relating to solicitors' accounts feature in the second of the SQE1 assessments (FLK2), and ethics and professional conduct relevant to the context of solicitors' accounts will be assessed pervasively in that assessment.

SQE ASSESSMENT ADVICE

As you work through this chapter, remember to pay particular attention in your revision to:

- the obligation to safeguard client money and assets
- maintaining trust and acting fairly when operating solicitors' accounts
- complying with service and competence obligations when operating solicitors' accounts
- cooperation with and accountability to the SRA when operating solicitors' accounts.

WHAT DO YOU KNOW ALREADY?

Have a go at these questions before reading this chapter. If you find some difficult or cannot remember the answers, make a note to look more closely at that area during your revision.

1) True or false? A solicitor must safeguard money belonging to clients but not money belonging to third parties.

   [Safeguarding client money; page 193]

2) What should a solicitor do if she becomes aware that a colleague is using client money to fund his purchase of an expensive new home for himself and his family?

   [Maintaining trust and acting fairly; page 194]

3) True or false? A newly qualified solicitor should keep themselves up to date on any changes to the Accounts Rules and Codes.

   [Service and competence; page 197]

4) True or false? A solicitor can refuse to speak to the SRA over an SRA investigation into suspected breaches of the Accounts Rules.

   [Cooperation and accountability; page 198]

INTRODUCTION TO ETHICS AND PROFESSIONAL CONDUCT IN SOLICITORS' ACCOUNTS

Ethics and professional conduct are central to good practice in solicitors' accounts and there are many overlaps between the SRA Principles (see **Chapter 1**), the SRA Code of Conduct for Solicitors, RELs and RFLs, the SRA Code of Conduct for Firms (collectively referred to as 'the Code' - see **Chapter 2**) and the SRA Accounts Rules 2019 (the Accounts Rules). It is for this reason that this chapter should be read in conjunction with ***Revise***

SQE: Solicitors' Accounts. In that guide, you will find many **Key terms** and important substantive topics to assist you in furthering your understanding of your ethical and professional obligations.

For example, a solicitor who breaches the Accounts Rules will often have simultaneously breached one or more of the Principles, and one or more paragraphs of the Code. This is demonstrated by the high number of Solicitors Disciplinary Tribunal (SDT) judgments, published on their website each year, that record overlapping breaches.

Revision tip

When answering questions in the SQE1 Assessment that might involve professional conduct and ethics in the context of solicitors' accounts, take a step back from the question and use your common sense to identify if something suspicious has happened, for example, with client money. You can often trust your instincts to help you identify breaches of the Accounts Rules, Principles or Code.

This chapter will consider how the relevant headings of the Code of Conduct operate in the context of solicitors' accounts. The headings used reflect the headings of the Code of Conduct.

SAFEGUARDING CLIENT MONEY

Para 4.2 of the Code requires solicitors to safeguard money and assets entrusted to them by clients and others. This professional conduct requirement underpins the core purpose of the Accounts Rules, which is to keep client money safe (see ***Revise SQE: Solicitors' Accounts*** for a full discussion as to the meaning of 'client money'). It also reflects some of the SRA Principles, in that safeguarding client money requires solicitors to act:

- in a way that upholds public trust and confidence in the solicitors' profession and in legal services (Principle 2)
- with honesty (Principle 4)
- with integrity (Principle 5)
- in the best interests of each client (Principle 7).

Practice example 8.1 indicates how your understanding of the obligation to safeguard client money might be tested in the SQE1 Assessment.

Practice example 8.1

Caroline is a solicitor, instructed by the personal representatives of Oyin, a former client who has recently died. One of the personal representatives visits the office to drop off some diamond jewellery and £800 cash, found in Oyin's home. She asks Caroline to take care of the jewellery and cash as she does not want to leave them in the empty house. Caroline leaves the jewellery and cash on her desk in the open plan office before rushing home for a bank holiday weekend break.

Has Caroline acted appropriately, and if not, what should she do?

Caroline has not acted appropriately to safeguard client money and assets belonging to Oyin's estate. Both the cash and the jewellery are at risk of being stolen. Caroline should ensure that the cash is paid into the firm's general client account promptly (and kept locked in the firm's safe over the bank holiday if needs be). She should also ensure that the jewellery is placed somewhere safe (for example, in a bank deposit box in the name of the personal representatives) as soon as possible. If necessary, this should also be kept in the firm's safe over the weekend until the banks reopen.

MAINTAINING TRUST AND ACTING FAIRLY

The Accounts Rules provide a road map to help solicitors and firms to be trustworthy when handling client money. This reflects their obligation to act fairly and maintain public trust in compliance with Para 1 of the Code. One example is complying with any undertakings that involve payments of client money (see **Undertakings, page 35**).

However, occasionally solicitors act dishonestly to steal client money or to commit fraud against their clients, third parties or their own firm. Such behaviour can lead to criminal prosecutions as well as to professional disciplinary sanctions, imposed by the SDT, such as being struck off the roll of solicitors.

Dishonest handling of client money

Dishonest handling of client money breaches many of the SRA Standards and Regulations at the same time. For example, **Table 8.1** highlights multiple breaches that occur if a solicitor steals client money from a firm's client account or withdraws client money fraudulently.

Table 8.1: Breaches when dishonestly handling client money

Which Principles, paragraphs of the Code and Accounts Rules have been breached?	What is the breach?
Principle 2	Undermining public trust and confidence in the profession
Principle 4	Acting dishonestly

Table 8.1: (continued)

Which Principles, paragraphs of the Code and Accounts Rules have been breached?	What is the breach?
Principle 5	Acting without integrity
Principle 7	Not acting in the best interest of the clients from whom money has been stolen
Para 1.2	Abusing position of trust (in handling client money) to take unfair advantage of their clients (by stealing money or defrauding clients or others)
Para 1.4	Misleading clients and others, including colleagues and firms
Para 4.1	Failing to safeguard client money entrusted to them by their clients
Accounts Rule 5.1	Stealing client money from a client account or withdrawing it fraudulently. This is *not* the purpose for which it was being held, and the withdrawal was *not* in accordance with the client's instructions

Revision tip

SQE1 Assessment questions may test your understanding of either how solicitors should act to comply with both the Code and Accounts Rules so that they maintain trust and act fairly; or what solicitors should do in a situation where both the Code and Accounts Rules have been breached, for example, by the actions of a dishonest solicitor.

When considering a SQE1 question about a dishonest solicitor who steals client money or commits fraud, correct answer options might focus on:

- correcting the breach of the Accounts Rules, for example replacing any client money wrongly withdrawn from the client account *immediately* (to comply with Accounts Rule 6.1), using business money if necessary (see ***Revise SQE: Solicitors' Accounts,*** **Chapter 3** for more information on correcting breaches of the Accounts Rules)
- taking action against the solicitor to prevent any further risk to client money
- reporting the matter to the firm's Compliance Officer for Finance and Administration (COFA - see **Chapter 2** for the **Key term**), to the SRA and/or to the police (see **Cooperation and accountability, page 61**).

Practice example 8.2 indicates how your understanding of how to deal with a dishonest solicitor might be tested in the SQE1 Assessment.

Practice example 8.2

A solicitor, Rupa, is managing the files of a colleague, Bedat, while he is on leave. She notices lots of suspicious payments from client ledgers to a property company, Granting Properties Ltd. The payments do not appear to relate to any of the client matters. On checking at Companies House, she discovers that Bedat is the sole director of Granting Properties Ltd. This leads her to believe that Bedat has been committing fraud.

What action, if any, should Rupa take in response to her suspicions?

Rupa should report the matter to the firm's COFA. They must ensure that the money withdrawn from the client account to pay Granting Properties Ltd is replaced, with business money if needs be (Accounts Rule 6.1). The COFA should also report the matter to the SRA as there is a significant risk to client money. As it appears that Bedat has committed fraud, it is appropriate to report the matter to the police as well. While investigations are under way, Bedat should be suspended from his job to avoid any further risks to client money.

Undertakings (Para 1.3)

The Code of Conduct places great emphasis on undertakings being performed in accordance with agreed timescales or within a reasonable time. Undertakings are essential to the smooth running of the solicitors' profession as a whole and reflect the underpinning SRA Principles of integrity and honesty.

Many undertakings given by solicitors involve payment of money to third parties and therefore fall within the context of solicitors' accounts. Examples include the payment of completion monies in a property purchase on the completion date, and the transfer of an agreed sum in settlement of a dispute on a prescribed date.

Practice example 8.3 illustrates how your understanding of this issue might be tested in the SQE1 Assessment.

Practice example 8.3

A solicitor acts for a client in a property purchase transaction. At completion, the solicitor gives an undertaking to the seller's solicitors that she will transfer the outstanding balance of £300,000 to them by the end of the day.

What accounting entries are required in the firm's ledgers when the solicitor complies with this undertaking?

The solicitor is obliged (and is personally liable) by Para 1.3 of the Code of Conduct to comply with the undertaking given to the seller's solicitors. Therefore, she must ensure that she authorises the withdrawal of the completion monies as soon as possible, and by the end of the day at the latest. The required accounting entries will be debit (DR) £300,000 client ledger client account and credit (CR) £300,000 cash sheet client ledger (see *Revise SQE: Solicitors' Accounts,* Chapter 3 for more details on the accounting entries required for a withdrawal from client account).

SERVICE AND COMPETENCE

In the previous section we considered the obligations on solicitors to be trustworthy when handling client money. Here, we will focus on their obligations to act competently and to ensure that there is appropriate supervision in the context of solicitors' accounts.

Sometimes solicitors or other employees of law firms make genuine mistakes when handling client money. The Accounts Rules provide for regular checks and balances to help identify mistakes quickly. These include both internal checks (such as the bank reconciliation process of checking bank statements for client accounts against the firm's internal accounting records at least once every five weeks - Accounts Rule 8.3) and external checks (such as obtaining an accountant's report within six months of the end of an accounting period - Accounts Rule 12.1) (see ***Revise SQE: Solicitors' Accounts,*** **Chapter 8** for more details on bank reconciliation and accountants' reports). Accounts Rule 6.1 also provides that any breaches of the Accounts Rules should be remedied promptly upon discovery.

However, the Code provides key standards to help minimise accounting errors happening in the first place. This is especially important where such errors may place client money at risk.

Para 3 of the Code for Individuals (see **Chapter 2)** governs solicitors' competence and supervisory responsibilities. This encompasses the way in which they operate their firm's accounting procedures. For example, solicitors should be competent in dealing with client money (Para 3.2) and should keep up to date with any changes in the Accounts Rules so that they maintain this level of competence (Para 3.3). Solicitors with supervisory or management responsibilities must provide effective supervision (Para 3.5) and must ensure that those they supervise or manage are also competent and up to date (Para 3.6) when dealing with accounts.

Equally, Para 4 of the Code for Firms requires firms to ensure that they provide competent services to clients (Para 4.2), to ensure their managers and employees are competent and up to date (Para 4.3) and to ensure that they have an effective system for supervising clients' matters (Para 4.4). These obligations encompass managing client money as part of the legal services offered to clients.

Practice example 8.4 indicates how this topic might be tested in the SQE1 Assessment.

Practice example 8.4

Oksana is a trainee solicitor. She receives a cheque for £2,000 from a client. £1,200 is in payment for an interim bill that Oksana sent to the client last week. The remaining £800 represents money on account of future costs and disbursements. Oksana is supervised by Joyce, one of the firm's partners. Oksana asks Joyce for advice on how to deal with the money, but Joyce is too busy to answer her questions and tells Oksana to go away and sort it out herself. Oksana therefore takes the cheque to the bank and pays it into the firm's business account before going on leave for the next fortnight. Joyce forgets about the matter and does not check the client ledger to see if the money has been paid in correctly.

Have there been any breaches of SRA Standards and Regulations, and if so, what action should be taken?

The cheque is a mixed receipt as it includes both business money (£1,200 in payment of a bill delivered to the client) and client money (£800 on account of future costs and disbursements). Although a mixed receipt can be paid into either the client account or the business account initially (so Oksana has not breached the Accounts Rules at this stage), it is important that the £800 client money element of the mixed receipt is transferred promptly into the client account to keep the client money separate from the business money (Accounts Rule 4.1) (see *Revise SQE: Solicitors' Accounts,* Chapter 6 for more details on mixed receipts). Oksana has no plans to make this transfer, probably because she does not realise she should do so. This may indicate that she has not maintained her own competence in this context (a breach of Para 3.3). Joyce is also in breach of her supervisory responsibilities (Para 3.5) as she did not answer Oksana's question or ensure that Oksana understood how to deal with mixed receipts properly. She also did not check the client ledger to see whether the money had been allocated to the correct bank accounts. As a manager, she should also ensure that Oksana receives proper training to keep her knowledge and understanding of the Accounts Rules up to date (Para 3.6).

COOPERATION AND ACCOUNTABILITY

Many of the provisions relating to cooperation and accountability can be assessed within the context of solicitors' accounts. **Table 8.2** summarises some of the different types of obligations on solicitors and firms within this context.

Table 8.2: Cooperation and accountability obligations

<table>
<tr><th>Proactive provisions (placing positive obligations on solicitors and firms)</th><th>Reactive provisions (placing obligations on solicitors or firms to react to, for example, requests from the SRA)</th><th>Negative provisions (placing obligations on solicitors or firms not to do something)</th></tr>
<tr><td>Reporting to the SRA anything that they consider amounts to a serious breach of the Accounts Rules (Para 7.7). A solicitor can satisfy this obligation by reporting the issue to the firm's COFA (Para 7.12), as the COFA should then escalate the matter to the SRA. This is illustrated in Practice example 8.2.</td><td rowspan="2">Cooperating with any SRA investigation that is already underway and responding promptly to SRA requests for information and documents etc. (Paras 7.3 and 7.4). This is illustrated in Practice example 8.5. Solicitors and firms may need to make careful decisions as to what to disclose by balancing their duty of confidentiality to their clients with their duty to act in the public interest in assisting the SRA with their regulatory function.</td><td rowspan="3">Where somebody is planning to report a serious breach of the Accounts Rules to the SRA, or where they have already done so, there is a negative obligation on solicitors and firms to refrain from any detrimental treatment of that person (Para 7.9). This protects whistleblowers from potential harassment, whether or not the SRA decide to investigate the matter or to take action against the firm.</td></tr>
<tr><td>Informing the SRA if they consider a matter should be investigated to see whether a serious breach of the Accounts Rules has occurred (Para 7.8). Again, if a solicitor informs the COFA, that is usually sufficient.</td></tr>
<tr><td>Being honest and open with the client if things go wrong and putting matters right if the client has suffered loss (Para 7.11). This may overlap with Accounts Rule 6.1. For example, if a client's money has been lost or stolen, the firm must tell the client what has happened and ensure that the money is replaced in the client account immediately, even if that involves using business money to do so.</td><td>Acting promptly to take any remedial action requested by the SRA (Para 7.10) – this may overlap with Accounts Rule 6.1 requiring solicitors to remedy any breach of the Accounts Rules promptly on discovery.</td></tr>
</table>

Practice example 8.5 illustrates how the SQE1 Assessment might test your understanding of how solicitors and firms should cooperate with the SRA.

Practice example 8.5

EFG Solicitors receive a cheque to settle a costs claim which they pay into the firm's business account. However, some of the costs are due to another firm, Hussain Law LLP, who acted previously for the client in the same claim. Hussain Law LLP report EFG Solicitors to the SRA after they are unsuccessful in persuading EFG Solicitors to pay them what is due. The SRA decide to investigate the matter.

How should EFG Solicitors respond to the SRA investigation?

EFG Solicitors must cooperate with the investigation and respond promptly to provide explanations, information and documents as requested by the SRA (Paras 7.3 and 7.4). This might include, for example, copies of the relevant ledgers and bank statements, costs settlement documentation and correspondence between the two firms. They must balance their duty of confidentiality to the client with their duty to act in the public interest by cooperating with the SRA when deciding whether or not to disclose confidential information.

FINAL ADVICE

This chapter has covered ethical issues and professional conduct matters as they arise in the context of solicitors' accounts, but you must remain vigilant and aware of more general conduct issues that may occur. Using ***Revise SQE: Solicitors' Accounts***, you should review the substantive law relating to solicitors' accounts and identify occasions when ethical and professional conduct issues may arise.

■ KEY POINT CHECKLIST

This chapter has covered the following key knowledge points. You can use these to structure your revision around, making sure to recall the key details for each point, as covered in this chapter.

- Safeguarding client money: Solicitors must safeguard client money in accordance with their obligations under the Principles, the Codes and the Accounts Rules.
- Maintaining trust and acting fairly: Solicitors must comply with the Accounts Rules to maintain trust and act fairly when handling client money. For example, they must comply with the terms of any undertakings involving client money.
- Dishonest handling of client money: Solicitors must report to the COFA, the SRA and/or the police if they suspect that other solicitors, employees or firms have stolen client money or acted fraudulently while handling client money.

- Service and competence: Solicitors and firms have obligations to act competently in handling client money, including keeping up to date with the Accounts Rules and ensuring appropriate supervisory and training arrangements are in place.
- Remedying breaches of the Accounts Rules: Solicitors and firms must take action to remedy any breaches of the Accounts Rules promptly on discovery.
- Cooperation and accountability: Solicitors and firms must liaise with the SRA appropriately if they are being investigated. They must also report any serious breaches, or suspicions of serious breaches of the Accounts Rules to the SRA, especially where client money has been put at risk.

■ KEY TERMS AND CONCEPTS

There are no key terms for this specific chapter.

■ SQE1-STYLE QUESTIONS

QUESTION 1

A solicitor completes a property transaction for a client and sends them a bill totalling £350 (inclusive of VAT and disbursements). The client sends a cheque for £350 in payment of the bill and the solicitor pays it into the firm's general client bank account.

What action, if any, should the solicitor take now with respect to this matter?

A. The solicitor should wait for the cheque to clear before closing the client's property file and ledger.

B. The solicitor can close the client's property file and ledger without waiting for the cheque to clear.

C. Once the cheque has cleared, the solicitor should transfer £350 from the client account to the business account promptly.

D. The solicitor must transfer £350 from the client account to the business account immediately, even if the cheque has not yet cleared.

E. The solicitor must report the matter to the Solicitors Regulation Authority immediately as the cheque has been paid into the wrong bank account, placing client money at risk.

QUESTION 2

A trainee solicitor works for a sole practitioner firm specialising in private client work. The sole practitioner leaves the trainee in charge of the firm's trusts and probate department while she is on holiday for two months. When the sole practitioner returns from holiday, she discovers that the trainee has made some errors. During the two month period, the trainee has paid over £5,000 business money into the firm's general client bank account, and over £800,000 client money into the firm's business bank account. The trainee has also stored £20,000 cash, found in the home of a deceased client, in his filing cabinet for over a month.

What action, if any, should the sole practitioner take with respect to these issues?

A. The sole practitioner should terminate the trainee's contract of employment immediately and then ensure that all money is paid or transferred into the correct bank accounts within two weeks.

B. The sole practitioner should leave the money where it is for now and report the trainee to the Solicitors Regulation Authority immediately for placing client money at risk.

C. The sole practitioner must ensure all money is paid or transferred correctly into the firm's client account immediately or business account promptly. She should also report herself to the Solicitors Regulation Authority for failures in supervision leading to client money being placed at risk.

D. The sole practitioner should ask the trainee to pay or transfer all money into the correct bank accounts within two weeks.

E. The sole practitioner should ensure all the money is paid or transferred correctly into the firm's business and client accounts promptly, and then train the trainee solicitor how to keep client money safe in the future.

QUESTION 3

A firm acts for several big educational trusts in managing their legal affairs. A junior solicitor notices some anomalies on the client ledgers of several of these trusts. There are unexplained payments to the personal bank account of one of the firm's senior partners, totalling approximately £600,000. The solicitor alerts the firm's Compliance Officer for Finance and Administration (COFA), but the COFA appears frightened and tells the solicitor to forget about the payments, without providing any explanation as to why they have been made.

What action, if any, should be taken by the junior solicitor considering the COFA's response?

A. The junior solicitor should report the matter to the Solicitors Regulation Authority promptly so that they can investigate the matter.

B. The junior solicitor should take no further action beyond alerting the COFA.

C. The junior solicitor should ask the senior partner about the unexplained payments and request that he returns the money from his personal bank account as soon as possible.
D. The junior solicitor should transfer money from the business account into the client account within the next six months to replace the unexplained payments made to the senior partner.
E. The junior solicitor should take no further action for now and leave the matter for the firm's accountant to check at the end of the firm's accounting period.

QUESTION 4

Two solicitors are setting up a new law firm, in which they will become partners. Neither has had experience of managing a firm before and they are concerned about the regulatory requirements for safeguarding client money.

Which of the following statements best describes the legal position of the solicitors?

A. The solicitors do not need to appoint a Compliance Officer for Finance and Administration as the firm will only have two partners.
B. The solicitors should appoint a Compliance Officer for Finance and Administration so that they can pass on their responsibility for safeguarding client money to them.
C. Each solicitor is only responsible for her own actions when safeguarding client money.
D. Both solicitors must update themselves and provide training for their employees so that everyone has sufficient understanding of the regulatory requirements for safeguarding client money.
E. The regulatory requirements for safeguarding client money only apply to the solicitors and any of the firm's employees responsible for giving legal advice to clients.

QUESTION 5

A solicitor tells a senior partner in his firm that he has reported her to the Solicitors Regulation Authority (SRA) for serious breaches of the Accounts Rules amounting to a serious failure to safeguard client money. In response, the senior partner threatens to terminate his contract of employment.

What action, if any, should the solicitor now take?

A. The solicitor must look for another job as the SRA will intervene shortly to stop the firm from operating.

B. The solicitor should explain to the senior partner that terminating his employment contract as a response to him reporting her to the SRA would be a further breach of the SRA's regulatory requirements.
C. The solicitor should take no action for now and wait to see if his employment contract is terminated. If it is, he must report this to the Solicitors Disciplinary Tribunal.
D. The solicitor must resign from his job immediately to avoid any further confrontations with the senior partner. He should then start a claim against the firm for constructive dismissal.
E. The solicitor should contact the SRA to retract his earlier report to protect his job, stating that he was mistaken about any risks to client money.

■ ANSWERS TO QUESTIONS

Answers to 'What do you know already?' questions at the start of the chapter

1) False. Para 4.2 Code for Individuals and Para 5.2 Code for Firms require solicitors to safeguard money and assets entrusted to them by *both* clients and others. This would include money held on behalf of a third party, such as deposit money held as agent or stakeholder in a property sale transaction, or money held to the order of a third party.
2) Using client money to fund an expensive personal property purchase is a breach of principles 2, 4, 5 and 7. It is also a breach of Paras 1.2, 1.4 and 4.2 Code for Individuals and Paras 1.2, 1.4 and 5.2 Code for Firms; and Accounts Rules 5.1 and 5.2. The solicitor should report these breaches to the firm's Compliance Officer for Finance and Administration (COFA) urgently. As the nature of the breaches is such as to cause a significant risk to client money, the COFA should report their concerns to the SRA (Para 7.12 Code for Individuals provides that the solicitor has satisfied any obligation under the Code to notify the SRA by providing information to the COFA on the understanding that they will do so). The firm should transfer funds from the business account immediately to replace the client money wrongly withdrawn from the client account (Accounts Rule 6.1). The firm should also take steps to prevent any further wrongful withdrawals (for example, by taking urgent disciplinary action against the colleague and suspending him from his job pending investigation). The firm should also report the matter to the police.
3) True. The Accounts Rules apply to all employees, including newly qualified solicitors (Rule 1.1). The solicitor also has an obligation under the Code to maintain their own competence and to keep their professional knowledge and skills up to date (Para 3.4 Code for Individuals). Their managers also have an obligation to ensure that this

is the case (Para 3.6 Code for Individuals), for example, by organising appropriate training for all staff. The Code for Firms includes similar provisions in Para 4.3.

4) False. The solicitor must co-operate with the SRA in this investigation (Para 7.3 Code for Individuals). They should provide full and accurate explanations, information and documents in response to any request from the SRA and, where appropriate, ensure that relevant information is available for inspection by the SRA (Para 7.4 Code for Individuals). In doing so, they will need to balance their duty of confidentiality to their clients with their duty to act in the public interest in assisting the SRA with their regulatory function.

Answers to end-of-chapter SQE1-style questions

Question 1:

The correct answer was C. This is because the cheque represents business money as it is in payment of a bill already delivered to the client. The money should have been paid into the firm's business bank account instead of the general client account. This is a breach of Accounts Rule 4.1 that requires client money to be kept separate from business money, and should be corrected promptly by transferring £350 from the general client account to the business account (Accounts Rule 6.1). However, the transfer must wait until after the cheque has cleared. If the client to business transfer is made before the cheque has cleared, the transfer will be from other clients' money, which is a clear breach of the Accounts Rules. Option D is therefore incorrect. Options A and B are both incorrect as they treat the cheque as client rather than business money. Option E is incorrect because it is business money, rather than client money, that has been paid into the wrong account. Therefore, no money belonging to clients, or third parties, has been placed at risk, such as to justify reporting the matter to the SRA.

Question 2:

The correct answer was C. This is because the sole practitioner should have ensured that the trainee solicitor had adequate supervision while she was on holiday. This lack of supervision (and the trainee's lack of awareness of the relevant regulations) has led to large amounts of client money being placed at risk (for example, client money in the business account might be wrongly used to pay business expenses or creditors; or cash in the filing cabinet is at risk of being stolen). This is sufficiently serious to warrant a report to the SRA, even if action is taken as required to pay client money into the client account *immediately*, and business money into the business account *promptly*. Option A is incorrect because the sole practitioner should take some of the blame for the errors, so firing the trainee is unlikely to be appropriate. It is also incorrect because the time limit of two weeks is too long. Option B is incorrect because the money cannot be left where it is, it must be placed in the correct accounts in accordance with the relevant regulations (*immediately* for client money and *promptly* for business money). Further, even if the trainee's errors are reported to the SRA, the sole practitioner also bears responsibility for failing to train or supervise him properly. Option D is incorrect because the time limit of two weeks is too long. It may also be wiser for the sole practitioner to allocate the money to the correct accounts herself. Option E is almost correct in that the business money should be transferred promptly into the business account and it would be sensible to train the trainee. However, the client money must be paid or transferred into the client account *immediately,* rather than promptly, so the answer is incorrect. Watch out for time limits in questions. You must select the correct one carefully.

Question 3:

The correct answer was A. This is because in the absence of any other explanation, it appears that the senior partner may be stealing large sums of client money from the educational trusts. If this is the case, client money is at risk, constituting a serious breach of the Accounts Rules which should be reported to the SRA promptly so that they can investigate and take action (Paras 7.7 and 7.8). It is also suspicious that the COFA appears frightened. It may also be appropriate for the solicitor to report the matter to the police at the same time. Option B is incorrect because although alerting the COFA in the first instance is appropriate, if the COFA cannot provide an explanation and will not take any action, the solicitor must protect client money by reporting to the SRA. Option C is not the best option as it is inadvisable to confront the senior partner as it may give them a chance to cover their tracks. The COFA's fear may also indicate some potential threat from the senior partner. Option D is incorrect because although it is appropriate to replace any client money withdrawn wrongly from the client account with money from the business account, this should be done promptly on discovery of the breach of the Accounts Rules, rather than within six months. Option E is incorrect because there may be an ongoing risk to client money, so leaving the matter to the end of the accounting period and waiting for the accountant's report is too late.

Question 4:

The correct answer was D. This is because everyone working in the law firm, whatever their role (Accounts Rule 1.1), must comply with the regulatory requirements for safeguarding client money (Para 4.2 Code for Individuals, Para 5.2 Code for Firms and the Accounts Rules). The solicitors should only employ staff who are competent for their roles and should make sure they are trained appropriately (Para 3.6 Code for Individuals and para 4.3 Code for Firms). Option A is incorrect because all law firms must have a COFA. Option B is incorrect because the solicitors cannot escape responsibility for safeguarding client money. Option C is incorrect because the solicitors will be jointly and severally responsible for compliance with the Accounts Rules (Rule 1.2) so that client money is kept safe. Option E is incorrect because all employees of the firm, not just those responsible for giving legal advice, must comply with the Accounts Rules (Rule 1.1).

Question 5:

The correct answer was B. This is because it is a breach of both the Code for Individuals and the Code for Firms for the senior partner to subject the solicitor to detrimental treatment (such as terminating his employment contract), for reporting her to the SRA. Option A is incorrect as there is no obligation on the solicitor to seek employment elsewhere unless he wishes to do so, and although the SRA may investigate the firm for breaches of the Codes and Accounts Rules, it cannot be assumed that the SRA will intervene to stop the firm operating. It may be inadvisable for the solicitor to wait and see whether his employment contract is terminated (Option C), but in any event, any report he makes should be to the SRA rather than the Solicitors Disciplinary Tribunal (making option C wrong in this respect). Option D is incorrect because there is no obligation on the solicitor to resign and bring a claim for constructive dismissal unless he chooses to do so. Option E is incorrect because it would be a breach of the regulatory requirements to tell the SRA that client money is not at risk when this is not true (for example, Principles 2, 4, 5 and 7; Paras 4.2, 7.7 and 7.8 of the Code for Individuals).

■ KEY CASES, RULES, STATUTES AND INSTRUMENTS

The SQE1 Assessment Specification has identified that candidates are required to understand the purpose, scope and content of the SRA Principles, Codes and Accounts Rules, although you are not required to know the relevant numbers. Make sure that you understand the application of the SRA Principles and Codes to practice in the context of solicitors' accounts.

The SQE1 Assessment Specification does not require you to know any case names, or statutory materials, for the topic of ethics and professional conduct in solicitors' accounts.

Index